THE MAKING
OF AN
ECONOMIC
SUPERPOWER

Unlocking
China's Secret
of Rapid Industrialization

THE MAKING
OF AN
ECONOMIC
SUPERPOWER
Unlocking
China's Secret
of Rapid Industrialization

Yi WEN
Federal Reserve Bank of St. Louis, USA
& Tsinghua University, China

World Scientific

NEW JERSEY · LONDON · SINGAPORE · BEIJING · SHANGHAI · HONG KONG · TAIPEI · CHENNAI · TOKYO

Published by

World Scientific Publishing Co. Pte. Ltd.

5 Toh Tuck Link, Singapore 596224

USA office: 27 Warren Street, Suite 401-402, Hackensack, NJ 07601

UK office: 57 Shelton Street, Covent Garden, London WC2H 9HE

Library of Congress Cataloging-in-Publication Data
Names: Wen, Yi, author.
Title: The making of an economic superpower : unlocking China's secret of rapid industrialization /
    Yi Wen (Federal Reserve Bank of St. Louis, USA & Tsinghua University, China).
Description: New Jersey : World Scientific, 2016. | Includes bibliographical references and index.
Identifiers: LCCN 2015048899 | ISBN 9789814733724 (hc : alk. paper)
Subjects: LCSH: Industrial policy--China. | China--Economic policy. |
    Economic development--China.
Classification: LCC HD3616.C63 W46 2016 | DDC 338.951--dc23
LC record available at http://lccn.loc.gov/2015048899

British Library Cataloguing-in-Publication Data
A catalogue record for this book is available from the British Library.

Desk Editors: Harini Lakshmi Narasimhan/Dong Lixi

Typeset by Stallion Press
Email: enquiries@stallionpress.com

Printed in Singapore

For JIN Baoli (金宝丽) and WEN You Ricardo (文又), with love

About the Author

Yi Wen

Research Division, Federal Reserve Bank of St. Louis, USA
&
School of Economics & Management, Tsinghua University, China

The author is a senior economist and assistant Vice President in the Research Department of the Federal Reserve Bank of St. Louis and CCB Chair Professor in the School of Economics and Management (SEM) of Tsinghua University. The views expressed are those of the author and do not reflect official positions of the Federal Reserve Bank of St. Louis, the Federal Reserve System, or the Board of Governors. I would like to thank Costas Azariadis, Ping Chen, Justin Yifu Lin, and Bill Gavin for strong encouragement and insightful comments on an earlier version of this project. Thanks also go to Jess Benhabib, Michele Boldrin, Roger Farmer, Belton Fleisher, Hong Ma, Carlos Marichal, Nancy Stokey, Peer Vries, Yong Wang, Yang Yao, Xiaobo Zhang, and Tian Zhu for kind comments and criticism, and Maria Arias and Jinfeng Luo for research assistance. My greatest gratitude goes to George Fortier, who has carefully edited the entire manuscript and provided numerous suggestions to improve the exposition of the ideas presented herein. Several ideas presented in this paper also exist in the related literature, and I have cited the original sources for all previously published content that I am aware of. But limitations in my knowledge and survey of the literature may have caused unintended omissions. Therefore, I welcome and appreciate feedback from readers who can identify any omitted or incorrect citations.

Abstract

The rise of China is no doubt one of the most important events in world economic history since the Industrial Revolution. Mainstream economics, especially the institutional theory of economic development based on a dichotomy of extractive vs. inclusive political institutions, is highly inadequate in explaining China's rise. This book argues that only a radical reinterpretation of the history of the Industrial Revolution and the rise of the West (as incorrectly portrayed by the institutional theory) can fully explain China's growth miracle and why the determined rise of China is unstoppable despite its current "backward" financial system and political institutions. Conversely, China's spectacular and rapid transformation from an impoverished agrarian society to a formidable industrial superpower sheds considerable light on the fundamental shortcomings of the institutional theory and mainstream "blackboard" economic models and provides more-accurate reevaluations of historical episodes such as Africa's enduring poverty trap despite radical political and economic reforms, Latin America's lost decades and frequent debt crises, 19th century Europe's great escape from the Malthusian trap, and the Industrial Revolution itself.

Quotes from the Book

"*Poverty or backwardness or the lack of industrialization is always and everywhere a social coordination-failure problem. The problem arises because of the enormous costs of creating market and its fundamental pillar — social trust.*"

"*The 'free' market is not free. It is a fundamental public good that is extremely costly to create. The ongoing industrial revolution in China has been driven not by technology adoption, per se, but instead by continuous market creation led by a capable mercantilist government.*"

"*The Glorious Revolution did not make British government more 'inclusive' in the sense of sharing political power with the working class (as glorified by Acemoglu and Robinson (2012, pp. 1–5) in their appraisal of the Arab Spring movement). It simply made the government more authoritarian and powerful in levying taxes, creating markets and commercial networks, promoting manufacturing and mercantilist trade, and reigning over the British economy.*"

"*The market for mass-produced industrial goods cannot be created by a single 'big push' under import substitution or 'shock therapy.' It can only be created step by step in the correct order (sequence). China's rise to global economic supremacy has been unstoppable because it has found*

*and followed the correct recipe (sequence) of market creation, in contrast
to its earlier three failed attempts at industrialization between 1860 and
1978 under different political systems."*

*"The degree of industrialization is limited by the extent of the market. The
fundamental reason the United Kingdom, instead of the Netherlands, kick-
started the First Industrial Revolution was because of its successful creation of the world's largest textile market and cotton-supply chains in the
18th century, which made the nationwide adoption of the spinning jenny
and factory system profitable and inevitable. Likewise, the fundamental
reason the United States, instead of France or Germany, overtook the
U.K. to become the next economic superpower was the U.S. government's
help in creating an even larger manufactured-goods market in the 19th
century, which nurtured the world's greatest inventors such as Thomas
Edison and industrial giants such as Andrew Carnegie, Henry Ford, J.P.
Morgan, John D. Rockefeller, and Cornelius Vanderbilt. Today, China
(instead of India) is well-positioned to overtake the United States in
manufacturing and technological innovations in the 21st century because
the Chinese government has helped create a gigantic market that is several times larger than the U.S. market."*

*"Democracy cannot function without industrialization. Industrialization
is impossible without a strong state."*

Yi Wen (*The Making of an Economic Superpower*)

Table of Contents

Chapter 1

Introduction

China's sudden emergence as an economic superpower has astonished the world. Even as recently as 15 years ago (say, around the 1997 Asian financial crisis), few would have predicted China's dominance as a regional industrial power, let alone a global superpower. In fact, many were betting on China's collapse, citing the Tiananmen Square incident, the collapse of the Soviet Union and Eastern European communism, the Asian financial crisis, and the 2008 global recession (which cut China's total exports almost permanently by more than 40% below trend). But reality has repeatedly defied all these pessimistic predictions: With a 35-year run of hyper-growth, China came, saw, and prospered — in merely one generation's time, China has created more massive and more colossal productive forces than have all her preceding 5,000-year dynasties together, and transformed from a vastly impoverished agrarian nation (with per capita income just one-third of the average Sub-Saharan African level) into the world's largest and most vigorous manufacturing powerhouse.

China today, for example, with less than 6% of the world's water resources and just 9% of the world's arable land, can produce in one year 50 billion t-shirts (more than seven times the world population), 10 billion pairs of shoes, 800 million metric tons of crude steel (50% of global supply and 900% of the U.S. level), 2.4 gigatons of cement (nearly 60% of world production), close to four trillion metric tons of coal (burning almost as much coal as the rest of the world combined), more than 23 million vehicles (more than a quarter of global supply), and 62,000 industrial patent applications (150% times that in the United States and more than the sum of the U.S. and Japan). China is also the world's largest producer of ships, speed trains, robots, tunnels, bridges, highways, electricity, chemical fiber, machine tools, cell phones, computers, bicycles, motorcycles, air conditioners, refrigerators, wash machines, furniture, textiles, clothing, footwear, toys, fertilizers, agricultural crops, pork, fish, eggs, cotton, copper, aluminum, books, magazines, newspapers, television shows, as well as college students.[1]

China's astonishing 30-fold expansion of real GDP since 1978 was unexpected, not merely because of its pervasive backwardness after centuries of turmoil and economic regress, but because of its enduring "extractive" and authoritarian political institutions — which, according to the institutional theories of economic development, would predict nothing but dismal failure for China's industrialization.[2]

These theories overly glorify the modern Western political institutions that China lacks, but ignore the not-so-glorious historical paths Western powers once traveled themselves. By asserting that democratic political institutions and the rule of law are prerequisites for economic development, such theories overlook the endogenous and evolutionary nature of institutions and the frequent disconnections between rhetoric and practice, between the rule of law and its actual enforcement, and between political institutions

---

[1] China contributed about one-third of the world's economic growth in recent years, according to an IMF estimate.
[2] See, for example, D. Acemoglu and J. Robinson (2012), *Why Nations Fail — The Origins of Power, Prosperity, and Poverty.*

and economic policies.[3] Thus, these theories end up confusing consequence with cause, correlation with causation, political superstructures with economic foundations, and open access to political power with open access to economic rights.[4] Specifically, universal

---

[3]Acemoglu and Robinson (2012) view the lack of democracy (or the lack of "inclusive" political institutions) as the root cause of poverty and stagnations around the world. For example, they not only agree with the protesters on the Tahrir Square during the Egyptian Jasmine Revolution that "Egypt is poor precisely because it has been ruled by a narrow elite that have organized society for their own benefits at the expense of the vast mass of people," but also argue that "this interpretation of Egyptian poverty [by the people on the Tahrir Square] ... provide[s] a general explanation for why poor countries are poor." The entire thesis of their popular book "Why Nations Fail" is to "show that poor countries are poor for the same reason that Egypt is poor" (Acemoglu and Robonson, 2012, p. 3). It is then not surprising that such theories are highly inadequate in explaining Russia's dismal failure in economic reform after adopting democracy and the shock therapy in the early 1990s, China's miracle growth since 1978 under an authoritarian political regime, as well as Japan's rapid industrialization during the Meiji Restoration, South Korean's economic takeoff in the 1960s–1980s, and Singapore's post-independence economic miracle. Such theories cannot even explain why with identical political institutions in American cities, such as Chicago or St. Louis, there are both pockets of extreme poverty and blocks of extreme wealth, both violent crime and obedience to the rule of law; nor can they explain why Southern Italy is significantly poorer than Northern Italy; or why the Dutch Republic failed to kick-start an industrial revolution in the 17th century despite having more liberal institutions than England.

[4]Consistent with my point, prominent economists such as Michele Boldrin, David Levine, and Salvatore Modica (2014) view the institutional theory of Acemoglu and Robinson (2012) as a tautology: "Explaining the entire history of humankind by dividing the world into 'extractive' and 'inclusive' institutions is a daunting task. At one level the notion that 'extractive' institutions fail and 'inclusive' ones succeed can be a tautology — if we mean that 'extractive' institutions are ones that successfully block growth and 'inclusive' ones are those that do not." For critical views from economic historians against the institutional theory's explanations of the British Industrial Revolution and economic development, see Robert Allen (2009), Gregory Clark (2007), Deirdre McCloskey (2010), and Kenneth Pomeranz (2001), among many others.

suffrage was the *consequence* of the Industrial Revolution instead of its *cause*, and modern sophisticated Western legal systems and the ability to enforce them were the *outcome* of centuries of economic development under colonialism, imperialism, mercantilism, the slave trade, and painful primitive accumulations.

Such confusion is at the root of the Western enthusiasm in advancing Western-style democracy in backward, developing countries regardless of their initial economic-social-political conditions. The consequence of such a political top-down approach to economic development has been clear: Look at the economic stagnation and continuous political turmoil in Afghanistan, Egypt, Iraq, and Libya and the situations in Ukraine and other parts of Eastern Europe where democracy advances only to collapse, living standards progress only to regress, and the hopes of prosperity rise only to burst.[5]

Thus, despite nearly 250 years since the publication of "The Wealth of Nations" and all the ink spilled on general-equilibrium models of economic growth, economists are still in the dark searching for the key — the "double helix" — of economic development.

---

[5] Ironically, after four years of economic stagnations in Tunisia following its overthrow of dictator Zine El Abidine Ben Ali that kicked off the Arab Spring in 2011, a 88-year-old former minister from Tunisia's old dictatorship regime, Mr. Beji Caid Essebsi, won the country's first ever democratic election for president on December 22, 2014. The reason is simple. Democracy has nothing to do with the driving forces of economic development; it can be just as ineffective as dictatorship in ending corruption and poverty and is even more likely to breed political instability in developing countries. In fact, Tunisia since 2011 has become a breeding ground for jihadists and is now the largest source of foreign fighters joining the Islamic State (ISIS) and other extremist groups in Syria and Iraq (see, e.g., http://www.theguardian.com/world/2014/oct/13/tunisia-breeding-ground-islamic-state-fighters. Hence, prematurely adopted democracy in developing countries tends to produce not only a failed market system, but also a failed state. Yet, as will be argued and demonstrated throughout this book, a strong state has been one of the single most important agents in market creation throughout the history of economic development and industrialization.

Adam Smith was perhaps closer to finding it than his modern neoliberal followers. He explained the wealth of nations by the division of labor based on the size of the market, using examples from early 18th century pin factories, but his modern neoliberal students mix democracy with free markets, free markets with property rights, and property rights with incentives. They assert that the British Industrial Revolution could still have run its course as long as democracy prevailed, without the great voyage and discovery of America, and without England's hegemony over global textile markets, its colossal wealth generated from the Trans-Atlantic slave trade, its powerful state assistance in creating and coordinating market activities, and its endorsement and fierce military protection of the East Indian Company's global commercial interests and monopoly power.[6]

---

[6]Even as early as late 1600s around the Glorious Revolution, a century before slave trade peaked (in late 1700s), nearly three-quarters of the value of trade goods bound for Africa to pay for slaves were in textiles, mostly of English manufacture (see William J. Bernstein, 2008, *A Splendid Exchange: How Trade Shaped The World.* pp. 274–276). The British government and merchants understood very well that "[W]e cannot carry on trade without war; nor war without trade," as declared by Jan Pieterszoon Coen in 1614, a famous Dutch merchant and warrior, the founder of Batavia and an officer of the Dutch East India Company in Indonesia (VOC) in the early 17th century, holding two terms as its Governor-General of the Dutch East Indies (see Stephen R. Bown, *Merchant Kings: When Companies Ruled the World, 1600–1900.* Macmillan, 2010, p. 7) Most economic historians would agree that "For England, which was politically and militarily the most successful country, the 'virtual monopoly among European powers of oversea colonies', established during the phase of proto-industrialization, was one of the central preconditions which carried proto-industrialization beyond itself into the Industrial Revolution" (see Kriedte, Medick, and Schlumbohm, *Industrialization before Industrialization.* 1977, p. 131). Economic historians Pomeranz and Topik argue that the opium trade "not only helped create Britain's direct [trade] surplus with China, but made possible even the larger surplus with India. Without those surpluses, Britain could not have remained the West's chief consumer and financer, and the Atlantic economy as a whole would have grown much more slowly" (K. Pomeranz and S. Topik, 2013, p. 104).

At the other extreme, neoclassical growth models based purely on (government-free) resource allocations still face daunting challenges connecting rational individual choices with long-term economic growth: How could merely re-shoveling available incomes by self-interested individuals across different consumption bundles have enabled Europe's great escape from the Malthusian trap and yielded unprecedented waves of technological changes and industrial revolutions? In such growth models not only is the state redundant but the market and its creators automatically exist, so much so that the Ford automobile assembly line and the textile cartage workshop are the same thing as long as they have the same capital's share in an abstract production function.[7]

No wonder technological change remains a black box in neoclassical growth models. No wonder the "Solow residual" in neoclassical production functions measures nothing but our ignorance. No wonder the Industrial Revolution that took place roughly 250 years ago first in England remains a great mystery.

Even for learned economic historians, the Industrial Revolution is, at the very best, considered a "tacit" knowledge comprehensible only to a handful of "predestined" countries blessed with geographical locations or mysterious cultural genes. *"Explaining the Industrial Revolution is the ultimate, elusive prize in economic history. It is a prize that has inspired generations of scholars to lifetimes of, so far, fruitless pursuit"* (Economic Historian Gregory Clark, 2012).

---

[7] For neoclassical models proposed to explain the Industrial Revolution, see Desmet and Parente (2012), Hansen and Prescott (2002), Stokey (2001), and Yang and Zhu (2013), among many others. Such models try to capture some important features of economic development presented herein, but treat technological change as exogenous and assume that supply can automatically create its own demand. Such models ignore the enormous costs and social-coordination problems associated with market creation and the division of labor and overlook the fundamental force of market size (demand) in stimulating supply and technological innovations as well as the pivotal role of the government in creating markets (among others). Hence, such elegant mathematical models remain impractical for policy makers in developing countries.

But China has just rediscovered this "tacit" knowledge — the secret recipe of industrial revolution. This very fact has gone almost completely unnoticed and unappreciated by Western academia and media; hence, we see in the West the severe under-prediction and lack of clear understanding of China's rapid and pronounced rise to economic prominence.

In terms of industrial chronology, China already successfully finished its first industrial revolution during its initial 15–20 year rural-industrial growth after the 1978 reform. It is now already halfway through its second industrial revolution and on the verge of kick-starting a third industrial revolution — "deceivingly" and stubbornly, despite all the stereotypical and pessimistic views predicting China's collapse.[8]

What is industrial revolution? Why was it absent or delayed in China for more than 200 years? How did China eventually manage to detonate such an industrial revolution (or a sequence of industrial revolutions) soon after a 10-year-long Cultural Revolution that destroyed so much of its already scarce human capital and business/cultural genes? What are the roles that geography, property rights, institutions, the rule of law, culture, religion, natural resources, science, technology, democracy, education, human capital, international

---

[8] Perhaps the most well-known person who has been repeatedly predicting China's collapse in the past decades is Gordon G. Chang, author of the book "The Coming Collapse of China." Similar books and articles are abundant, and pessimistic predictions on China's rise still dominate the Western news media despite repeated failures (see, e.g., the most recent article on March 2, 2015, in the popular bi-monthly magazine, *The National Interest*, titled "Doomsday: Preparing for China's Collapse," http://nationalinterest.org/feature/doomsday-preparing-chinas-collapse-12343) For discussions and analyses on Western media's propensity to criticize China in publications such as *The New York Times, The Washington Post, Bloomberg, The Financial Times,* and *The Wall Street Journal,* see Dealing With the Scourge of 'Schadenfreude' in Foreign Reporting on China (October 3, 2014) by freelance writer (also an international banker and former U.S. State Department official) Stephen M. Harner; available at http://blog.hiddenharmonies.org/2014/10/04/western-medias-pervasive-bias-against-china-today/.

trade, industrial policy, protectionism, mercantilism, and state power play in industrialization? Are there secret recipes to achieve rapid, "engineered" industrialization? Can other developing nations such as India and Ethiopia emulate China's success and ignite their own industrial revolution in the 21st century?[9]

i. China's Perseverance and Unfaltering Attempts at Industrialization

The Industrial Revolution appears a mysterious process of dramatic social-economic changes that only a handful of Western countries (with just a small percentage of the world population) experienced in the 18th and 19th centuries. It is a process that many backward nations (with more than 90% of the world population) longed to emulate but have failed miserably and repeatedly in the 20th century. And it is a process that economists and economic historians are still struggling to comprehend and identify its ultimate cause and explanations.[10]

But if a perceptive Western observer could travel to China once every year over the past 35 years, without wearing ideological Eurocentric institutional glasses, she would have witnessed the Industrial Revolution unfolding vividly in front of her eyes. China compressed the roughly 150–200 (or even more) years of revolutionary economic changes experienced by England in 1700–1900 and the United States in 1760–1920 and Japan in 1850–1960 into one single generation. What the Western traveler might see in China are the ideas of Adam Smith (1723–1790), Alexander Hamilton (1755–1804), David Ricardo (1772–1823), Friedrich List (1789–1846), Karl

---

[9] India's new Prime minister, Narendra Modi, promised "to make the 21st century India's century." Can India succeed? What will it take? (See the analysis in the next two chapters).

[10] See, e.g., R. Allen (2009), D. Acemoglu and J. Robinson (2012), G. Clark (2007), D. Landes (1999), R. Lucas (2003), D. McCloskey (2010), J. Mokyr (2010), I. Morris (2010), D. North (1981), K. Pomerranz (2001), among many others.

Marx (1818–1883), and Joseph Schumpeter (1883–1950) unfolding and playing out vividly in the 9,600,000 square kilometers of Chinese theater with more than 1 billion real Chinese actors — hundreds of millions of organized farmers, craftsmen, peasant-manufacturers, engineers, entrepreneurs, merchants, textile producers, coal miners, railroad builders, industrialists, speculators, arbitragers, traders, innovators, the state, and business-minded government officials. They all wear Chinese costumes and thus look unfamiliar to the Western observers. Yet, China today is perhaps more "capitalistic" than any 19th or 20th century emerging Western power. With mercantilism on the one hand and market competition on the other, without any "Glorious Revolution," "French Revolution," "Orange Revolution" or "Jasmine Revolution," Deng Xiaoping and his successors made capitalism (or capitalistic materialism) China's Absolute Spirit (a la Hegel) in the new millennium. And they did so under China's so-called "extractive" institutions.[11]

---

[11] Mercantilism is economic nationalism for the purpose of building a wealthy and powerful state based on commerce and *manufacturing*. It seeks to enrich the country by restraining imports of *manufactured* goods and encouraging exports of *manufactured* goods. In short, it emphasizes and promotes manufacturing over agriculture, and commercialism over physiocracy. However, most of the literature on mercantilism views it simply as a form of protectionism or pure pursuit of trade surplus or gold reserves, and overlooks the key point of commerce and *manufacturing*. An economy relying solely on agriculture has nothing to benefit from mercantilism. But a nation intending to build on manufacturing can benefit greatly from mercantilism because manufacturing stimulates the division of labor and generates the economies of scale. The historical importance of mercantilism in the 16th–18th century Europe as the prototype of capitalism and the key step leading to the English Industrial Revolution can never be emphasized enough. Indeed, the promotion of manufacturing inherent in mercantilism has seldom been appreciated by classical economists, including Adam Smith and David Ricardo, unlike Friedrich List (1841). One example of the impact of mercantilism on economic development is the 19th century American Industrial Revolution based on the "American System," which was an economic development strategy envisioned by Alexander Hamilton (1755–1804) in 1791 and vigorously implemented throughout

But what is "capitalism," exactly? Is it a new way of living (McCloskey's "bourgeois dignity"), a new system of belief and ideology (Joel Mokyr's "enlightened economy"), a new work ethic (Max Weber's ascetic Protestantism), a new configuration of civilization, state power, and social order (a la Samuel P. Huntington), or a new mode of production (a la Karl Marx)?

So many economists and economic historians have preoccupied themselves with the "ultimate and elusive prize" of explaining why the industrial revolution took place 250 years ago in late 18th century England instead of 18th century China or India. But, isn't it equally or even more intriguing to ask why China and India remained unindustrialized more than 200 years later despite ample opportunities to emulate the British industrialization? In other words, the fundamental reason the Industrial Revolution took place first in England instead of India may be found by asking why India remains unindustrialized even today. The lack of democracy and property rights is clearly not the explanation: India has been the largest democracy for decades, with one of the longest histories of private property rights on earth. Nor does the shifting of comparative advantage in cotton textiles from India to England in the 18th century (Broadberry and Gupta, 2009) explain India's failure to embark on the Industrial

---

the 19th century to win global competition with Great Britain (Hamilton's idea was not immediately adopted in 1790s and the initial decade of 1800s). It consisted of several mutually reinforcing parts: High tariffs to protect and promote the American infant Northern manufacturing sector; a national bank to foster commerce, stabilize the currency, and rein in risk-taking private banks; a maintenance of high public land prices to generate federal revenue; and large-scale federal subsidies for roads, canals, and other infrastructures to develop a unified national market — financed through the tariffs and land sales. Also see Ha-Joon Chang (2003), "Kicking Away the Ladder: Development Strategies in Historical Perspective," for many great examples of mercantilism and the historical role it played in Western economic development. However, many Latin American countries in the middle 20th century also adopted various forms of mercantilism (e.g., the Import Substitution Industrialization) but failed miserably. The reasons behind such successes and failures are precisely what this book is about.

Revolution: India had more than 200 years to observe, learn, emulate and reclaim the comparative advantage from England, just as China finally did in the 1990s (China became the World's largest textile producer and exporter in 1995). Equally intriguing is the proclivity of researchers to ask why the Industrial Revolution did not start in the 17th and 18th century China, given its superior technologies and Yangtze River delta region's hyper-economic prosperity,[12] instead of asking why China remained poor and unable to industrialize even hundreds of years later in the 20th century? Simply attributing this failure to the vested interests of the elite class and the lack of democracy (as the institutional theories do) is unconvincing at best and misleading at worst.[13]

Take note that the economic reform in 1978 was not China's first ambitious attempt to ignite industrialization on a vast and populous impoverished land. It was the *fourth* attempt in 120 years since the second opium war around 1860.[14]

The first attempt was made during 1861–1911, after China's defeat in the Second Opium War by the British in 1860.[15] Deeply

---

[12] See the large literature on the "Needham Puzzle" and the more recent literature on the Great Divergence between the West and the East by K. Pomerranz (2001). A good introduction to the Great Divergence debate is the article by Bishnupriya Gupta and Debin Ma (2010), "Europe in an Asian Mirror: The Great Divergence," and the article by Loren Brandt, Debin Ma, and Thomas G. Rawski (2012), "From Divergence to Convergence: Re-evaluating the History behind China's Economic Boom."

[13] See, e.g., Acemoglu and Robinson (2005 and 2012).

[14] For a vivid historical account of China's quest for national salvation since the late Qing dynasty, see Orville Schell and John Delury (2013), *Wealth and Power: China's Long March to the Twenty-First Century.*

[15] China fought two Opium Wars against the British Empire (around 1840 and 1860 respectively). In both wars, Britain relied on its mighty navigation technology and navy power and crushed China's effort to ban opium imports from British India, which the Britain government used as means to balance its large trade deficit with China and the loss of its silver reserve resulting from silk and tea imports. China lost both wars. The only country that has won wars against

humiliated by unequal treaties imposed by Western industrial powers, the late Qing monarchy embarked on an ambitious program to modernize its backward agrarian economy, including establishing a modern navy and industrial system. This attempt started 10 years earlier than the Meiji Restoration that triggered Japan's successful industrialization. But 50 years later the Qing monarchy's effort turned out to be a gigantic failure: The government was deep in debt and the "hoped for" industrial base was nowhere in sight. No wonder China was crushed in 1894 by the Japanese navy in the first Sino-Japanese war. Much like earlier conflicts against the British, the war was a lopsided defeat for China. Even a semi-industrialized Japan severely outmatched the still-underdeveloped China.[16]

The incompetence of the Qing government to defend China against foreign aggressions triggered nationwide demand for political reforms and escalating social turmoil and unrest, which ultimately led to the 1911 Xinhai Revolution that overthrew the "extractive" Qing monarchy and established the Republic of China, the first "inclusive" government in Chinese history based on Western-style constitutions.[17] This was a genuine revolution far more pervasive than the English Glorious Revolution: It did not simply restrict the power of the Qing Monarchy but instead completely eliminated it. The new republic government tried to industrialize China by a wholesale mimicking of the U.S. political institutions such as democracy and

---

international drug trafficking (opium trade) in history is the industrialized United States in the late 20th century against Latin American drug dealers.

[16] Technology matters. Spanish soldiers equipped with guns and steel easily slaughtered the unorganized agrarian Incans despite being outnumbered by several 100-fold. However, it takes more than pure technology to win a war or conquer a nation: Industrialization gives rise to national strength in human organizational capital and logistics capacity to project military forces and provide the required military supply chain of economic resources.

[17] The revolution arose because the Qing state had proven highly ineffective in its half century-long efforts to modernize China and confront foreign aggression; it was also exacerbated by ethnic resentment against the ruling Manchu minority.

the separation of powers (that is, legislative, executive, and judicial branches of government). The most famous slogans among Chinese at that time were "Of the people, by the people, and for the people" and "Only science and democracy can save China." The educated elite revolutionaries believed that the Qing monarchy's failure to industrialize and China's overall backwardness was due to its lack of democracy, political inclusiveness, and pluralism (exactly as the modern institutionalism has argued). The republic government established an inclusive government, based on open access to political powers (by including even the communist party in the government),[18] modern corporations, new private property laws, and public universities never seen before; these reforms encouraged free trade, welcomed foreign capital, and fully embraced the bourgeois life style throughout China, especially in large commercial cities such as Shanghai. But 40 years passed and, in 1949, China remained one of the poorest nations on earth in terms of average living standard and life expectancy.[19]

The second failed attempt at industrialization in China also explained Japan's almost effortless yet ruthless invasion and conquest of China in 1937, as manifested in the *"Rape of Nanking"* (the Nanking Massacre).[20]

The Republic government's ineffectiveness in solving China's poverty problem since its establishment in 1911 resulted in its defeat by the communist peasant army (the People's Liberalization Army)

---

[18] The inclusive Republic government was open to communists. For example, the young communism leader Mao, Zhedong was a high official member of the Republic Government in the early 1920s.

[19] In 1949, China's peasant population as a share of national total remained at more than 90%, not much changed since 1860. The average life expectance remained as low as 30–35 years.

[20] For documents and reports on the Nanking Massacre, see http://www.nanking-massacre.com/rape_of_nanking_or_nanjing_massacre_1937.html and http://www.csee.umbc.edu/~kunliu1/Nanjing_Massacre.html, and the references therein.

in 1949. With the support of 600 million impoverished peasants, Mao declared that "The Chinese People have [finally] stood up!" and initiated the third ambitious attempt to industrialize China — this time by mimicking the Soviet Union's central planning model instead of capitalism and democracy. Thirty years passed and the attempt failed again: In 1978, China remained essentially in the same Malthusian poverty trap with per capita income not significantly different from what it was around the Second Opium War.[21]

The third failure at industrialization led to Deng Xiaoping's new economic reform in 1978 — China's fourth attempt to industrialization over 120 years.[22] Boom! This time it worked and stunned the world (including China itself). The shock wave is still reverberating and penetrating economies around the globe. This industrial revolution, detonated by 1.3 billion people, has transformed China and the global economy. With its colossal demand for raw materials, energy resources, and access to the global commercial market, China is mobilizing and powering the entire Asian continent, Latin America, Africa, and even the industrial West

---

[21] To be correct, and fair, each attempt had made some progress but not been sufficient to set off an industrial revolution. For example, with the third attempt China managed to establish a basic (though highly unprofitable) industrial base, which relied heavily on government subsidies through heavy taxation on agriculture. Agricultural productivity, however, significantly improved (except during the Great Leap Forward), life expectancy significantly increased from 35 years in 1949 to 68 years in the late 1970s, infant mortality was slashed from 250 deaths to 40 deaths for every 1,000 live births, the malaria rate dropped from 5.55% of the entire Chinese population to 0.3% of the population (http://en.wikipedia.org/wiki/Healthcare_reform_in_China). However, the increased agricultural productivity was immediately translated into expanded population — from 600 million in 1950 to one billion in the late 1970s, leaving income per capita barely changed from 1949, when the communist regime took power. Hence, the third attempt provided no escape from the Malthusian trap and from the curse of food security.

[22] These repeated stop-and-go or start-and-fail cycles should sound familiar to Latin American countries, such as Argentina, and Africa countries, such as Egypt.

forward, with momentum 20 times the economic force of the emergence of the United States in the late 19th century and 100 times that of the United Kingdom in the early 19th century.[23] To get a sense of the power and scope of China's rise, simply look at China's production and consumption of cement, one of the most basic industrial materials since the Industrial Revolution: The United States consumed a total of 4.5 gigatons of cement in 1901–2000; but China consumed 6.5 gigatons in 2011–2013. China used more cement in those three years than the U.S. has used in the entire 20th century.[24]

ii. China's Legacy and the Plans of the Book

But, China's rise is astonishing not merely for its sheer size, its lightning speed, its absence of any large internal financial crisis that has plagued the 17th to early 21st century industrial powers, or its maneuvers through major political and international turmoil (e.g., the 1989 Tiananmen Square incident, the dramatic collapse of the Soviet Union and Eastern European communism, the 1997 Southeast Asian financial crisis, the 2008 Great Sichuan Earthquake, and the 2008 global recession). China's rise is astonishing also for its broadly peaceful manner.

---

[23] The population was about 10 million for the United Kingdom around 1810, 60 million for the United States around 1890, and one billion for China around 1980, and 1.2 billion for China around 1995.

[24] See http://www.gatesnotes.com/About-Bill-Gates/Concrete-in-China. However, it is worth noting that cement is the chief material of residential construction in China whereas its American counterpart is wood. During the rapid industrialization period of 1850–1910, America consumed 190 million acres of forest, equivalent to 42% of China's total forest reserves today (see http://www.foresthistory. org). Hence, heavy reliance on cement greatly slowed down China's deforestation process during its industrial revolution period (see http://www.natureworldnews. com/articles/13805/20150331/china-helps-reverse-global-forest-loss-with-a-little-bit-of-luck.htm).

China has nearly 20% of the world's population but only 6% of the world's water resources and 9% of the world's arable land.[25] No nation with such challenges has ever achieved industrialization purely through mutually beneficial international trade without repeating the Western industrial powers' historical development paths of colonialism, imperialism, slavery, and technology-led bloody wars against humanity and weaker nations. If anything, China has relied entirely on its own business instinct and inherited political institutions and on the greatest teacher of all — the development experiences of other nations and China's own past failures.

Such a special development path thus deserves an appropriate level of intellectual appreciation and impartial scrutiny. However, China is not and should not be treated as a special case or outlier of economic development. With 1.3 billion people and 56 ethnic groups and a geographic area similar to Europe, it would be too dubious an outlier of economic development. Hence, the case of China offers a golden opportunity to rethink about the entire theory of economic development, to re-ponder on the basic principles of political economy, and to regain insights into the very mechanics of the Industrial Revolution itself.[26]

The goal of this book is therefore two-fold: (i) describe and explain the key pattern of China's rapid industrialization and social-economic changes since 1978; and (ii) use the Chinese experience to shed light on the long-standing puzzle of the Industrial Revolution itself. The intention is to sketch a conceptual framework (called *New Stage Theory* (*NST*) of economic development) that illuminates

---

[25] Despite similar geographic size, arable land per person in China is less than one tenth of that in the United States.

[26] Acemoglu and Robinson (2012) attribute China's growth miracle under an authoritative government and extractive institutions to its severe backwardness and large technological gap from the frontier industrial countries. But the core question of all development economics and all the ink spilled on why nations fail is precisely to explain why backward nations fail to grow despite their backwardness and technological gaps.

the central historical developmental logic shared by both the Industrial Revolution and China's miracle growth.

The NST identifies missing markets and missing market-creators as the key problems of development and emphasizes the important role of government: Industrialization requires a sequence of distinctive stages of market creation, each with its own obstacles, and cannot be accomplished either by autarkic individuals through *laissez faire* (the invisible hand) alone or by the state through a one-time colossal national investment boom via foreign aid or a top-down approach (such as Big Push or Shock Therapy).[27]

Specifically, the NST characterizes economic development as a process of *sequential* market creation and market-structural transformation, from agrarian market structure to proto-industrial market structure and to light-industrial market structure and then to heavy-industrial market structure and finally to service-oriented welfare-state market structure. Each earlier developmental stage or market structure provides the necessary (but not sufficient) developmental conditions for successful (and successive) market creation and structural evolution in the later stages of development. Failure to go through the necessary developmental stages *sequentially* with the right industrial policies will result in developmental failures and disorders, or immature industrialization, such as the "poverty trap" and the "middle-income trap" symptoms, regardless of political institutions (which are endogenous to economic development).

In other words, NST emphasizes that for backward nations to catch up with developed nations, essential repetition of the *key* developmental stages of the British Industrial Revolution in earlier human history is necessary and the only way to achieve successful industrialization, as China's growth miracle has demonstrated once again after the success of the Asian tigers, Japan, West Europe, and

---

[27] The market can be defined as a set of economic and geographical and social conditions under which mutually beneficial (profitable) trade can take place.

North America. Similarly, the dissection of the recent successfully developed economies also sheds light on the secret of the Industrial Revolution itself (because they must share common underlying developmental logic and economic principles despite dramatically different initial social-political and international conditions).[28]

In sketching such a conceptual framework, I hope to find answers to the questions posed by economic historian David Landes when critically reviewing Gerschenkron's (1962) influential development theory of leaping forward via adopting capital-intensive modern efficient technologies:

> "How did backward countries, poor in capital and [skilled] labor, manage to create modern, capital-intensive industry? And how did they manage to acquire the knowledge and know-how? Finally, how did they overcome social, cultural, and institutional barriers to industrial enterprises? How did they create appropriate arrangements and institutions? How did they cope with the strains of change?" (Landes, 1999, p. 274).

---

[28] The conceptual framework embedded in NST is thus analogous to embryology or ontogeny in the field of evolutionary biology that studies the similarities of embryo development across species. Biologists have long noticed that an organism's development may contain clues about its history that biologists can use to build evolutionary trees. Embryos of many different kinds of animals: mammals, birds, reptiles, fish, etc., look very similar and it is often difficult to tell them apart. Many traits of one type of animal appear in the embryo of another type of animal. For example, fish embryos and human embryos both have gill slits. In fish they develop into gills, but in humans they disappear before birth. This shows not only that the animals are intrinsically related with common ancestors and that they develop similarly in history, but also that the basic plan for a creature's beginning remains the same and that it is necessary for the embryos of more advance species (such as humans) to repeat the basic stages (steps) of the earlier evolutionary history of the more primitive species. Analogously, the human race discovered mathematical knowledge sequentially over the past thousands of years: from numbers to arithmetic to algebra to calculus, etc. Yet today's children must repeat this evolutionary process to learn math, except with a faster pace. In this regard, the NST is also closely related to the tradition of the German historical school of economics.

These questions are intriguing because too many developing countries have too often fallen prey to the false development strategy suggested by Gerschenkron (1962),[29] or its variants offered by other schools — such as the institutional theory, the import substitution strategy, the Big Push theory, the shock (Big Bang) therapy, and the structural adjustment program based on the Washington Consensus. These development strategies and theories share one critical feature in common despite their drastically different appearances: They all take the roof of a building for its foundation and the effect for its cause. They take the consequence of Western industrialization for the prerequisite of economic development. They inspire or teach poor agrarian nations to start industrialization by building advanced capital-intensive industries (such as chemical, steel, and automobile industries), or by setting up modern financial systems (such as a floating exchange rate, free international capital flows, and fully-fledged privatization of state-owned properties and natural resources), or by erecting modern political institutions (such as democracy and universal suffrage).

Indeed, why bother to mimic the early 18th century British textile workshops when one can emulate a modern automobile assembly line? Why bother to repeat the old-fashioned 19th century American mercantilism when one can replicate modern Wall Street capitalism? Why bother to live through monarchy when one can enjoy democracy?

However, China's development success since 1978 (and even its previous failures) soundly rejects such naïve philosophies of economic development and views on how the world works. China's

---

[29] Gerschenkron (1962) was right in arguing that the continuously increasing scale and complexity of technologies would make it increasingly necessary for late-developing countries embarking on industrialization to rely more and more on centralized government assistance and powerful institutional vehicles in order to mobilize industrial financing and to catch up with the developed nations. However, he was incorrect to suggest that the way to catch up is to directly embark on modern efficient frontier technologies.

experiences (both good and bad, joyful and painful, successful and failed) show that *correct procedures* of development, *right sequences* of development, and *proper industrial policies and strategies* of development based on a nation's own initial social-political conditions matter. They matter a great deal. They matter not only for individuals' welfare, but also for a nation's survival, dignity, and destiny.

Industrialization is not only a revolutionary change in the mode of production at the firm level, but also an endeavor of state building. It requires the greatest coordination of all social classes and interest groups and the mobilization of all the grassroots population (especially the peasants) and untapped natural and social and political resources. Wrong development strategies and industrial policies can create disastrous and even irreversible consequences for a nation. The free market alone cannot do the job, democracy is not the recipe, whole-sale privatization and financial liberation is not the key, and the neoliberal Washington consensus is not the solution.

Why? Before we start telling the Chinese story, it is worth reemphasizing that China's development since the 1978 reform was very much outside the plan. Rather, it was the outcome of trial and error because no existing economic theories could advise China how to proceed.[30] Even though such theories and advice did exist in the West, China wisely refused to take them blindly without great caution (unlike Africa, Latin America, Russia, and Eastern Europe). To be sure, the path to development after 1978 was a bumpy one and the Chinese government made many mistakes; fortunately, none of them has been fatal, although some did inflict unnecessary pain on the Chinese people. But in its process of trial and error, the Chinese government under Deng Xiaoping's

---

[30] See B. Naughton (1995) for an in-depth description and analysis on China's seemingly chaotic yet systematic trial-and-error approach to reform and development.

leadership also made many correct decisions that turned out to be critical for setting off China's long-awaited industrial revolution. As the institutional theorist and self-proclaimed Chicago School economist Steven N. S. Cheung aptly put:

> "I can easily write a thick book in a week to criticize China. However, the fact that China's miracle growth has been lasting for so long despite so many hostile social-political conditions is truly amazing and unprecedented in human history ... . China must have done something so profoundly right ... . What is it? This is the real challenge."[31]

By reexamining the path traveled by China in the past three decades, we can answer questions such as those posed by David Landes or Steven Cheung. We can see clearly how the Chinese path actually followed the same iron logic of the English Industrial Revolution nearly 250 years ago despite a very different set of initial social-economic conditions and institutional environment. Underneath the superficial differences in political superstructures and institutional rhetoric, the Chinese model of development is essentially the same as the 18th century British model of development, the 19th century American model of development, and the 20th century Japanese model of development.

---

[31] Steven Ng-Sheong Cheung, *China's Economic Institutions* (in Chinese), quoted by Xiaopeng Li (2012, back cover page).

Chapter 2

Key Steps Taken by China to Set Off an Industrial Revolution

i. Food Security and the Malthusian Trap

Despite all the negative images of China's extractive institutions over its long history, China has never lacked innovation and technological changes, even during the late Qing dynasty and Cultural Revolution (1966–1976). But historically, such improvements in technology took place mostly in the agriculture sector and they immediately translated into a larger population instead of an improved average living standard. For example, between 1500 and 1900, China's population quadrupled from 100 million to 400 million, enabled mainly by its rapid agricultural technology innovations and partly by newly acquired arable land. Also, during Mao's communist regime (1949–1976), the life expectancy in China increased from 35 to 68 years and total population increased from 600 million to 1 billion despite no increase in arable land, enabled again by rapid improvement in agricultural productivity. But more crops from the land were used to support more mouths, and so food per mouth experienced no increase. More importantly, despite significantly improved irrigation systems and local roads, crop harvests were still constrained by draught, flood, pestilence, and other natural forces and geographical factors such that consumption fluctuated violently across seasons and years.

Why did the Chinese, unlike the 19th century Britons or the 20th century Americans, choose to use the dramatically increased food supply to support dramatically more babies rather than to get dramatically richer by accumulating dramatically larger amounts of wealth (such as financial claims on food and land)?

Food is a very special type of consumer good: People die (in several days) without it, but its marginal utility diminishes to zero quickly as soon as the stomach is filled. So the utility of possessing colossal amounts of food as a form of wealth is tiny except as insurance against natural disasters. Also, the availability of manufactured goods was extremely limited under the primitive craftsmen workshop mode of production. So, manufactured goods were extremely expensive and trading food for goods was not a viable option of accumulating wealth.[1]

---

[1] In agrarian societies, a piece of clothing may be worth a person's many, many years of labor income, hence very expensive in terms of its relative price to food. Economic historian Carlo M. Cipolla describes the Malthusian trap in preindustrial Europe vividly: "Having bought their food, the mass of the people had little left for their wants, no matter how elementary they were. In preindustrial Europe, the purchase of a garment or of the cloth for a garment remained a luxury the common people could only afford a few times in their lives. One of the main preoccupations of hospital administration was to ensure that the clothes of the deceased 'should not be usurped but should be given to lawful inheritors.' During epidemics of plague, the town authorities had to struggle to confiscate the clothes of the dead and to burn them: People waited for others to die so as to take over their clothes — which generally had the effect of spreading the epidemic. In Prato (Tuscany) during the plague of 1631 a surgeon lived and served in the pest house for about eight months lancing bubos and treating sores, catching the plague and recovering from it. He wore the same clothing throughout. (Carlo M. Cipolla (1994), *Before the Industrial Revolution: European Society and Economy, 1000– 1700*. W.W. Norton & Company. pp. 25–26).

What to do with the surplus good, then? In such an autarkic and unorganized agrarian society — without factories and cars and highways and shopping malls, or a very long life expectancy (only 30–40 years) — what would provide the most joy and utilitarian reward from the additional food? In this environment, it is only rational and optimal to use the extra food to raise extra babies (just like any other animal species). This is the Malthusian trap.

Industrial society is different. The bulk of the labor force is allocated to produce an array of industrial consumer goods — carpets, rugs, curtains, clothes, lingerie, outwears, coats, boots, high-heeled shoes, toys, perfumes, pots, pans, dishes, sofas, beds, chairs, tables, cameras, computers, cell phones, electronics, microwaves, refrigerators, CDs, movies, bikes, cars, airplanes, books, magazines, washing machines, swimming pools, apartments, residential houses, and all the related intermediate goods and machine tools — you name it. For each category of goods, there are also tens or hundreds of brands and varieties within the category to choose from.[2] People can get rich by accumulating an increasing variety of such durable material goods or financial claims on them (money, stocks, equities, and bonds). Money for the first time in human history became no longer simply the medium of exchange on existing goods but also claims on the future possibility of unknown goods yet to be produced and invented. Future(s) can be traded![3]

---

[2] For example, in China's famous square-mile Yiwu trade center for light consumer goods, there are more than 400,000 varieties of commodities on display for wholesale and retail trade. This trade center started as a small and short street with mom-and-pop candy bar shops in the late 1970s and grew into the world's largest trade center for household goods and light industrial commodities in the early 2000s.

[3] The Renaissance and its contemporaneous global exploration had already brought in for ordinary European households far more quantity and variety of consumer goods than they used to consume or afford, such as clocks, art, glasses, spices, tea, coffee, sugar, silk, cotton, wool, leather, rugs, textiles, curtains, clothes, garments, pottery, chinaware, porcelain, paper, prints, books, iron, gun powder, opium, and much more.

Hence, it is the discovery of how to mass-produce the ever-increasing amount and virtually unlimited variety of consumer goods in 18th–19th century England (starting with textiles) that ultimately shifted people's preferences and passions away from making babies to making goods, from accumulating children to accumulating material wealth. This discovery enabled the great escape from the Malthusian trap and defied the law of diminishing marginal utility. After all, it should have been easy for new generations of consumers during the Industrial Revolution to figure out that children and food form only a very tiny subset of the variety of goods and rewards (including affection and love) that people can enjoy, consume, and possess.

In other words, the law of diminishing marginal utility implies that it is optimal to pursue more variety of the same quantity rather than more quantity of the same variety.[4] This increase in the supply and demand of variety does not mean that a population will necessarily decline with income, but only that it will no longer grow as fast as income. Hence, when people's ability to purchase goods increased and the expanding market prompted mass production of a growing variety and quantity of durable consumer goods with rapidly declining prices during the Industrial Revolution in 19th century England, the Malthusian trap eventually ceased to exist.

To recap: The law of diminishing marginal utility applies only to the quantity of goods but not to the variety of goods. So adding new variety into the consumption basket is the only way to break the curse of the law of diminishing marginal utility and escape from the

---

[4] This phenomenon must have existed in any countries prior to their experience of the Industrial Revolution, such as in 17th–18th century England: "[T]here is little doubt that the range of consumer goods to be found in English households broadened considerably during the Restoration and throughout the 18th century" (Wrigley, 2010, p. 71). For more detailed historical analysis of the consumer revolution in 17th–18th century England, see McKendrick, Brewer, and Plumb, 1982; Shammas, 1990; and Weatherill, 1988.

Malthusian trap.[5] Therefore, the Industrial Revolution must be understood not just as a new mode of mass supply of quantities, but as a new mode of mass supply of varieties — far more varieties than Mother Nature had been able to provide in all of human history.

Indeed, demand-oriented mass production and innovation (discovering and inventing new varieties of new consumer goods and intermediate goods and even raw materials) were two prime drivers of capitalism and the Industrial Revolution.

Producing industrial goods also means dramatic changes in people's social-economic relationships and the organization of labor. The new mode of industrial production and its consequent dramatic increase in labor productivity depend critically on teamwork and the coordination among strangers of impersonal specific tasks during specific time units. In short, factory jobs and "[m]odern industrial technologies … are designed for labor forces that are disciplined, conscientious, and engaged. Products flow through many sets of

---

[5] In economic jargon, let U denote a concave utility function, N the number of varieties of consumption goods, and c the quantity of consumption goods for any specific variety. Then under the simplifying assumption of a unit price for both quantity and variety and that utility functions are additive, we can show easily that the total utilities of consuming more varieties with less quantity can exceed those of consuming more quantities with less variety; namely, $N \times U(c) > U(N \times c)$, if the variables $\{N, c\}$ are both sufficiently large. For example, with a square root utility function, we have $Nc^{0.5} > (Nc)^{0.5}$ if $N > 1$; and with a log utility function, we have $N \times \log(c) > \log(N \times c)$ if $c > 1$ and N sufficiently large; e.g., $N > 2$ when $c = 2$, $N > 1.5$ when $c = 3$, and so on. In other words, the larger c is, the smaller is the value of N needed to satisfy the above inequalities, and vice versa. This means that once consumer income reaches a certain level, it is better off to expand the consumption basket along the variety margin than on the quantity margin alone, or to use the same income to purchase more varieties with less quantity of each good than to consume more quantities with less variety. But the preconditions to enable people to make such choices are (i) the availability of new goods and (ii) a sufficiently high income. These two conditions were precisely what the Industrial Revolution created. Also see Desmet and Parente (2012) for a related argument.

hands, each one capable of destroying most of the value of the final output. Error rates by individual workers must be kept low to allow such process to succeed" (Gregory Clark, 2007, p. 15).

It is important to emphasize that such a revolutionary change in the organization of production is not a consequence of purely supply-side technological innovations by a handful of geniuses or inventors, but the consequence of a mass movement — a mobilization, if you will — of the grassroots population (peasants, craftsmen, and merchants) and their profit-driven responses to dramatically increased market demand for manufactured goods. Without sufficient purchasing power of the masses and a commercial network of timely delivery, no single peasant or craftsman or entrepreneur would dare to dramatically increase his/her supply of garments and yarns beyond his/her own consumption needs even if he/she had the technology (say, a spinning jenny) for mass-producing them. Hundreds of thousands of workers, craftsmen, and merchants must be simultaneously coordinated to engage in large-scale coordinated activities of mass production, mass distribution, and mass exchange. Hence, the emergence of a large-scale market with specialization and division of labor requires a society to pay for unprecedented social coordination costs. Such costs were initially borne by the profit-driven merchants but were ultimately paid for by the national economic system through the increased productivity of all social classes via the division of labor. Hence, the existence of a sufficiently large, organized, violence-free, robbery-free, credible, and unified market is the prerequisite of mass production and division of labor. Countries that fail to create such a politically stable market that supports specialization, division of labor, and mass production would remain in an autarkic agrarian equilibrium.

The *income elasticity of consumption* matters greatly in triggering such an epic revolutionary transition from family-based autarkic agrarian production to factory-based industrial mass production. The concept has to do with, first, securing what is necessary and then, if there is surplus (wealth, labor, time, etc.), obtaining what is useful. Consider some simple facts of biology: People do not die immediately if they go without consuming any of the industrial goods (as they do if they go without food) for weeks, months, years, or even a lifetime. In economic jargon, industrial goods are income elastic, which means there is some flexibility in the decisions to purchase industrial goods or not. Food is not income elastic; we need it. (By the way, children, or the love and affection received from and given to them are income elastic too).[6] Consider some simple facts of history: If Mao had allotted slightly more people to food production instead of steel production in 1959 during the Great Leap Forward, the Great Famine in China would probably have been avoided and tens of millions of lives would have been saved, precisely because the demand for food is not income/price elastic. Steel is not substitutable for food and crops cannot be produced in factories or at all times of the year (i.e., not only food demand is non-elastic but is also crop supply).[7]

So the question is how to supply an increasing amount and variety of new consumer goods (as imperfect substitutes for food and babies) with a finite labor force without jeopardizing food security? Peasants in agrarian societies must work continuously for long

---

[6] From a dynastic viewpoint, children are also income *inelastic*. The human race would become extinct without creating enough children, but more children beyond the need for survival need of the race have diminishing necessity.

[7] During the Great Leap Forward, farmers were organized like soldiers in the army, working and taking breaks together in the rice fields, eating together in collective dining halls, and counting on the government officials (much like military officers) to organize and manage food supplies (as during battles). Therefore, the social planners never considered the idiosyncratic needs for individuals to smooth individual consumption over the year through individual savings (self-storage of food). A sophisticated social insurance system was impossible and beyond the financial and organizational capacity of the government in 1950s China. This was what made the food shortage a grand-scale disaster. The Great Famine caused about 15–30 million deaths (including natural deaths), roughly 5% of the peasant population of 540 million.

hours on land to maintain subsistence-level living standards in the Malthusian equilibrium. In such societies, both leisure time and consumption levels are dictated by weather and seasons. Draught, flood, disease, natural disasters, famine, and wars fought over the monopoly rights and power to control and expropriate others are the norm in agricultural societies.

The Industrial Revolution means first that an increasing fraction of the population must stop producing food on farms and start producing industrial goods in factories. With the risk of food security, this labor reallocation is not feasible unless agricultural productivity can be simultaneously increased so that the same amount of land can yield no smaller amount of food but with less labor.[8] Mao probably understood this logic in 1959 when he allocated about 30–50 million farmers (10%–20% of China's then rural labor force) to produce steel.[9] But he overestimated the productivity of organized teamwork on farm land, overlooked the lack of *scale* effects of primitive agricultural production, and underestimated the rapidly diminishing marginal product of labor on land, resulting in a severe food shortage in 1960 and 1961.

But between 1978 and 1988, China gradually relocated from 30 to 90 million farmers each year to work in village-factories, yet

---

[8] Or alternatively, a country can rely on food imports if it has sufficient natural resources to trade in the world market. But this is a risky approach in terms of food security. Poor countries simply do not have the capacity and sophisticated distribution system to effectively allocate imported food across farmers and households. Even industrialized Japan today refuses to rely on food imports to reduce its expensive agricultural prices.

[9] About six million village firms were set up in the single year of 1958. If each firm employed 5–10 workers, the total number of farmer-worker would be 30–60 million. Also, statistics show that after the Great Famine in 1961–1962, the government relocated 50 million people back to rural land, the bulk of them were dismissed from village firms.

without suffering any food shortages and without importing food from outside the country. During that 10-year period, China's rural industrial output increased by nearly 15-fold, equivalent in magnitude to what Lucas (2003) and McCloskey (2010) have called the greatest, most mysterious increase in income in the World since the English Industrial Revolution. An even more dramatic increase in income in China is forthcoming in the next decade. But with just the initial 10 years of hyper-growth, China by 1988 had already successfully escaped from the Malthusian trap without jeopardizing its food security.[10] How did China accomplish this? What were its secrets to breaking the curses of food security and the Malthusian trap?

ii. A Primitive Agricultural Revolution

Agricultural production (for both traditional and modern techniques) is special. It has always required little teamwork and incorporation of individuals beyond the family members. In agriculture, the rate of return to the division, specialization, and coordination among a large body of labor force is low and extremely limited — unlike the pin factory visited by Adam Smith, or the labor-intensive mass-production textile factories in late 19th century England, or the Ford automobile assembly lines in early 20th century America. Crop growing is governed entirely by the natural biological cycle of plants, can hardly be arbitrarily divided into many intermediate stages or intermediate goods, and is land intensive and nature (weather, season, and daylight) sensitive, so it is subject to rapidly diminishing returns to labor and to any large-scale organizations of labor.

Hence, Mao's idea of organizing farming into large units or communes with hundreds and thousands of farmers in each working unit (as in the army) to boost agricultural productivity was a large

---

[10] China lifted all rationings on food, meat, and light industrial consumer goods such as garments and ended its "shortage economy."

and rather stupid mistake.[11] Because of the lack of complementarity among individual farmers' efforts in agriculture, free-rider moral-hazard problems can easily arise in large organized forms of teamwork regardless of property rights. Even in the development history of Western industrial countries, agriculture has always been the last sector to be industrialized (that is, mechanized) or to achieve the economies of scale with heavy machinery equipment. For example, fully fledged mechanized farming did not take place in the United States until the 1940s, compared with the mechanization of the textile industry in the middle 1800s.

Although a free market system would have naturally avoided Mao's mistakes under centrally planned collective farming, it by no means implies that a free market would have automatically solved China's food security problems and detonated China's agricultural revolution and industrial revolution. It did not in the Qing dynasty and the Republic era, so why would it do so in the 1950s or the 1980s?[12]

Deng's 1978 reform to tear down the large farming units and revert to the family-based natural units was the correct step to raise agricultural productivity regardless of the ownership of land. But this change meant going back to the production mode before communism. During the Qing dynasty (before 1911) and the Republic

---

[11] Due to the poor endowment of China's natural resources, Mao was compelled to use agricultural crops to exchange for heavy industrial equipment with the Soviet Union to jump-start China's industrial revolution. Also, Mao was impressed by Soviet Union's mechanized farming, yet China did not have machines except lots of labor. So Mao thought he could use labor to substitute for machines in large-scale farming, as also implied by the neoclassical Cobb-Douglas production function. But this is tragically wrong and misleading.

[12] Private land and alienable rights were very secure in the Qing dynasty and the Republican China (see, e.g., K. Pomeranz, 2001; and Taisu Zhang, 2011). However, such institutional arrangements did not help China solve its food security problem and render farmers immune to natural disasters; famine was quite common during the Qing dynasty and the Republic era.

era (1912–1949), agriculture in China was organized based on family units, but did not lead to agricultural self-sufficiency or break the curses of food security and the Malthusian trap. What was critically lacking in the Qing dynasty and the Republic era was not private property rights. Instead, it was (i) the lack of residual claim rights for the farmers in the so-called "market-determined" contracts between land owners and peasants; (ii) the lack of a network of village-level irrigation systems and public roads connecting villages and the townships (this lack of infrastructure and its associated market size for commercialized agricultural products made family-based farming highly unproductive in the Qing dynasty and Republic era despite private land ownership, because of the unbearable risk of agricultural specialization imposed on farmers from droughts and flood and other natural disasters); and (iii) the lack of any rural industrialization to promote demand for diversified agricultural goods and to absorb the surplus labor in the countryside (we will analyze this issue in detail later).

Mao's government built for rural China the local irrigation, hydro dam, and road infrastructure systems during the Great Leap Forward and his nearly 30-year rule of China. These infrastructure systems (based on Mao's notion of large collective farming units) actually provided a technological foundation that led to increased productivity for family-based agricultural system during Deng's agricultural reform era — despite the fact that land remained collectively owned under Deng's economic reform.[13]

---

[13] By 2009 China had 87,085 hydro dams, but more than 99% of them (86,258) were built between 1949 and 1978. In fact, Mao's communism period organized Chinese peasant-farmers to build more than 80% of China's existing rural canal and irrigation systems, which tremendously benefited Deng's family-based responsibility system (see, e.g., http://www.snzg.cn/article/2009/0210/article_13384.html). Ironically, Deng's family responsibility reform has greatly reduced the incentives of farmers and local village governments to invest in large-scale irrigation systems.

Moreover, under Deng's reform, farmers had the incentives to work harder than before because the payoff (the actual money reward) was linked to individual effort — again, despite public land ownership. Farmers were given a 15- or 30-year lease contract for land and the freedom to decide (i) what crops to grow based on market demand and (ii) when and how long to work. The productivity of land varies greatly depending on the type of soils and crops planted. This system allowed farmers to maximize output by growing diversified crops more suitable for the soil quality and type and be more responsive to market demand.

Second and more importantly, under Deng's new incentive-mechanism design, farmers became the residual claimers on the output they produced after meeting government quotas. So they worked harder and longer hours and could fully use evenings and seasonal leisure time as they desired. Women and children became an important part of the agricultural labor force in the family by doing sideline work, such as raising pigs and weaving cloth.

Again, some of these elements were also present in the Qing dynasty and Republic era. However, a critical difference is that, even though land was privately owned (by landlords) in the Qing dynasty and the Republic era, farmers did not have discretionary power and incentives to be entrepreneurial because they were not the *residual claimers* of the output produced from the land. They were much closer to wage earners in a firm. The landlords were the residual claimers. However, under Deng's reform, even though farmers did not own the land (it was only leased to them), they could do whatever they wanted with the land after achieving their government-specified quotas. (One exception is that they could not buy or sell land or the quotas in the market at that time.)[14] This new "institutional" arrangement was sufficient to provide the needed

---

[14] Today, Chinese farmers can re-lease their land to agricultural entrepreneurs through the market even though the ownership of land remains public. The entrepreneurs then make profits by applying mechanized farming method on the hundreds

incentives for efficient farming, profit seeking, entrepreneurship, and innovation in the agricultural sector without land privatization or a "counter-revolution."

Most importantly, because of better connections and access to bigger outside markets, agricultural-product specialization (primitive division of labor in the agricultural sector) became more profitable and less risky (in terms of jeopardizing food security under weather shocks and natural disasters), thanks to the irrigation, electricity, and road infrastructure system built before 1978 under Mao's collective farming era.

All these factors combined led to an unprecedented agricultural productivity boom in China in the early years of the reform after 1978.[15]

As a result of this primitive agricultural revolution, the aggregate agricultural output in China increased significantly and steadily. For example, crop output rose permanently by more than 20% in 1980 alone. However, as discussed earlier, this 20% permanent increase in agricultural output in 1980 could have been used to support an additional 200 million babies.[16] But the additional millions of new mouths did not come. One reason is the one-child policy implemented in 1979 by the central government. Another reason is that another revolution — the rural industrialization that offered an ever-increasing variety of consumption goods as substitutes for babies — was also underway.[17]

---

of land plots they collected (rented) from the individual farmer households. So both the farmers and the entrepreneurs are better off under the new contract.

[15] England experienced a similar primitive agricultural revolution from the 16th to 18th century that proceed the Industrial Revolution. See, e.g., http://en.wikipedia. org/wiki/British_Agricultural_Revolution and the references therein. For a critical review, see Gregory Clark (2002).

[16] China's agriculture was supporting one billion people in the late 1970s and early 1980s.

[17] China has significantly relaxed the one-child policy for years now but young people, even those in the countryside, no longer want more than one child. This

iii. A Proto-Industrialization in the Rural Areas

A well-documented phenomenon in China's early development stage after the 1978 reform was the emergence (even mushrooming) of the so-called township-village-enterprises (TVEs) across China's vast countryside.[18] Village industries flourished because (i) farmers wanted to find new ways to make money or to substitute for their subsistence-level farming income; and (ii) local village and township governments also wanted (and were required by Deng) to find ways to rapidly develop their local economies and help farmers become wealthier and escape from poverty and the Malthusian trap.

Even though the phenomenon of the mushrooming of collectively owned village enterprises in China is well known, its relation to the economic history of the West and its economic significance in triggering China's industrial revolution has not been well understood. But from a historical perspective, such a "Chinese-style" rural industrialization is in fact reminiscent of the proto-industrialization that took place in 17th and 18th century England for two hundred years right before the Industrial Revolution (see Franklin F. Mendels, 1972, for his seminal analysis of the phenomenon of proto-industrialization in history).[19]

Throughout the 17th century (1600–1700) and the first half of the 18th century that preceeded the English Industrial Revolution, a

---

unpredicted outcome is generating concerns for the government because of China's rapidly aging population.

[18] The literature on China's TVE phenomenon is vast. See, e.g., Xu and Zhang (2009), "The Evolution of Chinese Entrepreneurial Firms: Township-Village Enterprises Revisited" and the references therein.

[19] Also see Mendels' (1981) book, *Industrialization and Population Pressure in 18th-Century Flanders*, which was based on his doctoral dissertation in 1969 at the University of Wisconsin; as well as Kriedte, Medick, and Schlumbohm (1977), *Industrialization before Industrialization: Rural Industry in the Genesis of Capitalism*, translated by Beate Schmpp, and the references therein.

rural industrialization was also taking place in England. During this process, more and more English peasant families, including women and children, got involved in manufacturing, more and more peasant households opted to specialize in textiles and other products as the market deepened, and more and more family-based cartage industries were transformed into cooperation-based proto-industries (that involved specialization and long-distance trade) in the countryside. Over one and a half centuries of market fermentation and organizational development these part-time peasant workers and village firms eventually transformed into full-time workers and large-scale factories when mass production became the critical means for merchants and capitalists to win competition for domestic and international market shares.[20]

As noted earlier, a proto-industrialization was necessary for detonating the Industrial Revolution because mass production-based industrialization requires a deep and large market to render the further division of labor and large cooperations profitable, which in turn relies on sufficiently high incomes (wages) and purchasing power of the grassroots population, which in turn requires transforming and drawing a large pool of the autarkic peasants into the cooperation-based manufacturing and industrial organizations, yet without jeopardizing food security. Hence, starting from the countryside by utilizing rural surplus labor and farmers' spare time to produce primitive low value-added labor-intensive manufacturing goods *locally* is the economical and natural way to "ferment" the mass market, nurture entrepreneurship, develop a national ecosystem of supply chains and distribution networks and industrial

---

[20] The fact that early British industries all started in the countryside, instead of big commercial cities such as London, is also well documented by T. S. Ashton (1970) in his seminal book "*The Industrial Revolution 1760–1830*." In addition to the food security dilemma, setting up factories in the cities from the very beginning and hosting massive amounts of peasant workers and providing sleeping spaces for them would have been extremely costly and hence uneconomic in the early stages of development.

clusters, raise industrial demand and the productivity of a commerce-based agricultural sector, increase farmer income, generate government revenues for infrastructure, and eventually kick-start an industrial revolution.

The only critical difference between China's rural industrialization and the European or British proto-industrialization was that, in Europe or Great Britain, it was primarily the merchants that took the initiatives to facilitate, finance, and organize the village industries and trade: They engaged and recruited the peasants to work cooperatively; they coordinated the production systems and artisan workshops in the manufacturing of labor-intensive consumer goods (mostly textiles)[21]; and they distributed the goods nationwide and worldwide (e.g., from the emergence of the rudimentary "putting-out" system all the way to the emergence of large factories in rural areas).[22] So in Europe and Great Britain, the catalysts ("economic enzymes") of market creation and rural industrial organization were the merchants. In China, however, that entrepreneurial role of market creation and rural industrial organization was played in the early stages essentially by the local village-level and township-level governments. (A more detailed analysis on the formation of rural

---

[21] Other types of proto-industries included metal extraction and metal working, leather manufacturing, wood working, mining, and so on.

[22] The putting-out system was a system of family-based domestic manufacturing that was prevalent in rural areas of western Europe during the 17th and 18th centuries. It appeared even earlier in 16th century Italy. Domestic workers involved in this system typically owned their own primitive tools (such as looms and spinning wheels) but depended on merchant capitalists to provide them with the raw materials to fashion products that were deemed the property of the merchants. Semi-finished products would be passed on by the merchant to another workplace for further processing, while finished products would be taken directly to market by the merchants (see, e.g., http://www.encyclopedia.com/topic/Putting-Out_System.aspx at Encyopedia.com). Even independent domestic craftsmen working on their own account also relied on merchants to dispose their products in distant markets.

industries led by mercantilist Chinese governments will be provided later.)[23]

The "Chinese style" rural industrialization through the emergence of a massive number of (collectively owned) township and village firms since 1978 immediately ended China's shortage economy caused by central planning during Mao's era: In less than five years after the 1978 reform, China successfully lifted all rationings imposed on food, meat, textiles, and other light industrial consumer products.

But the rural industrialization also kick-started China's long-awaited industrial revolution and economic takeoff around the late 1980s and early 1990s. At that time, however, China still largely remained agrarian and poor; it still relied heavily on primitive technologies in the rural industrial sector. Hence, very few people (except maybe the architect Deng Xiaoping himself) were able to

---

[23] The key distinction between urban craftsmen workshops and proto-industries is that the former satisfied only local and restricted markets whereas the latter geared to national and international markets. Craftsmen workshops existed throughout Europe (as well as other parts of the world such as ancient China and India) long before the Industrial Revolution and were located mostly in towns where they catered for the demand of the local urban population and the agrarian community of the surrounding countryside. But such workshops would not be recognized as proto-industries and they did not evolve into factory production. Proto-industries compete for national and international markets and tend to be located in the rural areas because of abundant cheap labor. When the volume of demand (market size) is large, labor costs become the most critical concern for merchants in profit maximization, provided that the marginal cost of transportation does not increase significantly with distance — which is true for villages near rivers, canals, or national transportation networks. This explains why European proto-industries (or Chinese township-village enterprises) prospered more easily in a nation's coastal areas than inner mountainous areas. On the other hand, towns located in manufacturing zones served principally as centers of trade and commerce, and the merchants who organized proto-industries by supplying credit and distribution networks and raw materials to rural manufacturers lived in towns.

grasp or recognize the village industry's profound significance and the fact that China was at the doorstep of detonating an Industrial Revolution. This lack of recognition is not surprising, given that the initial phase of the Industrial Revolution is never as dramatic or revolutionary as people would have thought or imagined. Cases in point: Even Adam Smith, T. R. Malthus, David Ricardo, and John Stuart Mill were completely unaware of the English Industrial Revolution that was unfolding in front of their eyes between middle 18th century and early 19th century England, let alone the proto-industrialization in early 17th to middle 18th century Europe. It was not until the end of the First British Industrial Revolution and the start of the Second Industrial Revolution (i.e., around 1840s–1860s) that the full force and historical significance of the "primitive accumulation" and the Industrial Revolution itself was felt and recognized by a few insightful political economists, such as Karl Marx and Friedrich Engels.

Hence, following the same logical historical path of the British Industrial Revolution, China's industrial revolution also started primarily in the countryside with tens of millions of village enterprises in the vastly impoverished rural areas since the late 1970s and early 1980s; with the help of local governments these village firms were organized and managed by the uneducated peasants who were not much different from their Qing Dynasty ancestors in 17th and 18th centuries China (except maybe without the "pigtails"). Some economic historians and the human-capital school of development attribute China's failure to attain industrialization in the 17th and 18th centuries to the lack of education among these peasant farmers. But it was essentially the same type of uneducated peasant farmers who in fact ignited China's industrial revolution in the late 20th century.

The Chinese proto-industrialization was unprecedented in both scale and speed, compared with the 200 years for proto-industrialization to occur in Great Britain but even compared with the rapid proto-industrialization in Germany and the United States (about 100 years in the middle 18th to the middle 19th centuries). Between 1978 and 1988, within a 10-year period after the reform, the number of village firms in China increased more than 12-fold, from 1.5 million to 18.9 million; village industrial gross output increased more than 13.5-fold, from 51.5 billion yuan (14% of GDP) to 702 billion yuan (46% of GDP); village employment increased more than three-fold, from 28 million to 95 million; farmers' aggregate wage income increased 12-fold, from 8.7 billion yuan to 96.3 billion yuan; village firms' total capital stock increased more than nine-fold, from 23 billion yuan to 210 billion yuan. In the meantime, village workers as a fraction of the total rural labor force increased from 9% to 23%.[24]

This explosive growth continued throughout the 1990s and 2000s; like setting off a nuclear chain reaction, expansion leads to more expansion, and growth leads to more growth. By the year 2000, the number of village-firm workers had reached more than 128 million (not including the migrant workers in the cities), accounting for a remarkable 30% of China's entire rural labor force. Village industrial gross output reached 11.6 trillion, another 16.5-fold increase compared with its 1988 value, or 225 times higher than its 1978 value. The average growth rate of village-industrial output was 28% per year between 1978 and 2000, doubling every three years for 22 years. Even if we adjust for inflation,[25] the *real* growth rate would still stand at 21% per year (twice as fast as China's real GDP growth during that period, doubling every 3.7 years), and the total increase in *real* gross output of village industries was at least 66-fold over the 1978–2000 period. This scale and speed of long-lasting economic growth is unique in economic history.

With this immense scale and lightning speed of growth through a proto-industrialization (1978–1988) and a first industrial

---

[24] Data source: Appendix Table 1 in "A Short History of China's Village Enterprises," by Zhang Yi and Zhang Song-song, 2001, Chinese Agricultural Publication.

[25] The average CPI inflation rate in that period was 6.9% per year.

revolution (1988–1998), a Rostow (1960) moment of economic *takeoff* was bound to happen. This moment arrived around 1995–2000 when China's per capita GDP reached around $1,000 in year 2000. But $1,000 may be an arbitrary number, which the World Bank often uses it as a threshold measure for entering the middle-income country club, since many Latin American countries had per capita income several or even more than ten times as high as this, but yet lacked the dynamism to move forward. What really mattered for China was that by this point its capacity to mass-produce light consumer/industrial goods[26] and its domestic and foreign markets for "Made in China" goods were immensely large. So large in fact that the manufacturing sector's demand (purchasing power) for energy, locomotives, infrastructure, and machinery equipment was so great that the mass production of these heavy industrial goods became immensely profitable in China.

Hence, around 1995–2000, China was already at the doorstep of its second industrial revolution — which would involve the mass production of machinery (among other things) by means of machinery.[27] In particular, by the early 2000s after China joined the WTO, China formally entered the phase of heavy-industrial buildup (financed by its colossal domestic savings and international market demand for textiles and other light consumer/industrial goods) and kick-started the mass production of chemicals, cement, electricity, steel, metal products, combustion engines, trucks, automobiles, ships, highways, railroads, high-speed trains, and agricultural and textile machineries as well as assembly lines and machine tools for producing all sorts of light industrial goods such as electronics, computers, refrigerators, motorcycles, TV sets, washing machines, furniture, so on and so forth. The Asian financial crisis in 1997 did not stop China. The 2007 worldwide financial crisis (that nearly

---

[26] China became the world's largest textile producer and exporter in 1995.

[27] "It was one thing to spin and weave cotton; quite another to make the machines that did the work" (David Landes, 1999, p. 380).

permanently reduced China's export volume by more than 40% below trend) also did not stop China. An economy seems robust to crisis once it has finished the proto-industrialization, just like the United States in the 19th century: It experienced 15 financial crises and a four-year civil war, none of which stopped the robust rise of America to become the next world manufacturing center and superpower.

One way to formalize (in simple economic jargon) China's development experience in the 1980s and 1990s is to imagine two different technologies: (i) a primitive technology with the production function $y = n^{0.5}$ and (ii) an industrial technology with the production function, $y = 2n - 100$ where y is output and n is labor input. More specifically, assume that output is used only for trade in the market. The second technology involves fixed costs of 100, which may reflect the costs of daily operations or the amortization of costs in innovation, organization, or initial investment involved in setting up industries.

The first technology is subject to diminishing marginal product of labor (land intensive) and the second is not. Labor is obviously more productive in the second production technology in terms of its marginal product. However, when the market demand is small (say $y = 1$ unit), then using the first technology is clearly more profitable. The second technology would require at least 51 units of labor as input to break even with positive revenue net of the 100 units of fixed costs. But as soon as the market demand for y increases, say from 1 to 10 units of output, then using the first technology would require 100 units of labor whereas the second technology would require only 55 units of labor.

Now imagine that there are 200 families in a village with one unit of labor in each family. If they produce independently, the aggregate GDP of this village is 200 units. But if they can find a way to form a factory to engage in joint production through teamwork based on the division of labor by using the second technology, then the GDP of this village would be 300. More importantly, the more families the village has, the more extra output and productive force there is for using the second mode of production. Hence, the size of the market determines the extent of the division of labor (corporation) and new technology adoption.

But where does the mass market come from and who would create the market in the first place?

iv. Ideological Shift toward Commerce and Commercialism

"[I]t is ideas, not vested interests, which are dangerous for good or evil" (John Maynard Keynes, [1936] 1964, pp. 383–384).

Ironically, the proto-industrial revolution unleashed in China's rural areas after 1978 was attempted and envisioned first by Mao in 1958 and served as one of his fundamental development strategies during the Great Leap Forward movement. The initial 1.52 million village firms in 1978 were the legacy of the Great Leap Forward and served as the catalyst of China's long-awaited rural industrialization.

Mao was the son of peasants and a politician-turned military strategist who led the Long March and fought in the Sino-Japanese War and the civil war by organizing and mobilizing the peasantry and China's entire mass grassroots population. He understood well that the root cause of China's poverty was not merely the lack of capital, but the lack of organization. Mao told his government officials that China's industrial revolution must rely on disciplined and organized peasants in the countryside and start with a massive number of small rural manufacturing sites. Such rural manufacturing firms should produce basic farming tools and household goods to meet farmers' production and daily-life needs. He conjectured that gradual upgrading of technologies and the scales of operations in such rural industries would ultimately transform the countryside and greatly facilitate China's modernization and heavy industrial buildup in the cities.[28]

---

[28] See "A Short History of China's Village Enterprises," by Zhang Yi and Zhang Song-song, 2001.

But after the overenthusiastic farmers and local governments established 6 million village factories in 1958 and relocated approximately 50 million farmers to these village factories in a single year, a severe food shortage and famine soon followed (in 1960), causing a sharp three-year decline in China's agricultural sector specifically and recession throughout the entire economy. After the great famine, Mao's village-industrial movement was completely abandoned.[29]

Why did the Great Leap Forward generate results so different from those of the 1978–1988 rural industrialization? Notwithstanding the inefficient farming units and labor organizations on farm land, some of the differences are, at their core, philosophical (ideological). Under Mao, resources were allocated and production was determined according to government plans, rather than through a market-based demand-orientated mechanism. In short, there was no true commerce. And this was by design: Mao viewed commerce as the fundamental source of exploitation and inconsistent with Marx's labor theory of value; thus, he saw a market-allocation mechanism as a contradiction of the government's efforts to achieve an equitable industrialization for all.

But in 1978, China's leadership had gained a more expansive perspective. Deng Xiaoping had observed 20th century prosperity under capitalism and shortages (and worse) under socialism. Income equality was still a goal, but Deng came to believe that prosperity with income equality was not achievable in a single step. Some people were going to become rich ahead of everyone else. With an eye on future income equality, Deng put prosperity instead of equality as the first priority and viewed market exchange and central planning not as inherently contradictory but as plausibly complementary.

---

[29] The number of village firms declined sharply from 6 million to 117,000 in 1960, further down to 47,000 in 1970, but gradually climbed up to 1.52 million in 1978 after Mao secretly gave green lights to facilitate village firms toward the end of the Cultural Revolution.

Today, some capitalistic, developed economies in the West include elements of socialism and government-engineered development policies. Therefore, why couldn't socialistic China also adopt both a market-based allocation of resources and central planning as tools to achieve industrialization? The former (the market) would help achieve microeconomic efficiency based on individual productivity and competition, whereas social planning would help achieve macroeconomic efficiency based on strategic planning and aggregate management (similar to managing a giant company).

But the market relies on commerce. As the most critical microeconomic force to connect demand and supply, commerce builds, creates, deepens, and nurtures markets; channels goods to meet their demand; provides information about the two ends of the market; encourages profit-seeking and arbitrage behaviors to eliminate inefficiency and firm-level resource misallocations; and is thus the pathway of the market and the lubricant of the industrial wheel by materializing the market's fundamental "natural selection" mechanism for "good" and "bad" firms and serving as the "invisible" matchmaker between specialized demand and supply under the division of labor. However, absolutely free markets without regulations and macro management breed inequality and speculative behavior and can lead to macroeconomic instability and economic crisis. Absolutely free markets also encourage short-sighted self-interested behavior that inflict negative side-effects on society and may conflict with long-term social goals. Thus, markets require macroeconomic coordination, guidance, management, regulation, and planning. Considering all this, Deng hoped to introduce micro-level market mechanisms to resolve the rigidity of central planning (as manifested under Mao's era) while maintaining the government's ability and administrative power to coordinate, discipline, manage, regulate and supervise the macro economy, and design long-term development strategies for the nation.

Mao and Deng both saw market failures, the lack of long-term development strategies, the lack of state power in organizing the peasantry and grassroots population and providing social order and maintaining political stability as the root cause of the miserable failures of the Qing Dynasty and Republic era in achieving industrialization. Without such macroeconomic and political strength, China was unable to defend its national interests in the face of the Western imperial powers in the 19th century and Japanese military invasion in the 20th century, let alone competing with these imperial powers. Above all, Deng believed that a strong government and a powerful state would ensure political stability and social order and defend China's national interests and, in turn, that stability and social order would ensure China's industrialization under open-door policies and economic reform (including the introduction of free markets into segments of the national economy). Deng also believed that many heavy industries involving infrastructure and national security would need to continue to rely on a powerful government and national banking system to mobilize resources. Hence, Deng refused to throw the baby out with the bathwater when he introduced market competition into China's social planning model in the late 1970s. He fiercely rejected democracy and "shock therapy" amidst the collapse of the Soviet Union and Eastern European communism. He said frankly in private conversations with foreign leaders in the 1980s, before the Soviet Union's spectacular collapse, that the Russian political leaders were "naïve and stupid."[30]

How did Deng's strategy of (free market + central planning) complementarity unfold? From 16th to 18th century in Europe, commerce and long-distance trade flourished under strong state-supported commercialism and mercantilist ideology; this commerce was critical for Europe's proto-industrialization and a pre-condition

---

[30] See Ezra F. Vogel's 2013 book "Deng Xiaoping and the Transformation of China." Also see http://www.economist.com/node/21533354. Also see Chrystia Freeland's vivid descriptions of Russia's horrifying economic and political collapse under "shock therapy" (Chrystia Freeland (2000), *Sale of the Century: Russia's Wild Ride from Communism to Capitalism*).

for the English Industrial Revolution because it created and "fermented" the required mass market for supporting mass production.[31] Under Deng's gradualist and pragmatic economic policy and development strategies, commerce was not only *allowed* but also *promoted* by local governments. Deng's government not only encouraged commerce and merchant activities after the reform, especially in the countryside, but also subsidized and even directly participated in them using all sorts of government resources. Deng's analogy for this approach is straightforward: "It does not matter if the cat is black or white as long as it catches the rat." If rural commerce can make farmers better off, then the government should not only allow it but also support and facilitate it. So commerce flourished both across the countryside and within cities after 1978. In fact, China immediately became a nation of "shopkeepers." A popular slogan at that time for urban public employees was "Jump into the sea of commerce, Comrades!"[32]

---

[31] Historians and economists (including Karl Marx and Friedrich List) have long noted the intimate connection between the "commerce revolution" in 16th–18th century Europe and the subsequent British Industrial Revolution in the late 18th century (for the case of American development in commerce and its subsequent industrial revolution, see Alfred D. Chandler, Jr. (1977), *The Visible Hand: The Managerial Revolution in American Business*). Commerce creates mass markets, thus paving the way for an industrial revolution, which relies critically on mass markets to render mass production profitable. From the aggregate view point, a commerce revolution could by itself generate as much income growth as an industrial revolution except that the former is not driven primarily by technological change. This explains the puzzle that historians could not detect a significant breaking point and acceleration in GDP growth in the late 18th century at the point of the British Industrial Revolution. This also helps to explain why in the 1860s Japan was far more prepared and equipped than China to deal with the challenge of opening up to the Western industrial powers and benefiting from it. Japan experienced a long boom in commerce in the 18th and 19th centuries Tokugawa period, whereas commerce was severely restricted for several hundred years during the Qing dynasty and completely forbidden under Mao's communist regime.

[32] Napoleon was correct in seeing the United Kingdom as "a nation of shopkeepers." But it was precisely commerce that transformed the U.K. from an agrarian

Achieving this enthusiasm for commerce was no mean feat for communist China. It required a fundamental ideological shift in what people believed and in what people had perceived as "right and wrong" or "good and bad."[33] As economic historian Joel Mokyr points out:

> "Economic change in all periods depends, more than most economists think, on what people believe" (Joel Mokyr, 2009, p. 1).

The government-promoted commercialization and rural industrialization soon formed a colossal unified domestic market. Mom-and-Pop shops and commercialism in general (that is, commerce and competition for a higher living standards or "keeping up with the Wangs") were flourishing everywhere across the countryside and within cities. The awakened mercantile spirit and rapidly emerging commerce networks greatly facilitated commercial exchange, reduced market transaction costs, deepened and expanded the market size for all types of goods, and greatly stimulated village firms' division of labor and specialization in production as well as the demand for intermediate goods and raw materials available in rural areas. In fact, what had been a centuries-long natural "market-fermentation" process accomplished in 17th and 18th century England before the British Industrial Revolution was greatly compressed in China: It took merely a decade.[34]

Hence, what went wrong for the rural industrialization movement during the 1958–1962 Great Leap Forward was not only that

---

island to an industrial power, a fundamental process which laid the basis for a century of British hegemony after the Battle of Waterloo.

[33] Commerce has been perceived in communist China and elsewhere in history as naturally encouraging and justifying self-interested arbitrage behavior, materialism, and strategies for personal gain over public welfare.

[34] Today, Chinese merchants are distributed in all corners of the world, such as Europe, central Asia, Latin America, and Africa, to facilitate the creation of foreign markets and the export of "Made in China," very much similar to the British and European merchants in the 17th–19th century.

too many farmers were allocated to village factories that caused the food shortage, but also that village factories were set only to meet local village demand instead of broader market demand such as the national/international market demand (because there was no commerce and hence no market!). Given the colossal fixed costs (relative to income) involved in organizing and setting up firms (even at a relatively small scale compared with modern industry), the lack of markets necessarily implies very limited division of labor, very limited specialization of production and products, overcapacity and insufficient operational scale to cover the fixed costs; such village industries were thus unproductive and irresponsive to demand, thus impossible to have competitive pressure to correct production-decision errors, hence much less efficient than smaller-scaled family-based handicraft workshops.[35]

v. Mercantilist Governments as Market Creators and Commerce Organizers

As we mentioned earlier, mercantilism is in its essence an economic nationalism for state building based on commerce and manufacturing. It seeks to enrich the country by encouraging exports of manufactured goods. In other words, it emphasizes and promotes manufacturing over agriculture and commercialism over physiocracy.

In a primitive agrarian society, the family is the basic unit of production and exchange. The family members produce everything they need and there is little incentive to specialize and produce more than what is needed through the division of labor, because of the lack of an organized market. It is risky to specialize in producing just one type of household good and to depend on other sources for

---

[35] In 1958, the average size of a village firm was more than eight workers, whereas that in the 1980s and even 1990s it was less than six workers despite a significantly larger domestic and international market for village firms in the 80s and 90s.

other necessary goods: Food security is the highest priority, and the lack of any "insurance" for failed sales in the market is daunting. Yet, the division of labor and separation of demand and supply through specialization is the key to improving labor productivity. Hence, the emergence of mass commerce or large-scale trade beyond the sphere of local villages is a pre-condition for proto-industrialization and the Industrial Revolution itself.

Even the most primitive form of rural factories requires peasants from different families to be organized into a team (essentially, a corporation) to engage in coordinated production and to share the profits and business risks. Such an organization requires initial capital (more than a 100 or 1,000 times a farmer's annual family income)[36] as well as fundamental trust among the workers and the organizers; moreover, success depends critically on long-distance efficient distribution channels to ensure sales. During the proto-industrialization period in 17th–19th century Europe and England, this task of organization and financing and coordination was accomplished by merchants. These "middlemen" were the most important agents and catalysts in driving and facilitating the proto-industrial revolution.

Merchants throughout human history have been viewed negatively on religious (and other) grounds in agrarian societies. They have been labeled as profiteers, cheaters, greedy arbitragers, and opportunistic exploiters. They have been accused of calculating everything, including talents and friendship.[37] But since the Renaissance, conditions and perspectives gradually changed: Nation-states rose in Europe, and centuries of state building and military competition and international conflicts in controlling

---

[36]The average value of fixed capital stock of the rural factories was about 15,000 yuan in 1978, whereas the average rural family income was about 60 yuan in 1978.

[37]As Napoleon Bonaparte (1769–1821) once remarked on the English commercial culture, "The English have no exalted sentiments. They can all be bought."

global commerce and colonies among the emerging European powers followed. Mercantilist policies and practices and state-led and state-financed and state-engineered global trade (as with the East India Company and the Trans-Atlantic slave trade) produced for England a large wealthy class of "middlemen."[38] These entrepreneurial-spirited, risk-taking, profit-sensitive, business-minded merchants took the initiative in establishing and expanding markets, organizing and financing team production and sales (e.g., through the putting-out method), setting up workshops and cartage factories in rural areas, promoting the division of labor and technological adoption, nurturing the supply chain of raw materials and intermediate goods, distributing finished products to the final users, and supplying trade credits. These merchants (the early capitalists) were the catalysts for a new age. They competed fiercely with each other to accumulate wealth, and their self-interests and ethics were strongly supported by the state mercantilism ideology and protected by the state government in domestic and international affairs. After the Dark Ages, merchants finally earned their dignity and respect because commerce through merchants has become a much better source than agriculture and landlords to finance monarchs'

---

[38] England was a major participant in the transatlantic commerce of the 17th through 19th century. This highly profitable long-distance trade pattern involved coffee, cotton, sugar, rum, and tobacco from the New World (South, Central, and North Americas) to Europe; manufactured goods, particularly textiles, from Europe to Africa; and slaves from Africa to the New World. England was also the creator and architect of another triangular trade system (similar to that in the Atlantic Ocean) that involved sending British manufactured goods to India, India cotton and Opium to China, and Chinese tea and silk back to England. The vast international trade systems also demanded enormously large and sophisticated domestic commercial networks to absorb and distribute the colossal volumes of goods and raw materials across countless manufactures and consumers in cities and rural areas; hence, small wonder that England was called by Napoleon "a nation of shopkeepers."

continuous warfare among the European powers and over the natural wealth of overseas colonies.[39]

The emergence of this new and powerful merchant class thus provided a necessary economic and political condition for the *English* Industrial Revolution. But 17th and 18th century China and India did not create such a powerful wealthy merchant class because of the lack of both a state-supported mercantilism ideology and state-organized/protected domestic and global trade.[40]

Such a powerful merchant class was obviously lacking in 1978 China as well. Although Deng Xiaoping's pragmatism encouraged commerce, the time span was too short (two to three years compared with two to three centuries in Europe and England) to create such a powerful and wealthy merchant/capitalist class, especially in the absence of colonialism and imperialism and overseas windfall profits. How would China ignite its proto-industrial revolution almost as soon as the reform started in 1978?[41]

The secret lies in the village- and township-level governments and the collective land ownership in rural China.[42] With China's

---

[39] The 16th–18th centuries in Europe was an age of state building and intense national rivalry. "That was the nature of Europe, very different here from ecumenical China or anarchical India and Islam. Europe consisted of states big and small ... [a]ll knew the significance of money for standing and power." "The primacy of money in the service of power found expression in [mercantilism] ... Mercantilism was not a doctrine, nor a set of rules. It was a general recipe for political-economic management: Whatever enhanced the state was right. Even Adam Smith had his mercantilist moment: The navigation acts, he noted, may have cost the British consumer, but they worked wonderfully to put down the Dutch seapower" (David Landes, 1999, p. 443).

[40] This neglect of the government to promote trade and mercantilism was not caused by "extractive" institutions, but by bad economic ideas and policies.

[41] The number of village firms exploded and jumped up sharply by 450% in 1984 alone.

[42] For the literature on China's rural industries, see Barry Naughton (1995), Jean Oi (1992), and Xu and Zhang (2009) and the references therein. For insightful

institutional arrangement of public land ownership and the administrative power of local governments (a legacy of Mao's communism), farmers and peasants were able and willing to pool their savings to form the initial capital (cash and land assets) necessary for an initial investment in an establishment that by design was collectively owned with profits and work opportunities equally shared among village farmers.[43] Although land had been leased to individual families since 1978 under the family-responsibility system, the nature of the public ownership of land had not changed; acquiring land for industrial purpose, then, was not a great hurdle for the village farmers and the local governments. The managers of such collectively owned establishments were often the village officials, who were often democratically elected and viewed as natural leaders (China's earliest CEOs).[44] Although Deng disbanded the communes that had been created under Mao's regime, the legacy of the Great Leap Forward and its communization movement made it easy to reintroduce collectively owned organizations. The Cultural Revolution, while destroying human capital in the cities, nurtured the entrepreneurial spirits of farmers and village leaders in the countryside. The high degree of trust among these village families and the leadership of the local governments enabled Chinese farmers to overcome the prohibitive transaction costs of contracting in an agrarian society where the legal system and law enforcement were lacking. In essence, they trusted

---

analyses on China's land institutions, see Hua Sheng (2014), available at http://www.360doc.com/content/14/1210/21/14561708_431886261.shtml.

[43] In some villages the farmers use lottery to decide who get the chance to work in the collectively owned village firms (see Tiejun Wen (2011), *Understanding the Sunan Model of Village Industries*).

[44] Even during Mao's time, the commune or village officials were democratically elected by peasants. Only officials above the county level were appointed by the provincial or state government. For example, the current Chinese president Xi Jinping was democratically elected by local village farmers as their village leader in the 1970s when he was sent to the countryside by the Cultural Revolution movement.

fair income distribution and risk sharing and credit payments. In 16th–18th century England, the lack of trust in this regard and the associated transaction costs in forming corporations in rural areas were mitigated and overcome not by the local populous, but by the entrepreneurial, risk-taking, profit-seeking merchants, who were less financially constrained and more experienced in the putting-out system and long distance trade. But, again, it took Europe and England *centuries* to form such a powerful merchant class through commercialism, colonialism, imperialism, mercantilism, and the Trans-Atlantic trade. This process of forming markets in England, Europe, and elsewhere around the globe under colonialism can be thought of as "natural market fermentation," where the key agents are the powerful merchants. Any natural fermentation process these days (in making bread, cheese, and wine, for example) can be engineered to achieve better and faster results with modern biological technologies. China, in its market fermentation, found an analogous way to engineer a faster process of fermenting markets by using the local governments and their organizational capital as "enzymes." The local governments facilitated the creation of firms and sped up the process of creating markets. This is one of the keys to understanding China's rapid proto-industrialization and economic takeoff.

Deng's government imposed a national ideology: Economic development through all possible means conditioned on political stability and social order. If the communist party is unable to provide a decent material life to the peasants, it has no right to represent them. Any government official who was deemed incompetent in finding ways to bring material wealth to local people would be stripped of office under fierce intra-national competition for economic success in the villages, townships, counties, cities, and provinces. This pragmatism effectively turned all levels of Chinese government officials, through the powerful administrative networks established by Mao during his 30-year communism central planning experiments, into a highly motivated "public merchant" class. Through merit-based selections and competitions with neighboring villages or townships or cities or provinces, there emerged a new generation of very capable business-minded administrators who helped creating local, national, and international markets for local business through supporting village firms with low taxes and cheap land, attracting outside investment, advertising local products, negotiating business deals, and building distribution networks. These market creators did not bear the stigma of traditional merchants; there were not seen as profiteers, cheaters, greedy arbitragers, and opportunistic exploiters. They reinvented the European historical putting-out system except on a much larger scale and with an overly nationalistic mission: They provided critical entrepreneurial and middleman services to village firms by acting as the "board of directors" (a la Jean Oi, 1992), providing credit, enforcing payments, supplying commercial information, organizing industrial parks and trade exhibition forums, and engaging in the negotiation with out-of-region entities for the supply of raw materials and intermediate goods needed for production; they also sometimes even coordinated the absorption of inventories and the smoothing of supply and demand shocks to firms.[45] They also

---

[45] Consider the story of Gu Zhen, a town in Guangdong province on China's southeast coast. It was a poor village in the early 1980s but is now famous for its light fixture products. In the 1980s, the local government helped bring in two light-fixture assembly companies from Hong Kong, which also educated the local entrepreneurs on the production technology and business model. Once the local enterprises started to develop, the local government offered a variety of support in financing, information provision, worker training, and technology transfer assistance. Since 1999, as the local economy boomed and factories mushroomed and production scale expanded, Gu Zhen's local government organized annual international exhibitions each year to promote the products of local firms in the international market. These "middlemen" intermediation services offered by Gu Zhen's local government were extremely helpful in attracting business investment and enhancing the local economy and nurturing private enterprises by reducing their information and transaction costs (See Yang (2010), *Industrial Cluster and Regional Brand: A Study of Gu Zhen's Light-Fixture Industrial Cluster*, Guangzhou: Guangdong People Press House). In China, all levels of central and local government are motivated to provide similar facilities and services to help

helped organize farmers in their spare time to build roads, improve the irrigation systems, or obtain loans from provincial or national banks to build local infrastructure. According to political scientist Jean Oi (1992), "The impressive growth of collective rural industrial output between 1978 and 1988 is in large measure a result of local government entrepreneurship. Fiscal reform has assigned local governments property rights over increased income and has created strong incentives for local officials to pursue local economic development. In the process, local governments have taken on many characteristics of a business corporation, with officials acting as the equivalent of a board of directors."[46]

Agrarian societies and developing countries have trouble producing firms of an efficient scale, especially in the rural areas. It is hard to put together large tracts of land, to ensure reliable power supply, and to get goods in market quickly (which requires good roads and adequate ports). In China, the provision of such public goods came mainly from the local governments.

Facilitated by this large, powerful, and (perhaps most importantly) credible social class of "public entrepreneurs" or "public merchants," the size and number of village firms grew rapidly in China after the 1978 reform, despite the absence of a market-based financial system and traditional credit support from national banks.[47]

---

attract outside investment and local business formation. There is at least one government-built industrial park in each Chinese city to promote firm-formation, business investment, and economic growth. Also, when a local business requires raw materials, such as cotton, the government often helps buy back any excess supply from farmers to smooth cotton prices.

[46] Jean Oi (1992) provides an interesting analysis on the ways in which local governments in China coordinate economic activity and reallocate revenues from industrial production.

[47] The state banking system was responsible for financing only the large SOEs; so, most village firms were self-financed in the 1980s and 1990s by pooling farmers' savings and through the help of local credit unions.

The average size of the village firm, measured by average value of fixed capital stock, grew from 15,000 yuan in 1978 to 125,000 yuan in 2000, more than an eight-fold increase. An eight-fold expansion in fixed capital stock for an average firm is possible only if the market size also expands proportionally for each firm. On top of this, the total number of village firms increased by 14-fold in the same period. Hence, the total market size for village industrial output must have increased by about $8 \times 14 = 112$-fold between 1978 and 2000, implying a growth rate of 24% per year for the extent of the market. Indeed, the total value of village firm capital stock increased by 114-fold in that period (consistent with the figure of 112).[48]

This speed of China's primitive capital accumulation is unprecedented. The 17th and 18th century English primitive accumulation pales in comparison.[49] Yet, it was achieved in China without colonialism, slave trade, and imperialism. The size of China's domestic market must have helped. But a massive number of impoverished peasants without purchasing power and infrastructure to connect them are only a *potential*, not a *real* market. This potential market existed in the Qing Dynasty and the Republic era, but it did not materialize. Neither the Qing monarchy nor the Republic government cared about organizing the peasants. The former focused on

---

[48] Zhang, Yi and Zhang, Song-song (2001), Data Appendix.

[49] Some historians believe that slavery and trans-Atlantic trade helped finance the Industrial Revolution in England. Plantation owners, shipbuilders, and merchants who were connected with the slave trade accumulated vast fortunes that established banks and large manufactures in Europe and expanded the reach of capitalism worldwide. Most importantly, slave labor in the cotton fields across Africa and Americas made the mass supply of cotton required to feed the textile-led Industrial Revolution possible. For scholarly writings on the critical contributions of slavery and trans-Atlantic trade to the Industrial Revolution, see Sven Beckert (2014), *Empire of Cotton: A Global History;* and Eric Williams (1994), *Capitalism and Slavery;* among others.

state-built large-scale factories in the big cities, and the latter believed in *laissez faire* and private land ownership. Therefore, the simultaneous explosion in demand and supply in rural China since 1978 through the creation of a massive number of village firms and a unified colossal domestic market is largely attributable to one factor — organized peasants by the mercantilist Chinese government officials at all administrative levels. These mercantilist government officials (and administrative offices) served the same function as the English merchant class who helped create the pre-industrial English markets and proto-industries over centuries leading up to the publication of *The Wealth of Nations* in 1776.

This key point applies not only to China, but also to the agrarian nations in today's world. Hoping to rely on a "natural" *laissez faire* market fermentation process to kick-start an industrial revolution may no longer be feasible, if it ever was. At the very least, this process of market fermentation was an extremely slow and lengthy process that took the old industrial powers centuries to accomplish even under strong state support and mercantilism. It was also a process that had relied on colonial policies and slave trade. But, an "engineered" market fermentation led by the state and local governments (as was done in China) in today's peaceful postwar world order is the better way and maybe the only way to achieve rapid industrialization for agrarian developing countries.[50]

---

[50] When visiting or reading about the pin factories in early 18th century, Adam Smith noticed only the vastly increased productivity through the division of labor. But he did not ask how the dramatically increased output (the supply of pins) could create its own demand. He appealed to the market mechanism that already existed in his time through his assumption of the "invisible hand" principle. But he did not pay sufficient tribute to the hundreds of years of slow fermentation of the commercial markets and distribution networks and supply chains in Europe before his time that provided the pre-condition for product specialization, for the separation between demand and supply, and for the division of labor. No firm or family would dare to dramatically increase its productive capacity and supply to

There are logical connections to be made between China's township-village industrial boom in the 1980s, prior to its economic takeoff in the middle 1990s, and the English proto-industrialization in the 1600–1760 period prior to the English Industrial Revolution (1760–1850). The state and local Chinese government officials and the English merchants both played an active role in building the free market and its fundamental pillar — social trust, and in helping create the massive number of proto-industrial firms. So, the puzzle is no longer why a proto-industrialization was suddenly kick-started in China after 1978, but rather why it did not happen earlier in Chinese history, despite private property rights, such as those during its first and second attempts of industrialization in the 19th and early 20th century.[51] The answer to this puzzle is now much clearer: China did not have a well-fermented market and specifically a large number of market-creators and rural-firm organizers in the Qing Dynasty and the Republic Era. This missing-market or missing-market-creator problem could have been remedied only through a bottom-up approach to industrialization led by a strong pro-commerce and pro-manufacturing mercantilist government (as in Meiji Japan).

---

the market unless there was demand to match the supply. But how can a cottage workshop find or meet its buyers? How can one be sure of the constant flow of raw materials and stability of prices and market demand over time? The division of labor in one firm necessarily requires the division of labor in other firms. So this is a social coordination problem on a grand scale. Europe, and England in particular, solved this social coordination problem over centuries of natural market fermentation under commercialism, colonialism, imperialism, slave trade, and mercantilism before the Industrial Revolution.

[51] Proto-industries exist in many agrarian societies, especially in China's Yangzi Delta Region. But, without a strong mercantilist state and a large merchant class to help build a unified domestic market and a well-organized commercial network in the international market, they can never grow to the critical level or density to be called a "proto-industrialization." See more discussions in Chapter 3. (iii) "The Rise of the Textile Industry and the Logic of the English Industrial Revolution."

vi. Corruption, Chinese Style

A fundamental question for countries that may decide to adopt the Chinese-style engineered market fermentation strategy is *reward*: Specifically, how are the massive numbers of government officials to be rewarded for their "middleman" services and when and how should they "exit" after accomplishing their tasks?

China's response to this question is intriguing. But first, let's consider what rewards have been bestowed upon other government leaders in history. What material rewards did George Washington and Abraham Lincoln receive for their services to America? What did Deng Xiaoping receive for his services to China? The same questions can be asked about Ito Hirobuma in Japan, Park Chung Hee in South Korea, and Lee Kwan Yew in Singapore and so on down the line for the many leaders who have served their homelands.[52]

We might assume that these leaders may have been motivated by noble, perhaps nationalistic goals as opposed to self-interest and personal gain. Such issue of moral sentiment notwithstanding, there is the legitimate concern of corruption in the world. Conflict of interests occurs when government officials are deeply involved in business. It cannot be denied that corruption is rampant in China today, just as it is in nearly all developing countries, such as India, the Philippines, Mexico, Ukraine, and even late 19th and early 20th century America.[53] However, government corruption in China takes a distinctive form: Government officials actively provide productive "middlemen" services to the market participants and receive pay-

---

[52] For a profile of a typical Chinese local government official and his path to power after the 1978 economic reform, see the story of Xi Jinping at http://defence.pk/threads/supreme-leader-xi-jinping-personal-profile.226072/.

[53] See Carlos D. Ramirez, Is Corruption in China "Out of Control"? A Comparison with the U.S. in Historical Perspective, *Journal of Comparative Economics* 42(1), 2014. pp. 76–91.

ment ("rent") for these services. Although this type of "rent seeking" behavior is fraught with incentive-compatibility and conflict-of-interest problems, the behavior is actually more productive than "extractive."[54] This unique and creative role played by Chinese government officials at both the national and local levels may be one of the key sources of confusion and misunderstanding — and underestimation — of China by Western observers and the institutional theorists.[55] China has invented new political "institutions" and new types of public services for the government to provide. "Crony capitalism" is a known phenomenon, but it is not the essence of the critical role played in economic development by the Chinese government. True, there are aspects of crony capitalism involved in China's merchant government, as in all developing countries, but it is not the key function of China's merchant government and it does not capture the productive and innovative elements of Chinese government behavior.[56]

---

[54] Most of China's village firms were later privatized or merged by private enterprises since the middle 1990s.

[55] The institutional theorists and the Western media argue that all the economic development programs and reforms carried out in China since 1978 have been simply the means for the Chinese communist party to survive, as revealed in Ian Bremmer's article in *Reuters* (September 8, 2014): "But a prosperous economy is simply a means to an end-goal. Xi is [further] opening up the economy because, above all else, he wants to ensure the long-term survival and stability of the Communist Party leadership." But if all political parties and governments in developing countries could emulate the Chinese communist party, the poverty problem in this world would be much easier to solve.

[56] The "spoils" system (where public officers are allocated to the loyalists of the ruling party), and "nepotism" (the practice among those with power or influence of favoring relatives or friends, especially by giving jobs) were extremely popular and widespread in the 19th century Europe and the United States. Economic historian Ha-Joon Chang specifically points out that "open sales of public offices and honors — sometimes with widely-publicized price tags — was a common practice in most now-developed countries (NDCs)" before and during their industrialization stages (see, e.g., Ha-Joon Chang, 2003, p. 78)

To better understand the role of the Chinese government in China's economic takeoff, we must place economic development in the context of political economy, where no economic development is possible without the active involvement of the state. This was true in 18th and 19th centuries England, true in 19th and 20th centuries United States and Japan, and also true in today's China. The real question is *how* the government should be involved, not *whether* it should be involved. In a welfare state (such as modern-day United States and Europe) the main role of the government has changed: It has become redistribution of income, or how to divide the economic pie. But in China, the main role of the government has been to create business conditions (including infrastructures) so that poor people have the incentives and the means to work, to create income, and to grow the economic pie.[57]

The state is not just an institution that controls violence and provides social order (North and Wallis, 2009); it is also an institution that can eliminate or overcome market failures and solve the missing-market and missing-market-creator problems in developing

---

[57] This critical difference in the role of the government was also manifested in the fiscal stimulus programs of the U.S. and China after the 2007 financial crisis: Both nations initiated large fiscal stimulus programs (equivalent to more than 5% of their respective GDP) to combat the financial crisis and the subsequent economic collapse. But in the United States the money was spent mainly on income transfers, whereas in China it was spent mainly on infrastructures. Apparently, the stimulus programs were far more effective in China than in the U.S. (See Wen and Wu, 2014). In the case of Greece, for decades the government has directly subsidized citizens by providing well-paid government jobs with generous pensions and other welfare benefits, which led to an economy where one in five citizens of working age held a government job. This government spending was one of the root causes of the Greek debt crisis in the early 2010s. Greece entered a welfare state too soon, without even finishing its second industrial revolution, unlike Germany. So the 21st century Greek financial troubles actually started decades ago when political parties tried to win elections by competing for votes through increasing the size of the country's welfare program. This is one of the many key problems of democracy.

countries. A unified domestic goods market, labor market, and financial market fail to emerge in many agrarian societies not always because of "extractive" governments with vested interests, but rather because of the formidable costs of social coordination to create such markets. Hence, the missing-market problem typical for developing countries reflects the absence of the government and its services: Without a large powerful wealthy merchant class, the formidable coordination costs of transforming family-based artisan workshops into factories based on teamwork and the principle of the division of labor and specialization and the segregation of demand and supply can be overcome only through government assistance and leadership. Just a few capital-intensive enterprises or large international firms cannot bring about true industrialization. China demonstrated to the world (once again, after Japan and Singapore and South Korea and Taiwan) how to enact an industrial revolution through engineered market fermentation via the active involvement of the central and local governments. It is in this sense that the lack of firm growth and market formation in developing countries (such as Sub-Saharan Africa and even today's India) signifies more of a problem of missing government (government failures) than of missing market (market failures), *per se*.

Many local and village-level government officials in China conduct themselves like benevolent (Deng Xiaoping-style) leaders on the one hand and self-interested merchants on the other hand[58]: They are determined and empowered and necessary for developing their local economies and designing development policies based on local economic conditions (such as endowment and comparative advantages). They are motivated to work almost 365 days a year to attract outside investment, build bridges, repair roads, negotiate bank loans, provide trade information to local business, hold cross-regional economic talks, setup industrial parks, organize commercial exhibitions

---

[58] A Chinese joke tells it like this: "Chinese government officials are the most corrupt and yet the most efficient, productive, and hardworking CEOs on earth."

to establish trade links to the outside world, resolve business disputes, arrange land to facilitate firm entries, so on and so forth. Of course, many of them also accept bribes and receive rent for their services, paid by the local firms and even by international businesses. It is politically infeasible for their salaries to match all the value they add to the local economies. But their hard, creative, and entrepreneurial work as market creators (the "enzymes" of market fermentation) has allowed China to shorten the centuries-long natural market fermentation process in 16th–18th century England to a mere decade in China. This rapid process in China, as in the cases of all the Asian tigers, has proved that such an engineered market-fermentation in economic development is a legitimate formula, not a fluke.[59]

When asked by foreign leaders visiting China in 1985 and 1987 why China was doing so well and growing so fast after the 1978 reform,[60] Deng Xiaoping replied that the secret lies in village firms: "We have 7 million young people every year looking for new employment.[61] How to solve this problem? We have found our way, it is village firms … . The most unexpected consequence of our rural reform is the explosive growth of village firms, the sudden emergence of so many businesses and varieties of professions and specialized regional products created by village firms. This was not designed by the central government. It cannot be attributed to the central government. The nonstop over-20% per year real annual growth rate of village enterprises greatly solved our employment problem for the surplus labor in China's countryside; they created jobs for 50% of [new entrants] rural labor force each year. Such outcome means we have done something good and right for the

---

[59] Except Japan, local governments in the other Asian tigers are not as critical as in China because these are small economies.

[60] Of course they had not yet seen the even more dramatic changes in the 1990s and 2000s.

[61] In 2013 amidst global economic slowdown, China created 13.1 million jobs, compared with 2.2 million in the U.S.

people. This is totally out of my expectations. It just happened, what a surprise."[62] Deng was perhaps a bit too modest in his answers. He neglected to mention that his local county-level and village-level government officials were also pivotal for the rapid establishment of the village industries.

Another issue of government-related corruption is overinvestment in public infrastructure. A common observation of the enthusiasm and competition among China's local governments in boosting their local economies (and in rent-seeking) is the overbuilding of local infrastructures, as reflected in the phenomenon of "ghost towns" and "empty roads that lead to nowhere." This is indeed a problem, but different from corruption in developing countries where government officials simply took the money and built nothing.[63] And in general, this overinvestment problem must be viewed with caveats: Market forces also tend to generate overinvestment, including investment in infrastructures, as repeatedly manifested in the waves of periodic investment cycles and financial crisis in more traditional capitalistic economies.

The railroad boom in 19th century America is a case in point. Driven by the prospect of enormous natural monopolistic profits, the 19th century railroad companies in the United States built railroads at a furious pace to compete for the market shares in transportation. As a result, "the ton-miles carried by the thirteen largest lines

---

[62] Deng Xiaoping knew very well that the idea of village firms was first proposed and implemented by Mao in 1958 during the Great Leap Forward and that this effort failed miserably. Deng was the primary manager of dismissing and destroying the village firms after the Great Famine in 1961–1962. He was always an active advocate of the top-down approach to industrialization and a fan of setting up large high-tech firms … That is, until he observed the huge inefficiencies caused by central planning by the end of the Cultural Revolution. It never struck him that Mao's village firms were the way to break the curse of central planning, so it caught him by surprise when the village firms suddenly flourished after the rural reform in 1978.

[63] See Chapter 5 for more discussions on the issue of corruption.

rose 600% between 1865 and 1880, and mileage doubled just between the years 1870 and 1876 ... Competition was fiercest among the large trunk lines; these companies often overbuilt rail mileage and engaged in ruinous rate wars. There were, for example, twenty competitive routs between St. Louis and Atlanta in the 1880s" (Francis Fukuyama, "Political Order and Political Decay," 2014, p. 166).[64]

vii. Laws, Lessons, and the Central Questions of Development

Many developing countries, despite huge efforts to attract foreign direct investment and establish modern efficient manufacturing industries in major cities, have failed to emulate the Industrial Revolution because they all ignored the initial stage of the Industrial Revolution — the proto-industrialization. Instead of first laying the foundation for rural industrialization among the grassroots farmers in the countryside, many countries rushed into establishing modern and capital-intensive heavy industries in their big cities or commercial regions.[65] The process created many false alarms of industrial revolution. For example, W. W. Rostow in 1960 claimed prematurely that China and India had detonated their industrial revolutions and

---

[64] Coincidentally, many of the railroad workers were from late Qing dynasty China. They proved to be the most hard-working and skilled workers in the U.S. railroad construction history, in comparison with their Caucasian counterparts. But they and their descendants were also badly discriminated against in the United States even until the 20th century. For example, the Chinese Exclusion Act, a United States federal law signed by President Chester A. Arthur on May 6, 1882, was one of the most significant restrictions on free immigration in U.S. history, prohibiting all immigration of Chinese laborers, and was the first law implemented to prevent a specific ethnic group from immigrating to the United States. This law was not repealed until December 17, 1943.

[65] Such as Indonesia's automobile company Astra International, founded in 1957, and its Indonesia Aviation Industry built in the 1980s.

were at the doorstep of economic takeoff: He had seen rapid industrial growth and a high investment rate above 10% of GDP.[66] But he was proved wrong: China and India did not take off in the 1970s but instead remained in the Malthusian trap. Hence, GDP growth and investment rate, *per se*, do not presage (or tell the story of) an industrial revolution. It is the sequence and process of industrial buildup that matter. During 1750–1840, the English economy was growing at merely 1–1.5% per year in terms of GDP, but the country was truly undergoing the *first* industrial revolution.

In the middle of the 20th century, many Latin American and East and Southeast Asian nations had been growing around or above 5% per year for decades, yet they were unable to launch a full-fledged industrial revolution. In particular, China between 1953 and 1978 (its third attempt at industrialization) was growing almost as rapidly as South Korea between 1962 and 1992, at about 6.5% per year; but China did not take off, while South Korea did.[67]

---

[66] W. W. Rostow (1960), *The Stages of Economic Growth: A Non-Communist Manifesto*. Cambridge U.K.: University Press.

[67] GDP growth is not the right measure of economic performance and industrial dynamism for two reasons: It is highly uninformative with large measurement errors, and many of its components are irrelevant for measuring an industrial revolution. A better measure of economic strength is the growth rate of industrial output in the appropriate industries that correspond to a nation's development stage. For example, textile output growth is the right measure of economic health for nations experiencing a first industrial revolution. In the initial 20 years of the British Industrial Revolution, the amount of finished cloth produced by England's factories increased by more than 30-fold, from half a million pounds in 1765 to 16 million pounds in 1784 (William Bernstein, 2008, p. 263). As the Industrial Revolution continued, the number of looms in the U.K. increased from 2,400 in 1803 to 10,000 in 1833, growing at a spectacular rate of more than 13% per year for 30 years (see http://en.wikipedia.org/wiki/Textile_manufacture_during_the_Industrial_Revolution). Yet GDP in U.K. was growing at less than 1.5% per year in that same period. Similarly, when the United States was kick-starting its first industrial revolution between 1810 and 1830, the number of cotton spindles was

Therefore, China's industrialization experience since 1978 (as well as its earlier failures) teaches us once again that an industrial revolution cannot be detonated simply by a spurt of high investment rate in modern efficient technologies. Nor can it be detonated by suddenly switching to democracy or universal suffrage. It must start humbly in the rural areas and under a politically stable environment (that is, a lack of revolutions and riots and internal power struggles). It must be a bottom-up process — one that can tap the potential of the grassroots population, unleash their raw labor and entrepreneurial spirits, organize them and transform them from autarkic free atoms into organized and directed "electrical flows" and productive forces. This rural-industrialization process nurtures the division of labor and specialization, improves the grassroots class's wages and purchasing power, and "ferments" and deepens the market. This is a fundamental (and maybe the only) way to simultaneously escape from the Malthusian trap, break the curse of food security, and detonate a full-fledged industrial revolution first in the light industry.

The rush into establishing efficient large-scale modern heavy industries, either through the *Import Substitution Industrialization* strategy (Latin America or China in the 1950s–1970s), through relying heavily on foreign loans (Eastern Europe after the collapse of the Soviet Union), or through prematurely establishing modern financial and political institutions that tend to jeopardize financial and political stability, all violate the Smith principle that the wealth of nations hinges on the division of labor, which is limited by the extent of the market. In other words, such practices and theories fail to grasp that mass production requires a mass market with means of mass distribution and that it is extremely costly to create all this in the first place. So, in the simplest terms, behind these false development strategies lies the principle that supply does not automatically create its own demand.

---

growing at about 13% per year for 20 years, from 100,000 to 1.2 million (see David Landes, 1999, p. 300).

Between the 1860s (the Second Opium War) and 1894 (the first Sino-Japanese war), the Qing dynasty government set up more than 150 large-scale modern factories, including 16 shipbuilding and machinery-manufacturing firms, 97 mechanized textile mills, eight printing companies, and four steel enterprises. These modern firms were mainly state-owned and financed by government debt or foreign loans, but more importantly were all located in big commercial cities or regions, such as Shanghai (25%) and Guangdong (60%). Proto-industries and village workshops and active commerce in the vast rural areas were completely ignored and even discouraged by the government. The same top-down approach to modernization persisted in the Republic Era. The Republic government paid little attention to rural development. It instead focused on establishing large-scale modern manufacturing firms in big commercial cities. For example, in 1937, more than 40% of China's industrial capacity (including textile manufacturing) was located in Shanghai alone.[68]

Such a city-oriented, top-down approach to industrialization was in sharp contrast to Japan's development path and industrial policies before and after the Meiji Restoration in 1868. The Edo period of Japan (1603–1868) that preceded the Meiji Restoration was an important step in preparing Japan to fully embrace and import the first industrial revolution from Europe. It was a period of active commerce and trade, market fermentation, political stability, agricultural growth, national integration through communication and infrastructure buildup, the flourish of rural artisan manufacturing and craftsmen workshops, the emergence of a wealthy merchant class, official promotion of rural industries by both the national government and local governments, and the spread of education.[69]

---

[68] See, e.g., Li Zhou (2005), The Origin and Development of Rural Industrialization in China: A Case Study of Yong Village (1978–2004).

[69] See, e.g., Toyo Keizai Shimposha (2000, pp. 42–46), The Industrialization and Global Integration of Meiji Japan, Chapter 5 in *Globalization of Developing Countries: Is Autonomous Development Possible?* Also see David Landes (1999), *The Wealth and Poverty of Nations*, Chapter 22.

Japan's proto-industrialization was so impressive and successful that the historian David Landes believed strongly that "even without a European industrial revolution, the Japanese would sooner or later have made their own" (Landes, 1999, p. 368).

This proto-industrialization process was further reinforced and accelerated by the Meiji government. Their actions were motivated by nationalism to deter possible foreign invasion, colonization, or any loss of sovereignty. Just like the case of China since 1978, the Meiji government mobilized all of Japan's rural labor force to engage in proto-industrialization and carried out necessary economic and political reforms to facilitate commerce, infrastructure building, and international trade. What is critically important is that the Meiji government did not attempt to start its industrialization by establishing large-scale modern manufacturing enterprises in the large commercial cities (maybe due to the lack of a large sum of foreign loans at that time). It instead focused on labor-intensive small-scale textile and food-processing industries in the rural areas to build a light industrial base in Japan that could be internationally competitive.

"Throughout Meiji (1868–1912), Taisho (1912–1926) and pre-war Showa (1926–1936), Japan's top exports were raw silk yarn, tea, and marine products … . Virtually unseen in Japan nowadays, during Meiji all villages that could cultivate mulberries to rear silkworms, and many earned a good income from this activity. In this sense, silk was not only a traditional product that brought wealth to rural areas, but it also made an important contribution to Japan's industrialization by earning much coveted foreign exchange … . Japan exported primary commodities and imported manufactured [textile] goods — the typical vertical trade pattern of latecomer countries. However, as Japan's cotton industry grew, the import of textile products fell steadily and around the 1900s it was close to nothing. Furthermore, from the latter part of the 1890s, Japan began to export cotton yarn and clothes to neighboring Asian countries, and at the same time it started to import raw cotton in large quantities mainly from India. In other words, the industrialization of the Meiji Period was a light industrial revolution, which made its way from importing to domestic production and then onto exporting. Within this transition, cotton production played a central role" (Toyo Keizai Shimposha, 2000, pp. 51–52).

Japan did not start building its heavy industries until the end of the Meiji Restoration, especially after the First World War. Even by the end of the Meiji period, "[t]he iron and steel, shipbuilding and chemical industries, as well as the manufacture of electrical machinery and appliances were [still] in their infancy and the country was still in the process of learning by imitating the West. These industries were not yet in any condition to be called the main forces of production; they were not internationally competitive and importing the necessary machinery from the West was the norm" (Toyo Keizai Shimposha, 2000, p. 52). As Japan finished its first industrial revolution around the turn of the 20th century, its massive domestic demand for modern infrastructures and machineries necessitated a second industrial revolution. The Meiji government approached this development by first setting up state-owned heavy industrial enterprises, such as the Tokyo artillery factory, the Yokosuka naval arsenal, the Osaka artillery factory and the Kure naval arsenal, all of which used technology and machinery solely from the West and gradually privatized them as the engineers learned how to operate and reproduce such technologies on their own. The private heavy-industrial sector grew as a result.

Japan's government led the "big push" in industrial upgrading *after* finishing its proto-industrialization and its first industrial revolution. This state-led initiative in heavy industrial buildup based on the mass market and distributional networks and the savings accumulated through the earlier stages of development significantly shortened and flattened Japan's learning curve in heavy industrial buildup. So, "by late Meiji, private sector production in the areas of shipbuilding, railway carriages and machine instruments had slowly emerged. Meanwhile, engineers and workers who had handled new technology in the state-owned munitions plants began to transfer to private sector businesses or set up their own. In this manner, the production technology of the West propagated widely and small businesses and subcontractors began to form in Tokyo and Osaka. Thus, while heavy industry was in its infancy during the [late] Meiji period, it was preparing itself for a rapid leap in the period after the First World War" (Toyo Keizai Shimposha, 2000, p. 52).

Japan was the only Asian country to successfully kick-start an industrial revolution in the late 19th century and become an industrial superpower in the first half of the 20th century. This fact has puzzled economic historians and even sociologists and anthropologists, given Japan's relatively short history (compared with that of China and Europe) and its poor endowment in land and other natural resources. So most scholars attribute Japan's economic miracle to culture and personal character (as usual):

"The national character [of Japan] is strikingly marked, and strongly contrasted with that which generally prevails throughout Asia. The Japanese differ most especially from the Chinese, their nearest neighbors ... Instead of that tame, quiet, orderly, servile disposition which makes [the Chinese] the prepared and ready subjects of despotism, the Japanese have a character marked by energy, independence and a lofty of sense of honor" (cited by David Landes, 1999, p. 351).

But the truth is much simpler and economically easier to comprehend once the *historical logic* of the Industrial Revolution is grasped: Japan's economic miracle is attributable to its centuries-long overall political stability (thanks to its geographic isolation from the Eurasian continent) and correct mercantilist bottom-up development strategies of sequential market creation (mostly unintentional choices of the monarchs): Moving from commerce-based primitive agricultural revolution and rural proto-industrialization (mostly before and during the early phase of the Meiji Restoration), to export-oriented (or world-market based) labor-intensive mass production (during the later phase of the Meiji

Restoration), then to nationwide industrial-trinity buildup in energy/loco-motive power/transport infrastructure, and finally to capital-intensive heavy industrial catchup, all led by strong-willed mercantilist monarchy or state governments.[70]

Not surprisingly, even the United States also kick-started its 19th century industrial revolution first in the rural areas (just like 18th century Great Britain), based on the mushrooming of count-less proto-industries; instead of in its commercial and financial centers and big cities (such as New York and Philadelphia) based on cutting-edge British technologies or capital-intensive large enterprises such as steel and railroad companies.

Unaware of the fact that England did not kick-start its Industrial Revolution by steam engines and coal and steel and railroads, Anthony F. C. Wallace (1978, p. 5) wrote about the economic pros-perity of a small American village along the banks of Chester Creek in Delaware County, named Rockdale, during the early phase of America's industrial revolution from the early to middle 19th cen-tury: "Unlike England where, because of the almost universal use of steam engines for power, manufacturing was concentrated in sooty cities like Manchester, the American manufacturing districts were rural and dependent upon the new country's as yet unexploited resources of water power. The Rockdale manufacturing district was almost a self-sufficient rural community, like a plantation or a com-mune, tied economically to world markets and financial centers by the buying of raw cotton and the selling of yarn and cloth."

What are the lessons, then, based on the successful paths to industrialization taken by Britain, the United States (which will be discussed in more depth later), Japan, and China?

Do not start industrialization simply in the large commercial cit-ies. Do not blindly adopt modern, efficient production technologies

---

[70] See David Landes (1999, Chapters 22 and 23, especially pp. 364–368) for more detailed descriptions of Japan's proto-industrialization-based development path in the 19th century and its similarity to Europe's proto-industrialization in the 17th and 18th centuries before the British Industrial Revolution.

and liberal financial reforms (or systems) before the proto- and light-industrial markets, the distribution networks of proto- and light industries have been created, before mass demand (purchasing power) invites and initiates the mass supply of heavy-industrial goods such as steel and machinery. Do adopt a low-cost approach by starting industrialization in the rural areas. Do encourage humble, labor-intensive, low-value-added, but export-oriented (or large-market oriented) proto-industrial workshops and light industries. But to do these, there is the need of establishing a powerful mercantilist central government and its local administrative network that is willing and capable of creating national and international markets for rural industries, managing domestic savings and credit supplies for rural industries, and building infrastructures and trading posts and raw material supply chains for rural industries.

The opposite approach — through a "big push" or "shock therapy" or a "top-down" import substitution in the capital-intensive heavy industrial sector in big cities — will only achieve unwanted consequences: Inefficient industries (regardless of property ownership), misallocation of financial resources toward speculative assets such as land and natural resources, a high level of wealth and income inequality in ill-developed cities (which tend to attract massive numbers of poor and unemployed, such as Mumbai, Bangkok, Jakarta, Sao Paulo, Mexico City, and many others), and unbearable government debt and trade deficits that can ultimately bankrupt the nation. Most of these consequences did in fact occur in China during its first three failed attempts at industrialization and in many Latin America and Southeast Asia countries. Yet we do not observe massive numbers of poor and unemployed gathering in large commercial, industrial cities in 18th and 19th centuries England, late 19th century America, early 20th century Japan, or in today's China, *precisely because* these countries all went through a successful process of massive rural proto-industrialization (1600–1750 for U.K., 1700–1830 for US, 1800–1890 for Japan, 1970s–1990s for China), which, again, led to their first industrial revolution mainly in the countryside and small towns instead of in the large commercial and financial cities.

As mentioned earlier, Mao also focused on heavy industries especially in the 1950s. With the help of the Soviet Union, China established many industrial centers to produce heavy industrial goods such as automobiles, steel, machine tools, large precision instruments, and so on. Such industries by nature could only be established in big cities. To finance the heavy industrial buildup, Mao heavily taxed the agricultural sector during the 1950s and 1960s (hence the economic motive for the Great Leap Forward). But not only that the intermediate goods and parts could not be mass produced domestically, but the factories' output levels were also often less than 30%–50% of their potential production capacity — which was not merely a matter of efficient operations, but of the limited extent of the domestic and international markets for the products. For such industries to make a profit or even to cover the sunk-investment and fixed-operation costs, the market size must be extremely large, at least 70%–80% of the potential mass-production capacity. The existence of the excess production capacity was due not only to the miscalculation of market demand, but also to the incorrect belief that supply can create its own demand under central planning.[71]

---

[71] The Soviet Union was able to establish a heavy industrial system based on intra-national and international specializations across the communist Eastern European countries. But that system was not designed to respond to market demand and market competition, hence it lacked the internal driving force of innovation and creative destruction. Its heavy industrialization under the Big Push policy of Stalin was possible because Russia had basically already finished its proto-industrialization and first industrial revolution by the turn of the 20th century under the autocratic Tsarist government. For example, the reforms embraced by Alexander II in the early 1860s were designed to stimulate transitions in the Russian economy. In the 1870s, the Russian government initiated several large infrastructure programs, particularly the construction of railroads. By 1900 Russia already had a well-developed railroad system including the Trans-Siberian railroad, and the Russian empire was already the world's fourth-largest producer of steel and the second-largest source of petroleum. See more at: http://alphahistory.com/russianrevolution/russian-industrialisation/#sthash.DcvGO nuL.dpuf.

Regardless of property ownership or some other institutional factors, industries are not profitable if the market is too thin or the scale of operations too much below capacity. Establishing a Ford automobile assembly line in 1930s America would not have been viable if it produced only a dozen (instead of 100,000) cars per year. It would not have been any benefit to invent and adopt the spinning jenny in late 18th century England if there were demand for only a few (instead of hundreds of thousands) pounds of yarn per day. And what good would it have done to adopt the division of labor in Adam Smith's pin factory if the market demand were only one pin per day instead of 40,000 per day.

Thus, the famous English manufacturer Matthew Boulton (1728–1809) wrote in 1769 to his business partner James Watt (1736–1819) who invented the steam engine:

"It is not worth my while to manufacture your engine for three counties only, but I find it very well worth my while to make it for all the world" (Eric Roll, 1968, p. 14).

In the 1960s, China's state-owned enterprises (SOEs) were guided by self-reliance and self-sufficiency principles and produced only to meet the very thin and limited domestic demand. Thus, they appeared highly unproductive and inefficient. But in sharp contrast, today's SOEs in China are guided by the Smithian market-size principle and produce to meet well-developed and well-enriched domestic *and* international markets. Thus, they appear highly efficient and productive. Indeed, modern Chinese heavy industries (mostly SOEs) are very profitable because they have the market to support their large-scale mass operations, whereas they were unprofitable in the 1960s because they did not. For example, today after market-oriented reform, after China finished its first industrial revolution and kick-started its second industrial revolution, SOEs (enterprises with more than a 50% state share in equities) are about four to five times more profitable than privately owned enterprises

(POEs) in terms of profit per unit of enterprise; they are more than twice as profitable as POEs in terms of profit per employee.[72] Such a high profit margin cannot be attributed exclusively to monopoly power, since SOEs also had absolute monopoly power under Mao's central planning regime and yet were absolutely unprofitable. Hence, the inefficiency of SOEs in many developing countries is not due to ownership problems *per se* (as is commonly theorized by the institutional school), but rather due to the limited extent of the market, the scale of operations, the sophistication of distribution networks and supply chains, and the competitive pressure for profits.

However, governments in developing countries are often so eager to modernize their economy by adopting the latest efficient mass-production technologies (— why bother to use backward and outdated 19th century technology?) without finishing a proto-industrialization and first industrial revolution. Again, their misunderstanding of the relationship between mass production and the size of the market is their downfall. Thus, the heavy industries under these conditions (thin market, etc.) must be financed and subsidized by the government, national debt, or foreign loans; and often end up with unbearable financial burdens, bankruptcy, and defaults.[73]

> "Large-scale production required not only division of labor and specialized appliances, but also the support of an organized system of transport, commerce, and credit" (Economic Historian T.S. Ashton, 1970, p. 34).

Many economists attribute China's success in becoming the world's largest manufacturing powerhouse merely to its large pool of cheap labor. True, China had a large pool of cheap labor in the

---

[72] See Li, Liu, and Wang (2014) for detailed data analyses on the profitability of Chinese SOEs.

[73] See Justin Yifu Lin's (1996, 2009, 2011, 2012, 2013) many excellent analyses on the failure of China's heavy-industry-based development strategy under communism in the 1950s–1970s.

1980s, but so did China in the 18th century Qing Dynasty and early 20th century Republic era. So why was China unable to become the manufacturing powerhouse of the world a century earlier?

The answer is now clear: China, since 1978, has chosen (albeit unintentionally in the beginning) not to focus on heavy industrial buildups or a rapid full-fledged modernization, maybe because of both financial constraints and lessons learned from earlier failures, but instead to set up a low-key goal of a *xiaokang* (moderately prosperous) society, and began with a massive number of small-scale proto-industrial factories in the countryside that produced only primitive labor-intensive low-quality low-value-added light consumer/industrial goods (such as chopsticks, tooth-brushes, plastic plates, paper cups, buckets, containers, buttons, pins, nails, textiles, yarns, silk, sweaters, skirts, shirts, shoes, hats, gloves, pottery, china, tables, chairs, curtains, sofas, kitchenware, office furniture, bicycles, tricycles, motorcycles, simple farming tools, fertilizer, commercialized agricultural products, school supplies, toys, black-and-white TV sets, low-quality watches, so on and so forth) to meet the needs of the grassroots populace. These village factories nonetheless absorbed a massive number of the rural labor force which accounted for more than 80% of the nation's total labor force in the late 1970s and early 1980s; and in return such factories supplied to families an increasing variety of affordable new consumer goods, which served as substitutes for surplus food and babies. Thus, farmers' income and opportunity costs associated with how they used their time rose, and their utility function over the spectrum of consumption goods gradually shifted away from exclusively enjoying children to enjoying an increasing variety of industrial consumer goods produced by the proto-industrial factories.[74]

---

[74] Actually, China did attempt to kick-start its fourth industrialization in 1978 by massively importing modern efficient technologies to upgrade its outdated heavy industries built in the 1950s and 1960s, but was quickly forced to abandon the ambitious development program because of the rapid pile-up of financial burdens and

China's rural industrial boom was long noticed by economists worldwide as well as observers in China. But its relation to Western economic history and its economic significance in kick-starting China's industrialization was never clearly conceived by most development economists. Many (including Chinese economists) thought of it as a unique Chinese phenomenon due to China's economic transformation from central planning to a market economy, as a consequence of its lack of private property rights.[75] No. Not true.

---

an unsustainable level of national debt. China's lack of sufficient foreign aid and international loans at that time made Deng Xiaoping and other Chinese leaders realize that China must rely on exports to earn desperately needed foreign currency to pay for the foreign supply of heavy industrial technologies. Therefore, starting in 1984, after seeing the rural industrial boom, the Chinese government started to encourage rural industries to target foreign markets without realizing that it was precisely the rapid growth of these rural industries that was revolutionizing China's economy and detonating its long-awaited industrial revolution. Had China been endowed with massive amounts of oil, like countries in the Middle East, or easily obtained foreign loans, like many Latin American countries in the second half of the 20th century and Eastern European countries after the collapse of the Soviet Union, China might have not taken the hard (but correct) road of proto-industrialization it has taken. Without the needed proto-industrialization, as explained here, China would have failed for a fourth time at industrialization and today's world history would be much different. But like Meiji Japan and South Korea, Singapore, and Taiwan in the postwar era, China did not have the luxuries of oil endowment and cheap foreign loans, so it relied on hard labor to export labor-intensive manufactured goods to accumulate the needed foreign reserves to import the needed modern machineries from industrialized nations. (This process is akin to Britain's 18th and 19th centuries primitive accumulation.) The now-familiar undergraduate international economics textbook story is that China must exchange 100 million t-shirts with the United States for one Boeing airplane. But this story is told only as an example of the classical Ricardian principle of international specialization based on comparative advantage. It is more than that. It is also an example of China's profound development strategy — finishing the first industrial revolution of mass producing light consumer goods before jump-starting the second industrial revolution of mass producing heavy industrial goods.

[75] See, e.g., Jinglian Wu (2005), *Understanding and Interpreting Chinese Economic Reform*; and Tiejun Wen (2011), *Understanding the Sunan Model of Village Industries*.

China's village-firm phenomenon is not unique to China, but a feature shared by nearly all successfully developed nations in their early stage of industrialization, except the superficial difference in ownership: China's village firms in the beginning were largely collectively owned instead of privately owned. However, regardless of ownership, the "great spurt" (a la Gerschenkron) of a massive number of rural industries across the countryside has been the chief characteristic of pre-industrial economies in many successfully industrialized nations prior to their industrial takeoff: As noted, England in the 17th to late 18th century, the United States in the middle 18th to early 19th century, and Japan in the early 19th to late 19th century. This widely observed rural industrialization phenomenon was first noted and analyzed by Franklin Mendels (1972) and it is he who coined the term "proto-industrialization."

The economic significance of this initial phase of the Industrial Revolution, as a necessary transition from an agrarian society toward a mass-production economy, is as follows: (i) It stimulates agricultural commercialization, increases the productivity and utilization rate of agricultural labor in manufacturing (e.g., during idle seasons), and raises farmer income without jeopardizing food security; (ii) It trains and transforms atomic and autarkic peasants (including women and children) into a pre-industrial labor force, preparing the "reserve army" (called *non min gong* or migrant workers in China) for the first industrial revolution; (iii) It creates and deepens the mass market (purchasing power of the grassroots) for the adoption of the factory system; (iv) It overcomes the financial and technological barriers of setting up firms and reduces the entry costs and average costs of manufacturing through acquiring cheap land and avoiding labor relocations, thus facilitating primitive capital accumulations; (v) It stimulates regional specialization and domestic and international trade based on each village's local comparative advantage, helps expand foreign markets through the supply of low-value-added goods no longer produced in developed nations, and accumulates valuable foreign reserves needed for importing advanced technologies, and enhances government revenues for local infrastructural development; (vi) It nurtures entrepreneurship and skilled labor through learning by doing; (vii) Above all, it creates conditions for the formation of a commercial distribution system, supply chains, and industrial clusters to prepare for the era of mass production — the Industrial Revolution.[76]

Through "natural selection" based on market competition and Schumpeterian creative destruction, through entry and exits, and through learning by doing, village firms and proto-industries grow and evolve to form a labor-intensive ecosystem of industrial clusters, industrial supply chains, and industrial input–output networks based on the division of labor. The most successful village enterprises will eventually evolve to become modern firms and big players in international markets (such as China's Haier and Hua Wei companies). Such successful firms are normally multi-product firms because of capital abundance. The well-to-do villages and towns will grow into cities or satellite cities, such as Dong Guan City in Guangdong Province. The prosperous and well-connected mom-and-pop shops will evolve into trade centers such as the giant world-famous Yiwu City in East China, which was honored by the United Nations, the World Bank, Morgan Stanley, and other world authorities in 2005 as the "largest small commodity wholesale market in the world." The areas with abundant natural resources, such as coal and iron, will develop into industrial towns (such as Datong and Anshan in China, analogous to Pittsburgh in the United States). The demand for electricity, transportation, water supply, and other forms of infrastructure rises continuously, but such infrastructures become affordable because of the proto-industrialization and the dramatically increased government revenues and government initiatives to finance such projects.

---

[76] For patterns of China's industrialization through concentration, specialization, and clustering, see Long and Zhang (2011, 2012).

A rapidly expanding domestic and international market during proto-industrialization will eventually render labor-intensive mass production of light consumer goods profitable. Hence, China's first industrial revolution was set-off around the end of 1980s, after about 10 years of hyperkinetic rural industrial boom and commercial revolution.

From this viewpoint, the root cause of many African nations' poverty is the lack of a full-fledged proto-industrialization. Without proto-industrialization, these nations are unable to escape from the Malthusian trap and the curse of food security and enter the next stage of mass production. Without mass production, everything from agricultural crops, processed foods, clothing, cookware, simple farming tools, and fertilizers to basic means of transportation, are going to be too expensive to afford and possess, let alone modern irrigation systems and power grids. Hence, any extra food due to good luck (weather) would be immediately allocated to producing more babies.

China's first industrial revolution was financed by savings from its proto-industrialization and powered mainly by foreign technologies (the imported machine tools from advanced countries). But China was able to finance the massive imports of expensive technologies through its exports of mass-produced labor-intensive light consumer goods. This export-led growth process forms a positive feedback loop: Using mass-produced exports to support technological upgrading and using imports of advanced technologies to generate even more exports. This loop of industrialization is in sharp contrast to Latin America's development strategies, which relied heavily on the exports of agricultural products to sustain its industrialization. But the returns to scale in agriculture are quite limited because it is land intensive. More importantly, mechanized agriculture reduces the demand for labor, unlike mass-production-based light industries. Hence, although such a development strategy — that relies on exports of agricultural products or natural resources such as minerals and oil — utilized Latin America's comparative advantages in the abundance of arable land and other natural resources, it did not generate mass employment and failed to create a class of entrepreneurs and a mass market to support continuous industrialization through technological upgrading. As a result, most Latin American countries were able to rapidly modernize their agricultural sector, but unable to fully industrialize with competitive light and heavy industries, thus becoming trapped as middle-income nations.[77]

The rapidly accumulated national production capacity during an industrial revolution based on the mode of mass production often forces state governments to help create and look for new and broader international markets to absorb the mass-supplied goods and ensure a stable supply of raw materials. This explains the two Opium Wars the British Empire imposed on China to force open the Chinese market for mass-produced British goods in the 1840s and 1860s after finishing the first industrial revolution. This also explains why the Chinese government today becomes an advocate of free trade itself (but a non-violent one) and is so active in all continents seeking (i) markets to export "Made in China" as well as (ii) raw materials to feed the giant machine system behind "Made in China." Capitalism is expansionary by nature because an economy can produce more than it needs under the mode of mass production.[78]

---

[77] According to World Bank data (http://data.worldbank.org/indicator/NV.AGR.TOTL.ZS), many Latin American countries' shares of agricultural value added in GDP are as low as, or even much lower than those in developed OECD countries, but their manufacturing sector's shares of valued added in GDP have never been high enough (say above 20%–30% for a sustained period of time) to support full-fledged industrialization.

[78] According to Friedrich List ([1841] 1909, *The Natural System of Political Economy*), Adam Smith's principle of free trade makes sense only in a theoretically ideal frictionless world without national boundaries. In the real world of competing nation-states, free trade becomes a tool used by the powerful to promote their interests; and the less powerful are thus best served by having a strong state to guide economic development and protect domestic industries until they

Our analyses so far have raised and (partially) answered two central questions of development: (i) How to make mass production possible and *profitable* in a backward anarchic agrarian society with autarkic and unorganized peasants (who have zero purchasing power except their raw labor), yet without jeopardizing food security? (ii) Why some countries (mostly European) started to make this great transition 250 years ago while most nations are still unable to emulate such a transition, despite repeated attempts? In what follows, we will continue our quest and show that China's development experience can shed much light on these questions, which are central to economics and many branches of the social and political sciences.

---

are able to compete on an equal footing (see, e.g., Shaun Breslin (2009), "State Led Development in Historical Perspective: From Friedrich List to a Chinese Model of Governance?"). However, Both Smith and List missed the point that even without national boundaries the economy may still fail to prosper and organize according to the principle of the division of labor despite free trade, because of the enormous costs involved in creating the mass market to support the division of labor and mass production.

Chapter 3

Shedding Light on the Nature and Cause of the Industrial Revolution

i. The Nature of the Firm

The Nobel Prize winner Ronald Coase (1937) argued these points: The reason that firms emerge is they reduce or internalize the transaction costs of the market, which may be too high for individuals alone to accommodate. Firms will not emerge if the costs of market transactions are zero. And the optimal size of the firm is therefore proportionate to the size of the transaction costs. But such a theory of the firm cannot explain the Industrial Revolution; nor can it account for the miraculous growth of China's village firms.

My view is that the primary function of the firm is not to internalize trade (or the demand side of the market), but rather to initiate and provide organized mass supply. The Industrial Revolution is characterized not by the merger of market demand and supply to reduce or avoid market transactions. On the contrary, the Industrial Revolution is characterized by the separation between demand and supply through specialization and the division of labor, by the phenomenon of moving from autarkic craftsman workshops with limited supply capacity to large-scale mass-production factories with colossal supply capacity.

Hence, to explain the emergence of mass production or the dramatic increase in firm productivity is the key to understanding the nature of the firm and the Industrial Revolution in general. But to explain the emergence of large-scale mass-production factories based on the Coase theory, one would have to assume that the costs of market transactions had dramatically increased in 18th century England so that it became optimal for capitalists to dramatically expand the size of firms to internalize (avoid) the increased market-transaction costs. This would then also imply that the lack of industrialization in developing countries must be due to the *lack* of large market-transaction costs, thus making the emergence of large firms unnecessary or not worth the investment.

Such implications make no sense. In fact, the market transactions costs are formidable in developing countries; yet, there are no large firms emerging. Why? Because the fundamental nature of the firm manifests itself in the division of labor, and the division of labor is limited by the extent of the market (Adam Smith, 1776).

So the absence of modern firms and mass production in agrarian societies is not because there are no market transaction costs and thus no need for firms to emerge (as implied by the Coase theory). Rather, if modern firms do not exist, it is because of such prohibitive transaction costs — largely due to large business uncertainty and the lack of social trust and commercial infrastructure — that markets are non-existent. If there is no large market (insufficient demand), there will be no large firms (no need for supply).

Hence, the emergence of large factories has always been a response to the emergence of a large market, true in 18th century England and also true in post-1978 China. In short, the lack of firms by no means implies the lack of market transaction costs, but rather the lack of the market itself.

It is this lack of understanding of the more fundamental nature of the firm that has led to Ronald Coase's failure to fully grasp the mechanisms of the Industrial Revolution in general and China's rapid industrialization in particular.[1] Of course, Coase consistently and correctly emphasized the inability of today's dominant macroeconomic paradigm and institution-free neoclassical growth theory to explain China's rapid industrialization.[2]

ii. The Indian Textile Syndrome

After England's successful proto-industrialization that created the pre-industrial market, their Industrial Revolution soon followed, starting first in the textile industry. The cotton textile industry was the flagship of the British Industrial Revolution (Allen, 2009). But all economic historians have pondered this question: If the cotton textile industry was so important for kick-starting an industrial revolution, then why didn't it first start in India? After all, India had the world's best cotton textile industry in the 17th and 18th centuries. In fact, the British colonizers learned and copied the cotton textile technology from India; and India was so advanced in cotton textile technologies that, even by the 1840s (after the first industrial revolution), the quality of hand-made Indian cotton products was still superior to machine-made English textile products.

India's textile industry also "appeared" to have a large accessible market to make mechanized production or the invention and implementation of the spinning jenny profitable. This industry not only satisfied India's huge domestic demand but also exported roughly half of its output to the rest of the world, especially to Europe and specifically England.

---

[1] For other insightful criticism on Coase's theories of industrial organization and his views on government, institutions, social contract, and the provision of public goods, see Xiaopeng Li (2012), Ping Chen (2007, 2010), among other Chinese economists.

[2] See Ronald Coase's (2013) new book, *How China Become Capitalist*, with coauthor Ning Wang.

Many theories have been proposed to solve this Indian Textile Syndrome puzzle, but a dominant one attributes India's failure in kick-starting an industrial revolution to its comparative (dis)advantage in cheap labor (Allen 2009, Broadberry and Gupta, 2009). The argument goes like this: India, like China, had an abundant supply of cheap labor with extremely low real wages in the 18th century. Hence, inventing machines to substitute for labor was not profitable. In contrast, England had the second-highest labor costs and real wages in Europe (behind only the Netherlands); this environment motivated English entrepreneurs to invent textile machines to substitute for labor.[3]

This argument that the Industrial Revolution could have started only in the high-wage England instead of low-wage India is not convincing. For one thing, it suggests that all late-developing countries must wait until real wages increase dramatically before they start industrialization. But this cannot explain why it was precisely the cheap labor in 19th century Japan that benefited and fulfilled Japan's industrial revolution and the modernization of its textile industry. China since 1978 also took great advantage of its cheap labor to successfully embark on its own industrialization and became the world's largest textile manufacturer in 1995, long before China's dramatic increase in real wages in the 2000s. In fact, most late-developing countries have relied on their cheap labor as the stepping stone toward industrial revolution. In addition, high wages do not simply mean high labor costs, but instead imply high labor productivity.[4] In fact, the continuously rising English wage in the

---

[3]An immediate question is why the Industrial Revolution did not start in the Netherlands, where labor costs and real wages were much higher than those in England. Robert Allen's answer was that the Netherlands did not have cheap access to coal. We will scrutinize this "coal theory" of Industrial Revolution in the next chapter.
[4] See Clark's (1987) empirical study and cross-country comparison of real wages and labor efficiency in the early 20th century. Also see Mokyr's (1976) careful comparative study of the labor markets and wage structures of the Low Countries in the late 18th and early 19th centuries.

17th and 18th century (1600–1750) documented by Robert Allen (2009) before the first industrial revolution reflected nothing but the consequence of the proto-industrialization. This initial industriali-zation greatly improved the English population's labor productivity through commerce, primitive specialization, and the division of labor.

If, as Robert Allen (2009) has hypothesized, the motive for adopting the spinning jenny was merely to reduce labor costs or substitute capital for labor, then how can one explain the fact that the British real wage and demand for labor increased more dramati-cally during the Industrial Revolution than during the proto-indus-trialization period? For example, British wages increased by less than 20% over the 100 years between 1675 and 1775, but increased by 50% in the next 50 years between 1775 and 1825, during the first industrial revolution (data from Allen, 2009, Figure 2.1, p. 34). In addition, as Allen (2009) noted, the Netherlands had enjoyed even higher real wages throughout the 17th and 18th centuries than England did, yet it did not invent or adopt the spinning jenny and kick-start the Industrial Revolution.[5]

Therefore, the invention and widespread use of the flying shuttle and the spinning jenny in middle to late 18th century England was driven not by the urge to cut labor costs (or energy costs). The busi-ness case for mechanization was first and foremost the *speed* of production to meet global growing demand for British textiles and their timely deliveries, with the additional advantage of eliminating (domestic and foreign) competition.

---

[5] Note that the spinning jenny and Arkwright water frame and other textile machineries adopted and invented during the first industrial revolution were origi-nally all powered by natural forces instead of coal. Thus, Allen's (2009) argument that the Netherlands failed to invent textile machines to detonate the first indus-trial revolution because it did not have access to cheap coal (despite the higher wages) is dubious. See analyses on the coal theory of the Industrial Revolution in the next section.

I fully agree with Robert Allen's (2009) general thesis that the Industrial Revolution was driven largely by the demand for new technology, not by supply of new technology. But in contrast to Allen's high-wage (and cheap coal) theory, I argue that the pivotal force of demand for new technology does not originate from the incentives to reduce the labor or energy costs of textile production *per se*, but rather from rising output demand and competition for market shares based on the principle of economies of scale. As economic historian Phyllis Deane (1979) keenly noted:

> "[I]t was only when the potential market was large enough, and demand elastic enough, to justify a substantial increase in output, that the rank and file of entrepreneurs broke away from their traditional techniques and took advantage of the technical opportunities then open to them."[6]

The English high wages in 17th and 18th centuries were the result of its proto-industrialization and thus simply a manifestation of the existing size (depth) of the English market and the purchasing power of the grassroots population in the pre-Industrial Revolution period. But the adoption of the flying shuttle, the spinning jenny, the factory system, and the methods of mass production during the Industrial Revolution, driven by growing market demand and competition for market shares among a rapidly growing number of textile producers and merchants, further dramatically increased the English wages and demand for labor instead of reducing them.[7]

The characteristics of wage growth in China since 1978 can also shed light on the issue. The average real wage in China grew only moderately during China's proto-industrialization period

---

[6] Phyllis Deane (1979), *The First Industrial Revolution*, Second Edition, p. 131.

[7] The dramatically increased English population during the first industrial revolution would have further greatly depressed the real wage had the adoption of capital in production been driven by the incentives of reducing labor costs. But in fact the English real wage increased much faster during the Industrial Revolution than before the Revolution.

(roughly corresponding to the period of 1978–1988), rising at a rate of 4.9% per year (comparing with its real GDP growth of 10% and rural industrial output growth of 28% per year). During China's first industrial revolution period (roughly the period of 1988–1998), nationwide wage growth was still at a modest rate of 3.9% when employment in private and jointly-owned enterprises experienced vigorous growth and the method of mass-producing light consumer goods was widely adopted. It was only after China kick-started a second industrial revolution around 1997–1998 (featuring the heavy-industrial boom and the adoption of mass-producing heavy intermediate goods such as chemicals and steel and machine tools) and joined the World Trade Organization (WTO) in 2001 did real wage growth start to accelerate and outpace real GDP growth. For example, in the period of 1998–2007, real wage growth accelerated to an astonishing 13.2% per year.[8]

Therefore, a more sensible explanation of India's failure and Britain's success in detonating the textile-based Industrial Revolution is not the high real wage in Britain *per se* that rendered it profitable to substitute capital for labor; nor was the low real wage in India that rendered Indian workshops profitable in their intensive use of labor. But rather it is the lack of (or failure to create) a large organized domestic and international market (credit, intermediation, payment enforcement, trust, and purchasing power), the associated market competition, and the effective means for the supply of raw-materials (cotton) and a distribution system for mass-produced output in countries like India (as well as China at one point). England by the middle of the 18th century had successfully created not only a colossal domestic and international market for mass-produced textile goods but also the well-diversified supply chains of cotton (from India and the American colonies) and the distribution networks for her textile products, thanks to her

---

[8] See Yang, Chen, and Monarch (2010).

advanced domestic and international commercial trading posts, navigation systems (turnpikes and canals), and powerful navy, which were all carefully and deliberately cultivated and nurtured by the government for centuries to win global competition in commerce (especially textiles) and military domination among the European powers. In other words, through centuries of state-led proto-industrialization under mercantilism, the existence of severe competitive pressure among proto-industrial firms in Europe (and from Indian cotton textile manufacturers too) and the rapid government-led creation and expansion of both domestic and international markets for textiles incentivized British entrepreneurs and merchants to seek better ways to improve productivity and speed and volume of production and overall profitability by exploring and exploiting the economies of scale; that is, to switch from small-scale workshops with simple tools and primitive division of labor to large-scale factories with reproducible machines (capital) and a sophisticated organizational structure for labor (even though it was far more costly to organize large-scale production in terms of credit and management).

In general, the market size of a product depends negatively on transaction and transportation costs, but positively on the sophistication of commerce and middlemen services, on the ability to maintain a steady supply of raw materials and low risk of failure in making sales, on the communication technology (information about market demand in remote places), and on the purchasing power of consumers. Because of the proto-industrialization and strong state support (mercantilist policies and the protection of long-distance trade by the navy), 18th century England had the required colossal domestic and international market size and raw material supply chains and low-enough transportation and transaction costs to absorb (support) mass-produced textile goods, to cover the fixed costs in machinery investments and labor organizations and transportation, and to reduce the risk in product specialization and division of labor. But 18th century India (and China) had none of these. Not even the

Netherlands created such a colossal domestic and global market and supply chains and distribution networks in textiles.[9]

Most economic historians have failed to sufficiently emphasize an important yet simple fact (related intrinsically to market size), or its importance in explaining and understanding the Industrial Revolution and economic development: that is, the connection between the economy of scale and sunk and fixed capital investment costs. Once the capital is installed, regardless of its installation costs, the marginal cost of using the capital is essentially zero. The production costs from then on consist only (or mainly) of the variable input costs such as labor, materials, and energy. In other words, capital (structures and equipment) are "free" to use once they are installed. Therefore, expanding the scale of production and intensively using the installed capacity (say by 24 hours a day) is the fundamental driving force of the capital-based (rather than land-based) production for all industrial nations (because capital is reproducible but land is not, and capital utilization is not subject to seasonal and day-night changes while land is). So the stream of future profits depends entirely on the size of the market. Too small a market cannot pay for the fixed cost of capital investment. But the market can never be too large for any establishment (the more the merrier).[10] Also, output prices decline with the size of the market

---

[9] This Smithian market-size theory also helps to explain one of the biggest puzzles in economic history: Why did the Netherlands fail to kick-start the Industrial Revolution? It did not even catch up and finish industrialization by the end of the 19th century (lagged behind France and Germany). The high-wage theory of Robert Allen (2009) cannot explain it because the Netherlands at the time had the highest wages in the world, nor can the institutional theory of Acemoglu and Robinson (2005, 2012) explain it because the Netherlands had the most liberal political and economic institutions in Europe.

[10] For example, both 19th century British firms and 21st century Chinese firms would like to run their textile machines 24 hours a day and 365 days a year. Workers' working hours were often stretched to the human biological limit during every nation's first industrial revolution period.

(precisely because of the fixed cost of investment and the zero marginal cost of using existing capital), making a larger firm more competitive while simultaneously creating additional disproportionately larger demand for the extremely income-elastic textile products.

Therefore, the English Industrial Revolution was not caused by the high wages of labor *per se*, but instead by the rapidly expanding textile market and the increasing preemptive competitive pressure among the massive number of English textile proto-industrial firms for market shares. The colossal market demand and severe preemptive competitive pressure made the adoption of the spinning jenny profitable because even semi-mechanized production can dramatically increase the speed and volume of supply despite the high wage costs of English workers. The high wages acted rather as a demand-side factor (the purchasing power of the population) than as a supply-side cost factor.

It's no wonder that ever since the use of capital in production (spinning jenny and steam engine), discovering new technologies and expanding new markets have become the single most important drive and ultimate goal of all capitalists and capitalistic production. Hence, the British government and merchant-capitalists vigorously promoted free trade after finishing the first industrial revolution in textile production and the railroad transportation boom.

Just as Rome was not built in a day, neither was the Industrial Revolution. The family-based craftsmen workshops cannot directly transform themselves into factory-based mass production because of the restrictions imposed by market size, which is measured not only by the population but also its purchasing power and more importantly the means of transportation, delivery, and merchant credit (known as "financial intermediation") to reach the customers (including wholesalers and retailers) and ensure raw material supplies. British textile industries had the means to reach their customers nationwide and worldwide and the colonies to provide the needed raw materials (cotton) in "arm's reach," but Indian craftsmen and artisans did not. In other words, Adam Smith's pin factories with fine division of labor and regional product specialization and low-cost commercial networks and resource-supply chains were the norm of English proto-industries but were exceptions in 17th and 18th century China and India.

What set English statesmen and merchants apart from their counterparts elsewhere was their ability to dominate the global textile trade and cotton supply chains. India (and China) did not even come close to such global dominance. And yet starting in the 16th century, European — and especially British — monarchies and their state-backed armed merchants had gradually created the largest and most sophisticated global textile market and cotton supply chains, which were unimaginable in earlier human history. It was this enormous market and the acute competitive pressure facing the European states and textile producers that laid the precondition for the Industrial Revolution. (Also see Sven Beckert, 2014).

This also explains why it was the European nations surrounding Great Britain and sharing the British global commercial market and cotton supply chains, instead of the Asian or Latin American nations, that successfully emulated the British Industrial Revolution by as early as middle 19th century despite the fact that cotton planting and production was never the comparative advantage of Europe but of Asia and Latin America.

David Landes (1999, p. 225) asked a great question when discussing India's failure to start its industrial revolution in the 18th century: "Who would have gained from mechanization and transformation [in India]?" He answered that it had to be the merchants or the middlemen, because the artisans and craftsmen in India were incapable of arbitraging the enormous profits from international trade, just as the Chinese tea growers or the Indonesia spice planters were unable to exploit the colossal price differentials between Asia and the European market. The family-based primitive textile workshops in India had very limited ability to create their own demand; hence, India would rely on rich and powerful merchants and middlemen to organize (and finance) larger-scale production and long-distance sales if it wanted to expand production capacity through teamwork, further division of labor, specialization of production, and adoption of capital-intensive technology. But mass production and long-distance trade also require a large amount of trade credit to support the supply of raw materials and finance capital investment, an advanced infrastructure to deliver goods without incurring prohibitive transaction costs and unpredictable time delays, and a deep and large market to absorb and ensure the massively enlarged volume of output supply. India lacked all of these facilitating factors: It did not have a powerful class of wealthy middlemen to ensure the smooth flow of raw materials, finance capital investment and trade credit, and tolerate losses from failed sales. Nor did it have sufficient infrastructure to reduce long-distance trade costs and ensure timely deliveries or a deep, large, and unified domestic market with enough purchasing power to absorb the colossal supply. Not only did India lack these facilitating factors 200 years ago, it lacks them even today, which explains why India remains unindustrialized. So the economic structure in the 18th century India was simply unprepared to detonate an industrial revolution, despite a then-advanced family-based textile sector and fertile land to grow cotton. As noted, that sector greatly helped the English Industrial Revolution, despite the lack of homegrown cotton, of course. The British could not have detonated the first industrial revolution without the textile technology transfer from India and its own relatively deep, large, and unified domestic and well-cultivated international markets (supported by millions of English bourgeois consumers and merchants and the British navy and trans-Atlantic traders, as well as well-developed infrastructure and commercial networks).[11]

---

[11] Neoclassical economists (maybe except Paul Krugman's New Trade Theory) seldom emphasize that the most important incentive for international trade is not about comparative advantages, but about the size of the market. Market size matters in capitalist economies because of the scale effect of operations under the

Therefore, despite its domestic market of nearly 1.3 billion people, India today is still largely outside of the global supply chains for mass-produced items: It must depend on China and other exporters for goods — from industrial machinery and mobile phones to more basic products such as light bulbs and toys. Why can't India produce even basic items, such as toys? In the 1960s the Indian economy was 20% larger than China's. Today China's economy is 500% larger than India's. The two countries have nearly identical populations, but China today attracts seven times more foreign direct investment (FDI) than India, and produces and consumes nearly 60% of world cement output, while India's share is only 7%.

What has prevented India so far from emulating China and detonating an industrial revolution? Is it the lack of access to technology? No. India is already capable of sending spaceships to Mars. Is it the lack of democracy? No. India is the largest democracy on earth. Is it the lack of property rights? No. India has had private property rights in place for thousands of years. Is it the lack of the rule of law? No. India inherited English common law in the 18th century. Why then does India choose to import toys instead of producing them on its own? To answer this question, we must forget about the rhetoric of extractive and inclusive institutions or the law of comparative advantages. We must think about market coordination failures. It is the lack of a well fermented market and intermediaries to organize India's massive number of autarkic and anarchic peasants to form organizations based on the principle of the division of labor that has led to India's failure to create its own supply of toys. It is this lack of market creators and state-backed powerful intermediaries that has prevented agrarian India from replacing small-scale autarkic artisan workshops with mass-production

---

essentially zero marginal cost of using installed capital once the sunk costs of investment are paid. In long-run growth as in short-run recessions, it is (market) demand that determines (firms') supply and the mode of production, not the other way around.

factories. In one word, India lacks *proto-industrialization* to jump start its own industrial revolution, to create and nurture a large and powerful merchant class, to raise the demand and purchasing power of its grassroots population, to transform its rural population into an organized work force, and to promote the division of labor and form supply chains and distribution networks nationwide.

To achieve all of these in a short period of time in a rapidly changing world with already-crowded industrialized powers and highly competitive international markets, India needs its central and local governments (not international investors or giant foreign corporations) to do more to facilitate the formation of domestic markets and proto-industries and to build better infrastructures. Big international corporations and manufacturers do not establish a presence in a country without an organized system of transport, commerce, trade credit, and supply chains. In fact, huge flows of international FDI from advanced industrial countries did not start pouring into China until the early to middle 1990s — after China successfully finished its proto-industrialization and embarked on its first industrial revolution. Then and only then did China become a real (instead of potential) market for profit-seeking international corporations, a target of Western FDI outflows; only then did China's colossal population become a real (instead of potential) purchasing power and source of cheap labor for cost-minimizing international giants.[12]

---

[12] China's FDI inflow grew slowly during its proto-industrialization period and was tiny in the 1980s. For example, in 1983, the inflow of FDI into China was 636 million U.S. dollars, accounting for 0.3% of China's GDP, and the figure remained below 1% even by the end of the 1980s. But in the 1990s during China's first industrial revolution period, FDI inflow to China increased more than 10-fold, e.g., from $4.37 billion in 1991 to $45.26 billion in 1997, accounting for 5% of GDP. The pace of FDI inflow to China further accelerated after China finished its first industrial revolution by the end of the 1990s and kick-started a second industrial revolution in the early 2000s. As a result, China has overtaken the U.S. in 2014 as the top destination for global FDI ($128 trillion for mainland

iii. The Rise of the Textile Industry and the Logic of the English Industrial Revolution

The Rise of China's Textile Industry

With rapid fermentation of a unified national market and nearly a decade-long flourish of proto-industries and commercial networks in its domestic and international trade, China reached the tipping point of its first industrial revolution in the late 1980s. The flagship industry of China's first industrial revolution was its textile and clothing industry.

With the rapidly improving living standard of the Chinese grass-roots population, local demand for textile and apparel goods continued to rise throughout the 1980s, thanks to the huge income elasticity of such goods. Fueled by the rising demand and intense competition, mass production of textiles and garments, based on mass organization of migrant peasant-workers, became profitable. Hence, China's total production of yarn and cotton fabrics increased from 330,000 tons and 1.9 billion meters in 1985 to 8,500,000 tons and 32.2 billion meters in 2002, respectively, with a 23-fold increase for yarn and a 15-fold increase for cotton fabrics over 17 years

---

China, $111 trillion for Hong Kong, and $86 trillion for the U.S.). In general, the specific nature of FDI inflow to China has gone through three phases (waves) analogous to China's stage of industrialization: In the 1980s FDI came mainly from low-tech and small-scale labor-intensive firms in Hong Kong and it mostly went to China's rural areas (especially Guangdong province, which shares the same dialect with Hong Kong). In the 1990s, it came mainly from large-scale labor-intensive firms from Taiwan and South Korea. Since late 1990s and early 2000s, it came mainly from modern efficient capital-intensive manufacturing firms in the more advanced developed nations, such as Japan, the United States, and Germany. Foreign firms, especially large-scale heavy-industrial firms, would never venture into a country if the country's market size and supply chains and commercial/transportation system were inadequate to support mass production and mass distribution. This explains why India lags far behind China in attracting FDI despite a similar-sized population to China.

(implying an annual growth rate of 20% and 17%, respectively). Total garment output increased from 1.3 (billion pieces) in 1985 to 9.5 (billion pieces) in 1996, with an average growth rate of 22% per year. Total chemical fabric production increased from 94.8 (thousand tons) in 1986 to 991.2 (thousand tons) in 2002, growing by 16% per year on average.[13] By as early as 1990, there were already tens of millions of spindles in the east and south of China with well-formed industrial production chains and clusters of textile manufacturing. By 1994–1995, the number of spindles reached 40 million, one for every 25 Chinese.[14]

The growth was driven initially by the large state-owned enterprises (SOEs) but then primarily by privately owned enterprises (POEs) as soon as the POEs caught up with the mass-production technologies with self-financing. The profits of POEs grew by 23.5% per year between 1990 and 1997.

Mass production requires mass mobilization of labor. Since the late 1980s and early 1990s, China entered an era of unprecedented mass flow of migrant workers from rural to urban factories. Each year, hundreds of millions of migrant workers poured into the relatively more prosperous and internationally better connected south and east coasts after spending the Chinese New Year back home, traveling thousands and even tens of thousands of miles through China's emerging highway and railroad networks. Just like 19th century

---

[13] Data source: Larry D. Qiu (2005).

[14] This number became 80 million in 2006, accounting for nearly half of the world's total spindles. In comparison, Lancashire had 1.7 million spindles by early 1780s. In 1813, there were about 240,000 looms in England, about one for every 40 British. But only 1% of them were power looms, the rest were looms operated by hands. On the edge of the American Industrial Revolution in 1831, there were 1.2 million spindles and 33,500 looms in the United States. Based on the rule of thumb that one Chinese year of growth and development roughly equals five Western years, and taking China's starting point of proto-industrial revolution as 1980 and the Britain as 1730–1750, then China in 1990 would be equivalent to England around 1780–1800, and China in 2000 would correspond to England in 1830–1850, the point when Britain finished its first industrial revolution and started the second Industrial Revolution with a booming industrial trinity of coal/steam engine/railroad.

Europe and England, where labor-intensive mass production in textile manufacturing rested on the ability to persuade, entice, or even force people to give up the activities that had organized human life for thousands of years and join the newly emerging factory system and industrial army, China needed to do something similar. This was not an easy task and required critical economic, legal, social, and political conditions. Such conditions were ripe in late 20th century China (but clearly not in the Qing dynasty or Republic era) after a decade of reform and rapid proto-industrialization.

As a result, the textile and clothing industry became the largest manufacturing industry and major source of foreign exchange in China during its first industrial revolution period (between 1988 and 1998). This industry had about 24,000 enterprises and employed about 8 million workers in the 1990s, and its exports accounted for more than 20% of China's total exports.[15] Small wonder China surpassed the United States and became the world's largest producer and exporter of textiles and garments in 1995, six to seven years before joining the WTO, and has remained this dominant position ever since.[16]

Again, the government has played a pivotal role in kick-starting China's textile-led industrial revolution. To assist China's economic reforms and open door policies, the government in 1979 wisely chose the textile and clothing industry as one of its primary target-industries for promotion, in sharp contrast with its earlier development strategy of focusing on heavy industries such as steel under Mao. The most important reasons for this choice were that (i) this industry was consistent with China's comparative advantage in its abundance in labor, (ii) it did not require very advanced technologies and had relatively low entry costs, and (iii) it had a huge domestic and international market.

---

[15] Total employment in the textile and clothing industry in China reached 20 million in 2007. In contrast, during the heyday of Western industrial revolution in the early 1860s, the number of textile workers was 446,000 in the U.K., 250,300 in Germany, 200,000 in France, 150,000 in Russia, 105,000 in Spain, and 122,000 in the U.S. (see Sven Beckert, 2014, p. 180)

[16] China remains the world's largest producer and exporter of textile and clothing products, including cotton yarn, wool fiber, cotton fabric, silk fabric, garments, chemical fibers, and knitted goods.

To promote the textile industry, the government launched a policy called "Six Priorities," under which the textile industry enjoyed favorable treatment in six areas: supply of raw materials, energy and power, bank loans, foreign exchange, imported advanced technology, and transportation (see, e.g., Larry D. Qiu, 2005).

Accordingly, sophisticated government organizations were established to facilitate, intermediate, and regulate the textile industry. For example, besides direct state involvement in managing national cotton inventories to hedge against global fluctuations in cotton prices, China had the following government agencies (long before joining the WTO) to supervise, regulate, and assist the textile and clothing industry in coping with international textile market rules and competition:

MOA — Ministry of Agriculture.

NDRC — National Development and Reform Commission.

MOFCOM — Ministry of Commerce.

SASAC — State-owned Assets Supervision and Administration Commission.

CCCT — China Chamber of Commerce for Import and Export of Textiles.

CNTIC — China National Textile Industry Council.

CPCIA — China Petroleum and Chemical Industry Association.

SEPA — State Environmental Protection Administration.

The specific functions of some of these government agencies are as follows:

1. *Raw Material Supply*

The MOA is responsible for key raw material industries including cotton, silk, and wool. However, the NDRC is responsible for the importation of raw materials, for which import quotas still apply.

2. *Production and Processing*

CNTIC guides the production and processing in the textile industry. CNTIC is the legacy agency of the now defunct Ministry of Textile

Industry. Its broad responsibilities include the implementation of industrial development guidelines for the sector.

3. *Export Quota License*

The NDRC's Department of Industry supervises the national textile industry. The Bureau of "Economic Operation" is responsible for formulating policies and controlling the export quota licensing system in the textile industry. However, the MOFCOM is in charge of actually issuing export quota licenses.[17]

4. *Standards-Setting*

The State Administration for Quality, Supervision, Inspection and Quarantine (AQSIQ) is the government agency responsible for setting technical, safety, and environmental protection standards for textile products in China. In the textile sector, AQSIQ functions as a standards-setting coordinator. When setting standards, it seeks technical support from the Textile Industry Standardization Institute (TISI) and consults with the CNTIC. AQSIQ is also the agency in charge of enforcing standards and providing certification of products and enterprises. AQSIQ is also involved in drafting laws and regulations governing industrial standardization in the textile sector.

The Logic of the English Industrial Revolution

The fact that the textile industry was so pivotal and instrumental in kick-starting China's first industrial revolution and has led the way

---

[17] Because trade protectionism from developed countries imposed a severe limit on China's total textile exports, China set up this agency to manage and select the number and type of firms entering the export market (to reduce vicious competition). Since 1974 the U.S., Europe, and other rich countries have formalized and greatly expanded a web of curbs to be imposed on developing countries for their textile products and producers, known as the Multifibre Arrangement (MFA). This system has not succeeded in its aim of stemming a steady fall in employment in the industry in the west, but has severely distorted trade and has cost western consumers, as well as developing economies, dearly.

into China's second industrial revolution (1998–present) resembles the pattern of the British Industrial Revolution. This phenomenon sheds considerable light on the long-standing puzzle and the internal *logic* of the Industrial Revolution itself.

The Industrial Revolution was detonated first in England and also first in the textile industry. It was triggered by the mechanization of textile production in the period of 1760s–1830s through a series of inventions of simple yet powerful wood-framed tools and machines; these tools and machines rapidly sped up spinning and weaving.[18]

However, the British Industrial Revolution was not merely driven by such technological inventions *per se*, as the conventional wisdom often assumes; rather, it was driven mainly by the colossal textile market demand created by Britain and the fierce competition among the proto-industrial textile firms for market shares.

In other words, the Industrial Revolution was detonated first in England and first in the textile industry because (i) among all the economic activities, the production of food, clothes, and shelter is the most basic, and cotton fibers are the most easily manipulable (amongst all natural fibers) and spinning and weaving are much less dependent on weather, season, and daylight conditions and much easier to be mechanized through the use of simple low-cost tools than growing crops and building shelters;[19] (ii) the textile market is

---

[18] According to the commonly accepted chronology, the first industrial revolution started around 1760–1780 and was finished around 1830–1840.

[19] Cotton's versatility allowed it to be combined with linen and be made into velvet. It was cheaper than silk and could be imprinted more easily than wool, allowing for patterned dresses for women. It became the standard fashion and, because of its price, was accessible to the general public. New inventions in the 1770s (such as the spinning jenny, the water frame, and the spinning mule) made many parts of Great Britain very profitable manufacturing centers. In 1794–1796, British cotton goods accounted for 15.6% of Britain's exports, and in 1804–1806 grew to 42.3% (see, e.g., http://en.wikipedia.org/wiki/History_of_cotton#British_Empire).

potentially the largest and most income elastic compared with other light consumer goods (such as jewelry, pottery, or furniture), hence can grow rapidly with income and easily support mass production and stimulate innovation under competition;[20] and (iii) before the British Industrial Revolution, England nurtured its textile market for hundreds of years at least since Elizabeth I (1558–1603) or even earlier. These interventions created Europe's largest textile market by the early 18th century, and Great Britain eventually possessed the largest number of early textile firms.[21] However, by the early and

---

[20] The income/price elasticity of textiles and garments are extremely high, compared with other consumer goods available in 18th and 19th century Europe or any agrarian societies, such as tea, coffee, sugar, glasses, arts, jewelry, pottery, watch, and furniture. As Phyllis Deane (1979, p. 66) amply put: "[Cotton textile] was cheap enough to come within the budget of the lowest income groups and fine enough to be desired by rich as well as poor; it was salable in tropical as well as in temperate climates; and it found a market ready-made for it in the regions which Britain had been supplying for a century with Indian calicoes." Such large income/price elasticity of cotton textile goods implies gigantic global market and growth potential, making the Industrial Revolution sustainable not only in 19th century England, but also far into the future of mankind. It is not an exaggeration to say that the textile industry has fulfilled all late-developed economies' industrial revolution after Britain, including France, Germany, Italy, the United States, Japan, Singapore, Hong Kong, Taiwan, South Korea, and China, among many others; and it will continue to play such a pivotal role for other developing nations in the future.

[21] According to Ha-Joon Chang (2003, p. 19) "Edward III (1327–1377) is believed to have been the first king who deliberately tried to develop local wool cloth manufacturing. He wore only English cloth to set an example to the rest of the country, brought in Flemish weavers, centralized trade in raw wool and banned the import of woolen cloth." Such mercantilist industrial policies (with a particular focus on textiles) continued almost uninterrupted for the following centuries leading up to the first industrial revolution. For example, "Daniel Defoe describes ... how the Tudor monarchs, especially Henry VII (1485–1509) and Elizabeth I (1558–1603), transformed England from a country relying heavily on raw wool export to the Low Countries into the most formidable wool-manufacturing nation in the world" (Ha-Joon Chang, 2003, p. 20). In order to protect the

middle of 18th century, after centuries of proto-industrialization and a boom in textile production across Europe (see, e.g., Franklin F. Mendels, 1972, 1981, and Ogilvie and Cerman, 1996), the global woolen and linen textile market for European and British textile products (based on artisan workshops) appeared virtually saturated. This immensely competitive situation was critical for stimulating technology innovation and discovery of new varieties to survive market competition by re-shaping the market and gaining new market shares, as exemplified by the government-promoted shift of the British textile industry from the traditional woolen/linen textiles to cotton textiles around the 1730s (e.g., as symbolized by the Manchester Act in 1736), and from workshops to cotton mills around 1740s, and the subsequent Industrial Revolution based on mechanized cotton textile mass production.[22]

English textile industry from international competition of the Low Countries, the Tudor monarchs passed a series of legislations in 1489, 1512, 1513, and 1536 to ban the exports of unfinished cloths ... According to Defoe, it was not until the time of Elizabeth I (1587), nearly a 100 years after Henry VII started his import substitution policy (1489), that Britain was confident enough about its raw wool manufacturing industry's international competitiveness to ban raw wool export completely. This eventually drove the manufacturers in the Low Countries to ruin ... In order to open new markets Elizabeth I dispatched trade envoys to the Pope and the Emperors of Russia, Mogul, and Persia. Britain's massive investment in building its naval supremacy allowed it to break into new markets and often to colonize them and keep them as captive markets" (Ha-Joon Chang, 2003, pp. 20–21). The English protectionism rose even more dramatically after the Glorious Revolution (see, e.g., Ralph Davis, 1966, The Rise of Protection in England, 1689–1786, *The Economic History Review*, Vol. 19, No. 2, pp. 306–317).

[22] "British craftsmen had spun fibers into yarn and woven cotton into marketable cloths for more than a century before Hargreaves' jenny appeared... By 1750, the British economy already produced a far greater volume of yarn, cloth, and finished textiles, manufactured wholly or partly from cotton fibers, than any other economies outside India." (Patrick O'Brien *et al.*, 1991, Political Components of the Industrial Revolution: Parliament and the English Cotton Textile

In addition, unlike agricultural activities such as crop growing, textile production are much easier to divide into many intermediate production stages and adoptive to an environment of division of labor. Textile production requires repeated body movements from workers and is simple enough that even unskilled workers (elderly women and young children) can easily accomplish. Also, textile production often involves long working hours, thus can absorb a huge amount of surplus labor in the rural areas.

Hence, it is not surprising that the Industrial Revolution started first in England and first in such a particular industry — because only a massive market with mature distribution networks and highly income-elastic demand could stimulate and sustain profitable mass production through mechanization.[23]

Industry, 1660–1774, *Economic History Review*, 44(3), pp. 395–423) John Kay (1704–1779) in Lancashire invented the flying shuttle in 1733 — one of the first of a series of inventions associated with the cotton industry. The flying shuttle increased the width of cotton cloth and speed of production of a single weaver at a loom. The first cotton mills were established in the 1740s to house roller spinning machinery invented by Lewis Paul and John Wyatt. The machines were the first to spin cotton mechanically without the intervention of human fingers. They were driven by a single non-human power source which allowed the use of larger machinery and made it possible to concentrate production into organized factories. The spinning jenny — the first symbol of the Industrial Revolution — was invented in 1764 by James Hargreaves in England. The device dramatically increased the speed of yarn production, with a worker able to work eight or more spools at once. This grew to 120 as technology advanced in subsequent years.

[23] Alternatively, it could be said that the industrialization also started in other industries (such as printing) but these industries had much smaller impact on the overall economy than the textile industry, precisely because the textile market was far larger than the other goods markets. Only with the tremendous amount of profits and revenues constantly flowing from the textile industry could the British economy finance its huge investment in coal and steam power and railroad expansion. In fact, the Netherlands applied the division of labor and machinery in the fishery industry in the 17th century, but that food-processing industry was too small to kick-start an industrial revolution.

Mechanization is the natural outcome of the division of labor based on large market. Through the division of labor, firms can identify the segments of the production process that require mechanical motion. Such repeatable physical movements are part of the production process most easily replaced by preliminary machines (tools) operated by natural power (the human body, animals, or water flow) such as the wood framed spinning jenny and Arkwright's water frame.

However, once the entire production process is divided into different segments, the mechanization of one particular production segment immediately creates *demand* for mechanization of other production segments to keep pace so that the demand/supply of intermediate-stage goods can continue. Eventually, the whole production process becomes mechanized. Karl Marx described the process this way: "Thus spinning by machinery made weaving by machinery a necessity, and both together made the mechanical and chemical revolution that took place in bleaching, printing, and dyeing, imperative. So too, on the other hand, the revolution in cotton-spinning called forth the invention of the gin, for separating the seeds from the cotton fiber; it was only by means of this invention, that the production of cotton became possible on the enormous scale at present required" (Karl Marx, Capita, Chapter 15).

Mechanization of spinning thus triggered other aspects of the industrial revolution: the productive power of men to meet a gigantic, ever-increasing, ever-diversified income-elastic market demand for textiles and for all sorts of related light consumer goods. The increased volume of trade and demand for the delivery and distribution of such goods at such a scale across such a vast geographic space in early 19th century England naturally called for revolutions in other areas of the economy, such as new energy sources (coal), new materials and intermediate goods (iron and steel), new motive power (steam engine), and new methods of communication (telegraphs) and transportation (turnpikes, railroads, and steam-powered ships). "In a society whose pivot [...] was agriculture on a small scale, with its subsidiary domestic industries, and the urban handicrafts, the means of communication and transport were so utterly inadequate to the productive requirements of the manufacturing period" (Karl Marx, Capita, Chapter 15). Thus the demand for more efficient forms of communication and transportation powered by new forms of energy and technology brought about new industries and new innovations and new applications of existing discoveries, such as replacing sailing vessels with a system of river steamers, railways, and ocean steamers and substituting human messengers with telegraphs. But the materials required to build such a colossal communication and transportation system implied "huge masses of iron that had now to be forged, to be welded, to be cut, to be bored, and to be shaped, demanded" (Karl Marx, Des Capita, Chapter 15).

As the economy grows and the market deepens, even these relatively new methods of manufacturing became "utterly inadequate." In other words, once the division of labor is established and demand and supply are separated, the demand and the supply sides of the market then entered a horserace to create (and catch up with) each other. Each step of mechanization raises the scale of production, thus requiring a bigger market to cover the fixed costs involved and to absorb the excess capacity created on the supply side. Each expansion of the productive capacity in turn calls for more demand, thus driving profit-seeking capitalists into continents to create new markets. The discovery of new markets makes another round of mechanization or new technology adoption profitable. Also, a radical change in the mechanization of production in one sphere of industry creates demand and incentives for a similar change in other spheres, so growth leads to more growth, and expansion leads to more expansion.

Interestingly, this economic logic has not changed since the British Industrial Revolution. Virtually, all recently developed nations followed the same path paved by the British to successfully kick-start their own first industrial revolution.

Specifically, the rise of China's light industries, particularly its textile and clothing industry, as well as its subsequent booms in coal and steel production and highway building since the middle 1990s and high-speed rail construction since the early 2000s clearly echoed the historical pattern and sequence of the British Industrial Revolution in the 18th and 19th centuries, and they shared the same *developmental logic*: These waves of industrialization in both 18th–19th century England and modern China were all powered by demand and sustained by supply in a dynamic feedback process with continuous technology adoptions and market expansions in new industries both up- and downstream.

Proto-industries to the Industrial Revolution were like yeast to sourdough or oxygen to fire. Only a few O_2 molecules in the air without a critical density is not enough to light a fire. All agrarian societies have some proto-industries, especially in textiles. But they do not grow to critical levels or densities and reach an ignition point unless the countries have (i) a unified domestic market with a well-developed middleman/merchant class and a commercial network with a massive number of trading posts; (ii) a powerful central government to favor and promote commerce and export-oriented manufacturing under the mercantilism ideology; (iii) an infrastructure for intra- and international trade with great shipping capacity and easy access to raw materials (e.g., wool and cotton supply); and (iv) the right industrial policy of focusing on key industries (such as textiles) with abundant domestic factor supply (such as rural surplus labor) and colossal global demand.

Among the affluent European countries with the capacity for ocean voyages and distant colonies, not the Netherlands, not Portugal, not France, not Germany, not Ireland, not Italy, not Spain, but only Britain had all of the above necessary conditions for an industrial revolution by the middle of the 18th century (when Adam Smith wrote *The Wealth of Nations*). After more than 200 years of market "fermentation," by the 1720s England had already developed a sophisticated proto-industrial base with a massive number of supply chains, industrial clusters, and regional specialization and product concentrations in textiles and other manufactured goods, such as metal goods in Sheffield, Birmingham, and the Black Country; woolens in East Anglia and the West Country; worsteds around Bradford; woolens around Leeds; cottons around Manchester; and pottery in Cheshire, as described by Daniel Defoe in his "Tour Through the Whole Island of Great Britain (1724–1726)."[24] By the 1750s in Lancashire alone there were already countless textile workshops (and even factories and mills) with maximal division of labor and tens of thousands of spindles standing ready to welcome the revolutionary spinning jenny. Fierce competition among European and especially British proto-industries for market shares in and outside of England and Europe and Africa and Asia (and indeed around the globe) was bound to lead to the profitable adoption of mechanized production and large-scale factories with organized labor and machines even if wages were cheap and coal more expensive.[25]

Traditional textile industries are not capital intensive, nor energy-intensive (still the case in modern textile industries with regard to the lower end of the value chain in textile and clothing production). The spinning jenny and Arkwright water frame and other textile machineries adopted and invented during the first industrial revolution can be powered by water and wind. But cotton fibers are most easily manipulable by machine tools, more so than any other natural fibers such as wool and silk; and textile goods are the most income elastic with the longest production chains for sophisticated division of labor, more so than any other light-industrial consumer goods such as shoes and pottery and furniture and cement. Thus, cotton textiles have the largest potential domestic and international markets to support and profit from mechanization. Whoever grabbed this particular market would be the winner in the race to the Industrial Revolution.

---

[24] Available online at https://archive.org/search.php?query=A%20tour%20 thro%20the%20Whole%20Island%20of%20Great%20Britain%20AND%20 mediatype%3Atexts. Also cited in David Landes (1999, p. 215).

[25] See the next subsection for the discussion on the role of coal in the Industrial Revolution.

The Netherlands had the most sophisticated pre-industrial ship-building technology, highly spirited merchants and commerce-promoting government, and the most advanced commerce-facilitating financial institutions. But it had no critical mass of proto-industries in textiles, especially cotton textiles, nor did it have a strong and centralized government to nurture and reign over a global cotton-textile input–output supply chain and a worldwide textile market as it lacked American and Indian colonies — so it did not have the opportunity to engage with an Indian colonial textile artisan to teach them cotton textile technology, and it did not have American colonial land to provide a virtually unlimited supply of cotton inputs. France, Spain, Italy, and Germany were no match for the Netherlands, let alone England. Hence, the first industrial revolution took place first in England and first in the textile industry. It had to be the case.[26]

Moreover, all later successfully developed countries (including today's China) also kick-started their first industrial revolution by relying heavily on the textile industry. The nature of textile products and their colossal income-elastic demand and world market has dictated this iron logic of the industrial revolution.[27]

---

[26] For the development and flourish of textile proto-industries in various European countries before and during the British Industrial Revolution, see Franklin F. Mendels (1981), Sheilagh C. Ogilvie and Markus Cerman (1996) and Sven Beckert (2014).

[27] The United States became the world's textile superpower (replacing Great Britain) around the middle of the 19th century before it became the global manufacturing superpower in the late 19th century; Japan became a textile superpower in the early 20th century before it became a manufacturing superpower around the middle of the 20th century; China became the world's textile superpower in 1995 before it launched its second industrial revolution in heavy industries. Throughout history, these same development steps were taken by France, Germany, South Korea, Taiwan, and many, many other economies regardless of their geographic locations, population sizes, or cultural and institutional differences.

iv. The Industrial Trinity[28] and Another Look at the "Nature and Cause" of the Industrial Revolution

Many economic historians also claim that it was the easy access to cheap coal that ignited the English Industrial Revolution (see, e.g., K. Pomeranz 2001; R. Allen, 2009). In particular, Pomeranz argues that the Industrial Revolution took place first in Britain, instead of China or Japan or India or other parts of Europe, because of Britain's fortunate abundance of coal. The Netherland, France, Italy, Germany, China, Japan, and India did not have that same abundance of coal; thus, they were unable to escape from the Malthusian trap as early as Britain did.

However, China's development experiences cast doubts on such theories. First, China in the past 35 years has indeed relied heavily on coal as its chief energy source to power its industrial wheels. But if it were the prohibitive costs of coal that prevented China from igniting the Industrial Revolution in the 18th century, why was such a difficulty suddenly removed or resolved 200 years later when the real cost of coal had increased worldwide 100- or 1,000-fold? International coal prices did not become cheaper in real terms in 1978 or afterward, nor did China rely on foreign coal for its economic takeoff. Also, the majority of small Chinese coal miners were still using backward technology to extract coal even in the 1990s and 2000s. So the real costs of coal in China could not have been cheaper in the 1980s than in the 18th century in either absolute or relative terms.

Second, the growth rate of coal consumption in China was only about 4%–5% per year in the 1980s and 1990s during China's proto-industrialization and first industrial revolution era

---

[28] Industrial trinity means three key industries: energy, locomotive power, and infrastructure. Infrastructure includes but not limited to transportation and communication.

(1978–1998). This rate did not nearly match China's phenomenal village-firm industrial growth rate of 28% per year and real GDP growth of 10% per year in that entire period. The growth rate of energy consumption (and energy production) in China reached 10% per year only after 2000; yet, by then, China had already finished its first industrial revolution and kick-started its second industrial revolution.[29]

Third, neither proto-industrialization nor the first industrial revolution is energy-intensive, whether in 19th century England or modern China. During the early 1980s and even up to the late 1990s, most village-firms in China used very primitive tools and machinery in production. For example, many tools and machines were self-made by the peasants, and sometimes they bought obsolete machines from nearby cities' state-owned factories, which were using rudimentary technology themselves. Of course, in the 1990s, more and more rapidly growing village firms imported better machinery from abroad but they were not the dominant cases until the late 1990s and early 2000s. This low level of technology explains why China's rapid industrial growth in the 1980s and 1990s was not accompanied or matched by the same level of growth in energy demand, as would be the case for modern technologies and capital-intensive industries. China's rapid pace of growth in energy demand and supply did not happen until 2000, after China started its second industrial revolution, in which capital- and energy-intensive industries were built up and improved to a great degree.

Fourth, historically the flagship industry of the British Industrial Revolution — the textile industry — in the late 18th and early 19th centuries (1750–1840) was powered mainly by wind and water despite widely available cheap coal. The steam engine was not widely applied to textile factories or widely used anywhere in the

---

[29] China's energy consumption and production data can be found at http://www.eia.gov/countries/country-data.cfm?fips=CH, and http://www.eia.gov/cfapps/ipdb-project/IEDIndex3.cfm.

British economy until the middle of the 19th century, when the first industrial revolution was nearing its end. It was only toward the end of the first industrial revolution around the 1830s that the rapidly rising volume of domestic and international trade — driven mainly by the mass production of textiles and the demand for mass distribution of textile outputs and colossal cargo transportation of raw production materials (e.g., cotton) and the associated trade in other goods and business travels — made the mass investment in coal-powered railroads and steam engines profitable. In fact, coal was discovered and used in Europe and China long before the English Industrial Revolution. But coal output did not see significant or explosive growth in England until after the 1820s or even the 1830s (see G. Clark 2007, p. 237, Figure 12.3). Only then did the demand and supply of coal energy rise rapidly and catch up with industrial growth overall. Such a boom in energy and transport infrastructure and the associated demand for motive power (the steam engine) signaled the finishing phase of the First Industrial Revolution and the initial phase of the Second Industrial Revolution — featuring the mass production of machinery tools and heavy industrial goods, such as coal, chemicals, iron, steel, railroads, steam engines, metal boats and wagons, and the machine tools that produce machines. It was also the Second Industrial Revolution that made the agricultural revolution possible by mass-supplying the heavy agricultural machineries and chemical fertilizers.

In other words, the first industrial revolution (led by the mechanization of the textile industry and the associated world textile trade) generated huge if not insatiable demand for more efficient and large-scale transportation powered by new energy. A colossal volume of cotton imports from India and the southern states of America was critical for Britain's textile industry. It was this unprecedented demand for efficient motive power to lift and move goods and large-scale cargos that made large-scale and long-distance coal mining/transportation and the adoption of new technologies in mining/transportation profitable.

This also explains the co-emergence of the Triple Industrial Boom around the middle 19th century in England: coal, steam engines, and railroads. This industrial trinity also had large-scale and multi-dimensional positive effects on the behaviors of households and firms as well as on the input–output networks in the new industrial economy. A common characteristic of the industrial trinity is that none of the components could on its own serve directly as a final consumption good (except for coal as a heating source for homes); they are *individually* nothing but a means to achieve greater productivity in meeting the demand for final consumption or producing final consumption goods. Hence, without the drive from large-scale final demand for mass-produced textiles and other light industrial goods, the business of coal mining, steam engine production, and railroad construction and operation could not be profitable on their own. Why would the massive production of tools (intermediate goods) be profitable without sufficient demand for the final goods in the first place? Coal was used to power the steam engine, the steam engine was used to lift coal from coal mines and transport coal on the rail from one place to another. The railroad was used to run the steam engine and ship coal over large distances. But, this industrial trinity could not have been profitable on its own unless it served the purpose of some kind of final consumption. Without final consumption demand, the industrial trinity could have not by itself have created the demand for textiles. So, economic historians have constantly committed the fallacy of Say's law that "supply creates its own demand." Once again: Not true. Putting on businessman's shoes to think about the real world, one would have to agree with Keynes that in a market-based economy it is demand that creates its own supply, not only in short-run economic recessions, but also in long-term development.[30]

---

[30] Only in centrally planned economies does supply determine its own demand. But such economies lack the power of creative destruction and the force of evolution through "natural" selection.

One more case in point is that, even by 1830 near the end of the first industrial revolution, the use of steam power in coal mining and manufacturing in England still accounted for much less installed power than water plus wind (Allen, 2009, p. 173, Table 7.1), despite the fact that the steam engine was invented in the early 18th century (by Thomas Newcomen) and first put in use in 1712 to drain a coal mine. Widespread use of the steam engine to power factories and land/water transportation did not come until 150 years later, the middle of the 19th century, stimulated by colossal demand generated by the first industrial revolution.

Time series data also indicate this causal linkage from demand to supply. Coal consumption per capita in England experienced only gradual increases between the middles of the 17th and 19th centuries, rising from about 5,000 units to around 40,000 units, an eight-fold increase in 200 years, growing about 1% per year. However, between 1850 and 1860, coal consumption per capita more than doubled, from 40,000 units to 90,000 units, growing about 8.5% per year for a decade. So the speed of change after the first industrial revolution (in 1850) was suddenly more than eight times faster (see Wrigley, 2010, p. 95, Table 4.1).

The initial slower-growth phase of energy consumption was driven mainly by population growth and urbanization (due to commerce and proto-industrialization) because in that period coal was used mainly as an alternative cheap source of heat for households. For example, at the beginning of the 17th century, the annual level of coal shipped to London was in the range of 125,000–150,000 tons. By the end of the century it was about 500,000 tons, growing by about 1.2%–1.4% per year on average. Over the same period the population of London rose from 200,000 to 575,000, growing slightly over 1% per year and suggesting little growth in per capita coal consumption. Also, by the end of the 18th century, London was importing a total of about 1.2 million tons of coal from the same north-east ports, growing about 0.9% per year, while its population had risen to 950,000 by 1800, growing about 0.5% per year. Hence, coal consumption per head changed only modestly in the entire 18th century (Wrigley, 2010, p. 106). However, after 1820 coal consumption increased far more rapidly than population growth and the absolute tonnage of coal shipped around England was almost doubling every 10 years (equivalent to the miracle growth rate of Chinese GDP today). To transport coal on this scale required very substantial shipping capacity; thus, no wonder the railroad and steam engine revolution occurred simultaneously in and after that period. So the critical difference after 1820 was that the demand for coal no longer came from households' heating needs, but instead from the burning need of steam engines and railroad transportation — forming the loop of the industrial trinity that fulfilled the rising demand for cargo transportation and trade.

These points suggest that Britain's easy access to cheap coal could not have been the prerequisite or cause of the first industrial revolution, regardless of the arguments of Robert Allen (2009), K. Pomeranz (2001) and others; it was surely a facilitator that enabled Britain to finish the last phase of the first industrial revolution and kick-start the Second Industrial Revolution at a lower cost through the rail transportation boom. Hence, neither coal, nor the steam engine, nor the railroad was the cause of the first industrial revolution (1750–1830).

What this means is that the Industrial Revolution would still have taken place first in England had its real wage been lower and coal been more expensive than, say, in France and Germany and the Netherlands. It would certainly not have happened in 18th century China or India even if the real wage there were much higher and coal much cheaper. The first industrial revolution would of course not have continued and turned into the Second Industrial Revolution without coal, steam engines, and railroads. But this scenario was unlikely because the industrial trinity was merely the consequence (demand) of the first industrial revolution — had coal and the steam engine not been discovered in England, it would still have been made available by importing or stealing from somewhere else.[31]

Why didn't the Industrial Revolution Start in the Netherlands, China, or India?

Once again, what caused the first industrial revolution in Great Britain was centuries of formation/fermentation of the world's largest domestic and global textile market (helped partly by other European countries' proto-industrial textile firms in terms of market creation and building up competitive pressure on the British textile firms), which made the adoption of the spinning jenny and other textile machines (and the mass production of textiles) profitable and an imperative for survival. To ferment and dominate such a market, the British government passed many laws to encourage or enforce the consumption and exports of domestically produced woolen products and restrict the import of foreign-produced textiles and limit the production and exports of woolen products by its colonies. As an example, the Wool Act of 1699 was not repealed until 1867, when Britain had long finished its first industrial revolution and was halfway through its Second Industrial Revolution.[32]

The Netherlands and other European powers did not create and control such a large domestic and global textile market by the late 18th century, despite the Netherlands' more advanced economy and financial institutions throughout the 16th and 17th centuries. The Netherlands occupied the bulk of the world market for spices but not textiles. Their hegemony in the spice trade did not help them

---

[31] Indeed, the four great inventions pivotal for modern Western civilization (paper-making, gunpowder, printing, and the compass) were all originated in China. Also, the colossal amount of coal that fueled Japan's industrialization in the late 19th and early 20th centuries was largely taken from China and other parts of Asia.

[32] See Chapters 5 and 6 for more information and discussions on British mercantilist policies.

industrialize even though it was the spice trade that kick-started the European Age of Discovery and stimulated Portuguese and Dutch shipbuilding technology. Spices are simply far less income elastic than textile goods and can hardly be mass-produced because they are land intensive instead of labor-capital intensive. Sugar production in the 17th and 18th centuries is a good example of the limitation of the economies of scale and the division of labor in agriculture. Only England built its economy almost entirely on textile production and trade and relied heavily on this industry to generate national power and wealth and government revenues. This lucky choice of industry or industrial policy ultimately led Great Britain to her industrial revolution. Had the Netherlands created the global cotton-textile market and monopolized the global cotton-textile trade like the British, the honor of the first industrial revolution would have gone to them.

Nonetheless, soon after the British discovered the power of mass production in textiles, other European nations followed and detonated their own industrial revolution by encouraging textile production and participating in the global textile market. In their early development stages, France, Germany, and the United States in the 19th century, Japan in the late 19th to early 20th century, Taiwan, Singapore, and South Korea in the middle 20th century all followed this road to prosperity paved with textiles. So did China. China became the world's largest textile producer and exporter in 1995, signaling its economic takeoff and ultimate success in detonating its long-waited industrial revolution.

Therefore, the explanation for the puzzle of the Great Divergence (a la Pomeranz) is clear: The cause of England's successful industrial revolution was not coal. Likewise, the cause of China's failure in industrial revolution in the 17th and 18th centuries was not coal. And the same applies to India. The causes must be found outside of coal and other geographic conditions. China in the 17th and 18th centuries never showed any special interest in coal, not even in the 19th century.

But Japan in the late 19th century and early 20th century, especially in the 1920s–1930s after finishing its first industrial revolution, showed tremendous interest in and appetite for energy — it looted a colossal volume of coal from China (and other parts of Asia) to meet its rising energy demand to power its industrial wheel (the industrial trinity).[33]

Two hundred years ago, China and India were similar. Both were incapable of industrialization. For India, this became even more evident in the 19th century after the British colonists built railroads in India, the most sophisticated railway networks in all of Asia at the time. But, even more than 100 years later, no industrialization has occured in India. The proto-industrial base and consumer-goods market in India (and China) at the time were simply too thin, too anarchic and unorganized to allow for any industrial revolution despite a huge population. If we look at what occurred in China since the 1980s and take that as the requirements for industrialization, among other things, the critical mass of proto-industries must reach at least 40%–50% of total agricultural value added, or around 25%–30% of total rural labor force in their employment share before a first industrial revolution can take place, or a nationwide adoption of large-scale mass production of light consumer goods can become profitable.[34] As I have discussed, market-oriented mass

---

[33] Many historians, such as J. Mokyr (2009) and D. McCloskey (2010), have also offered arguments against the coal theory of the Industrial Revolution.

[34] China reached this critical threshold value around 1992–1995. As a comparison, in 1800 England during its Industrial Revolution, 51% of its rural population was already engaged in non-agricultural activities, while this share was only 19% in 1500 (see Robert Allen (2009), p. 17, Table 1.1). In France, this share was 32% in 1800 and 20% in 1500. In Spain, this share remained low and stable at 20% between 1500 and 1800. Even for the Low Countries where the Industrial Revolution was most likely to occur, this share reached only 37% in the Netherlands and Belgium in 1800 (keep in mind that rural proto-industrial employment is only a fraction of non-agricultural rural labor force). This suggests that the share of non-agricultural population in total rural population must have reached 40% around 1700 in England at the outset of the Industrial Revolution.

production in textiles or any light consumer goods is never profitable if the market size is too small and the intermediation costs too large to match highly specialized demand and supply in long distance. India in the 17th and 18th centuries had a much bigger population than England but a much smaller market because the transportation costs in India across villages were so formidable and Indian textile family-workshops (cartage industries) were autarkic with many tiny isolated and highly localized markets; whereas, in the 18th century, British textile enterprises were well connected by a nationwide commerce and mercantile network with sophisticated supply chains and transportation (canal and turnpike) systems. Also, India lacked a powerful wealthy merchant class to take the initiative to establish factories with the division of labor and to aim for long-distance trade. And India lacked state power and military force to protect its organized commerce in domestic and international trade and its national interests in the global supply chain and distributional networks. The majority of Indian rural workshops and proto-industries remain autarkic and anarchic even today, poorly connected by industrial clusters and distribution networks, and little evolved over these 200 years after the English Industrial Revolution.[35]

---

[35] When Adam Smith (1776, Chapter III) tried to lay the foundation for his theory that the division of labor is limited by the extent of the market, he described market situations very similar to today's agrarian nations, including India: "In the lone houses and very small villages which are scattered about in so desert a country as the highlands of Scotland, every farmer must be butcher, baker, and brewer, for his own family. In such situations, we can scarce expect to find even a smith, a carpenter, or a mason, within less than twenty miles of another of the same trade. The scattered families that live at eight or ten miles distance from the nearest of them, must learn to perform themselves a great number of little pieces of work, for which, in more populous countries, they would call in the assistance of those workmen ... There could be little or no commerce of any kind between the distant parts of the world. What goods could bear the expense of land-carriage between London and Calcutta? Or if there were any so precious as to be able to support this expense, with what safety could they be transported through the territories of so many barbarous nations?"

Human beings organize in order to compete and compete to organize (paraphrasing Francis Fukuyama, 2014, p. 186). Who in the 17th and 18th centuries would organize India to compete when India was not even a unified nation-state?[36]

---

[36] Industrialization cannot take place without the rise of a unified nation-state and a powerful mercantilist government to create a unified domestic market and build the national infrastructure and global commercial networks. Hence, David Landes (2009) attributes Britain's success in detonating the Industrial Revolution to the fact (among others) that Britain was among the first in "the European world of competition for power and wealth" to become a modern nation-state: "Britain had the early advantage of being a *nation* ... Nations can reconcile social purpose with individual aspirations and initiatives and enhance performance by their collective synergy. The whole is more than the sum of the parts. Citizens of a nation will respond better to state encouragement and initiatives; conversely, the state will know better what to do and how, in accord with active social forces. Nations can compete" (David Landes, 1999, p. 219).

Chapter 4

Why Is China's Rise Unstoppable?

I have referred to China's industrialization and growth as "unstoppable" despite its current "backward" financial system and political institutions and the fact that China's per capita income is merely one-eighth of the U.S. level despite 35 years of hyper growth. What does "unstoppable" mean, exactly? What are the economic rationales for such optimism? Previous chapters have traced China's path to (and through) its first industrial revolution and explained how it was able to kick-start a second industrial revolution in the late 1990s and early 2000s through the market-demand determined but government-led "industrial trinity" programs. But what does China's future hold? Can China continue to grow as fast and ultimately surpass the United States not only in per capita income but also in major frontier technologies by the middle of this century? And what does this mean to the world economic and geopolitical order?

On the one hand, China's rapid development compressed the typical 250–300 years of Western industrial achievements (i.e., from proto-industrialization to kick-starting the second industrial revolution) into a mere 35 years. It must have also rapidly accumulated the typical 250–300 years' worth of major development problems and hurdles that the West encountered. These problems include but are not limited to rampant corruption, unprecedented pollution and environmental destruction, rapid breakdown of traditional family values and an accelerated sexual liberation, rising divorce and suicide rates, wide-spread business fraud, markets-full of "lemons" and low-quality goods, pervasive asset bubbles, rising income inequality and class discrimination, frequent industrial accidents, organized crime, economic scandals, and unemployment. Given these drastically compounded social/economic/political problems, it is no wonder so many predictions about China are pessimistic; some are even betting on China's dramatic collapse. Truly, the financial and institutional innovations necessary to cope with China's new economic reality are not easy to come by. Exacerbating these predictions are popular Eurocentric ideologies and antagonistic views on China.[1]

On the other hand, optimistic predictions for China also exist and have started to flourish especially since the early 2000s. One of the

---

[1]In addition to Gordon Chang's (2001) popular book, *The Coming Collapse of China*, also see James Gorrie (2013), *The China Crisis: How China's Economic Collapse Will Lead to a Global Depression*, and Peter Navarro and Greg Autry (2011), *The Death by China: Confronting the Dragon — A Global Call to Action*, among countless other China-bashing books and articles on China. Such widespread pessimistic and negative views on China can hardly be blamed given the Western population's ignorance on economic history and on the mainstream economists' failure to explain the industrial revolution as well as the powerful influence of the institutional theories. Four decades ago, President Richard Nixon himself once mused after visiting China in the early 1970s, "Well, you can just stop and think of what could happen if anybody with a decent system of government got control of that mainland. Good God ... There'd be no power in the world that could even — I mean, you put 800 million Chinese to work under a decent system ... and they will be the leaders of the world" (http://www.newsweek.com/henry-kissingers-prescription-china-67555). Today's communist party in China put 1.3 billion Chinese to work under a "flawed" and "lousy" system objected by the institutional theorists (Acemoglu and Robinson, 2012), while Russian, by far a much formidable economic force before the 1980s, has passed entirely from the scene after blindly adopting the neoliberalism ideology and Shock Therapy for economic and political reform.

earliest bold predictions of the rise of China was made by the previous World Bank chief economist Justin Yifu Lin and his co-authors (Fang Cai and Zou Li) in the book titled "The China Miracle," first published in 1994 in Chinese and since then translated into many foreign languages. In this seminal book, Lin and his co-authors provided the first systematic account of China's dismal failure of industrialization between 1949 and 1977 and the growth miracle since the 1978 reform, based on the notion of comparative advantage and late-comer advantage. They argue that China's growth miracle since 1978 was based on the correct development strategy of relying first on labor-intensive industries before gradually shifting to capital-intensive technologies.

But still, it took quite a while for a handful of Western observers to slowly realize China's "inescapable" rise. For example, former U.S. Secretary of State Henry Kissinger remarked in 2007 that "The rise of China is inevitable, and there is nothing we could do about it." Kissinger made this statement even though China's income per capita at the time was only 1/20th of the United States and 1/5th of middle-income Latin American countries such as Argentina, Brazil, and Mexico.

Jim Rogers (the co-founder of The Quantum Fund) remarked that "just as the future belonged to the British in the 19th century and the Americans in the 20th century, so the Chinese will own the 21st century."[2] The most optimistic prediction to date on China's rise and impact on the world geopolitical order can be found in Martin Jacques's (2009) influential book, "When China Rules the World: The Rise of the Middle Kingdom and the End of the Western World" and its second edition (2012) "When China Rules the World: The End of the Western World and the Birth of a New Global Order."

However, although these optimistic Western views on China have started to grow rapidly since the 2007 global financial crisis and become increasingly popular and influential, especially since

---

[2] See, e.g., https://www.youtube.com/watch?v=doMXl89Lur8.

the IMF and World Bank predictions of China overtaking the United States in 2014 in a purchasing-power-parity (PPP)-based measure of GDP, such views have all relied solely on the linear extrapolation of China's past growth and have provided few if any economic rationales or theoretical foundations. They are, therefore, just as baseless as the overly pessimistic views.

Indeed, former Treasury Secretary of the United States Larry Summers analyzed a large pool of cross-country data on the history of economic growth and argues that optimistic projections for future Chinese growth are way off the mark[3]:

"[H]istory teaches that abnormally rapid growth is rarely persistent, even though economic forecasts invariably extrapolate recent growth. Indeed, regression to the mean is the empirically most salient feature of economic growth. It is far more robust in the data than, say, the much-discussed middle-income trap. Furthermore, statistical analysis of growth reveals that in developing countries, episodes of rapid growth are frequently punctuated by discontinuous drop-offs in growth. Such discontinuities account for a large fraction of the variation in growth rates. We suggest that salient characteristics of China — high levels of state control and corruption along with high measures of authoritarian rule — make a discontinuous decline in growth even more likely than general experience would suggest."[4]

Hence, why would China's rise and international dominance be inevitable? How long and by how much can China continue to

---

[3] Lant Pritchett and Lawrence H. Summers, 2014, "Asiaphoria Meets Regression to the Mean." NBER Working Paper No. 20573 (http://www.nber.org/papers/w20573).

[4] Arguments based on statistics can be misleading, however: Statistically speaking, for example, the probability of the Industrial Revolution was zero in late 18th century England. Even today, 250 years after the British Industrial Revolution, pure statistics still teach us nothing about the nature and cause of the Industrial Revolution.

rise — rising to become a middle-income country like Brazil or Mexico, or to become a high-income country like Japan and the United States? What about the middle-income trap China will face in the next 10 years once its per capita income reaches the Latin American level? Even by the end of 2014, China's per capita GDP was only 1/8th of the U.S. level and its per capita consumption 1/15th; and China still has about 50% of its population living in the rural areas. And the layman's view is that China was once the world's largest economy, more than 200,000 years ago; so its rejuvenation is inevitable. But, think of the painful long development history of Egypt and India (both civilizations are older than China's) and the fact that China has remained in a stagnant position for at least the 200 years before the 1978 reform.

Based on Larry Summer's research, China-optimism is not statistically justifiable. In particular, China's high growth rate in the past decades and its remaining developmental gap with respect to Japan and South Korea are no bases for such (aforementioned) optimism. Also, simply having the world's largest population and a long history of agricultural civilization provides no justification for optimism either, just as the Ottoman Empire is no basis for the rejuvenation of Turkey, and just as the ancient Greek civilization and Roman Empire are no bases for predicting the English Industrial Revolution.

To recap: Despite the increasing popularity of the optimistic view in the West about China's inevitable rise, few economic rationales have been provided to back up such optimism (or perhaps "fear") about the rise of China. Since 1978, it has been growing rapidly and, so the story goes, can continue to grow so because of its backwardness and late-comer advantage, its large pool of cheap labor, its Confucianism tradition, and its political autocracy to facilitate unfair international competition and exchange rate manipulations. But those who make this claim do not ask themselves why so many old civilizations and developing countries failed to industrialize for centuries despite their backwardness, cheap labor, late-comer advantage, autocracy, and exchange rate manipulations? If China were still stuck in the poverty trap instead of growing as it does today, the same cultural and institutional factors would also have been cited as the "explanations" for China's failures.

Again, this book argues that it is only with correct insight on the internal logic of the Industrial Revolution and in-depth analysis of the rise of the West can one fully grasp why China's rise is unstoppable despite formidable future challenges in *institutional* innovations to protect the fruits of industrialization and further deepen the markets for goods, services, labor, capital, and ideas. From such a new perspective, the aforementioned social/political/economic challenges facing today's China are merely growing pains, and not the same daunting structural obstacles like the poverty trap or the middle-income trap faced by many developing nations in Africa, Latin America, Middle East, and South East Asia.[5]

i. Correct Development Strategies

The first explanation of China's inescapable rise is that it has found the right development strategy and followed the correct sequence of industrialization — which apply specifically to China,

---

[5] Although China has not yet reached and crossed through the middle-income trap, our analysis suggests that China will be able to overcome the middle-income trap if it can successfully finish its second industrial revolution — which looks extremely likely in the next 10–20 years despite all the "growing pains" (Tian Zhu's commentary shares similar views on this issue, see http://www.guancha.cn/ZhuTian/2014_10_17_274362.shtml.) The most important task of the second industrial revolution is to create the market base, distribution networks, and supply chains to support the technology of "mass-producing the means of mass production." As will be discussed in detail in Chapters 5 and 6, signs of successful completion of the second industrial revolution include the completion of agricultural mechanization (modernization) and financial industrial takeoff (financial capitalism). Such a society is then ready to enter a welfare state or post-industrial stage.

but also can apply to many other nations that have yet to industrialize. This development sequence is fully consistent with the *internal logic* of the Industrial Revolution in England and other successfully developed countries despite the fact that China's institutional conditions are different from those of the 18th and 19th century Western powers.

To recap what I have said throughout this book: The Industrial Revolution has its internal economic logic that unfolds sequentially in developmental stages. It starts with a proto-industrialization in the rural areas based on the division of labor, which kick-starts the great escape from the Malthusian poverty trap and breaks the curse of food security. At the end of the proto-industrialization, the enormously expanded domestic grassroots market and discoveries of international markets, the improved proto-industrial supply chains and commercial distribution networks, and the intensified competition among proto-industrial firms all make the adoption of mass production of light industrial goods profitable. This triggers the first industrial revolution — an English Industrial Revolution in its modern form under modern conditions, which features labor-intensive mass production of light consumer goods based on regional industrial specialization and clustering. These labor-intensive mass-producing industries have relatively low capital requirement and energy demands (compared with heavy industries) and are thus easier to finance with the accumulated domestic savings from the proto-industrialization stage.

But mechanization (mass production) in one segment of the production process creates demand for the mechanization in other segments of the production process and ultimately the mechanization in all segments of the entire production process and the associated industrial input–output supply chains. This continuous process of mechanization across production chains calls for more efficient provision of raw materials, intermediate goods, and machinery, and a better commercial distribution system and transportation infrastructure. Hence, once the first industrial revolution is kick-started, the rising demand for better, faster, larger-scale production and distribution systems and commercial networks ultimately calls for a revolution in the "Industrial Trinity" composed of energy, locomotion, and transportation infrastructure to sustain the continuously expanding economy and facilitate heavy cargo and long-distance trade.

Such a boom in the Industrial Trinity, triggered by market demand created by the first industrial revolution, generates colossal demand for heavy industrial goods and materials, which in turn provides economic forces and markets to support the second industrial revolution. The second industrial revolution features the mass production (supply) of machinery and various intermediate goods required for sustaining the growth of the "Industrial Trinity," thus calling for the mass provision of heavy industrial goods such as chemicals, cements, iron, steel, communications, automotive products, ships, cars, trucks, airplanes, and a large organized credit system. Any new discoveries that can facilitate the supply of these goods will necessarily be adopted or invented and ultimately mass produced, as long as their benefits outweigh their costs — such as any new forms of energy, motive power, transportation, communication, and materials. This process also calls for innovations in financial services and credit management to facilitate large-volume trade. A stable and well-managed national banking system is, hence, a plus.

The entire sequence of the industrialization is thus powered by demand and financed by savings from the previous stage of development. Each stage encounters the problem of new market creation, discovery, and expansion and thus requires the collective actions of new market participants to overcome the colossal social costs involved in higher-level market creation and the associated provision of public goods.

More specifically, the colossal social and private costs associated with kick-starting the first industrial revolution, such as the costs of creating the pre-industrial market and pre-industrial firms and technology adoption/innovation are financed by primitive accumulation during the proto-industrialization; and the even more colossal social and private costs associated with the buildup and upgrading of the industrial trinity (energy/motive power/infrastructure) and kick-starting the second industrial revolution must in turn be financed by the savings through the first industrial revolution.

The economies of scale (originated mainly from the enormously large fixed costs of installing private and social capital and the zero marginal costs of using the installed capital, as well as the externalities and spillover effects of manufacturing knowledge) imply that all social and private costs involved in each development stage will ultimately be compensated by the fruits of each successful industrial revolution and the enormously expanded market (purchasing power) and discoveries of new forms of raw industrial materials (wool, cotton, coal, iron, steel, oil, plastics, rubber, chemical fiber, rare earth, so on and so forth). For example, the second industrial revolution ultimately feeds back to the mechanization of the agriculture so that this primitive land-intensive and labor-intensive sector can be finally liberated and transformed into a capital-intensive industry and become the ultimate beneficiary of the industrial revolution, thus offering a permanent and complete solution to the food security problem that was the obstacle of the first industrial revolution and has haunted human societies since the loss of Eden.

Hence, industrialization is a bootstrapping and self-propelling dynamic process that unfolds in proper sequence. Each stage requires a "Big Push" and coordinated joint effort of the government and the private sector. The initial and intermediate stages cannot be skipped but can be accelerated and shortened by the government acting as the market creators. Skipping initial or intermediate stages, such as directly jumping to heavy industrial buildup under the top-down approaches suggested by Gerschenkron (1962) and the Big Push theory, can lead to severe development problems, because the lack of the earlier stages implies (among other things) not only the lack of scaled markets to render the heavy industries profitable, but also the lack of sufficient domestic savings to self-finance the technological adoption and upgrading, which can choke off the continuous process of industrialization and fall into the so-called "middle-income trap."[6]

The discovery of capital and its efficient reproduction lies at the heart of the industrial revolution and capitalism. But the extent of mass-producing capital or the speed and scale of reproducing capital, like the division of labor, depends critically on the size of the market, and the size of the market in turn depends on a nation's vision and willingness to create it and on the financial ability of the state to overcome the social costs associated with market creation.

Historically the market creators have been the powerful and wealthy merchants and financial intermediaries (bankers). But such a merchant-dependent natural market fermentation process, especially with regard to the pre- or proto-industrial market, can take centuries to accomplish, even under strong state support. China has (re)discovered that this slow and lengthy natural market fermentation process can be dramatically shortened into mere decades through engineered market fermentation by a powerful government (as Japan did during the Meiji Restoration and South Korea did in the 1960s–1980s).

How to maintain a high national saving rate to continuously finance the increasing fixed costs of market creation and climb up the industrial ladder is thus a key to continuous growth and unstoppable industrialization. Top-down approaches to industrialization that starts with heavy industries lack such a generous source of financing and must therefore rely heavily on foreign aid or taxation on the primitive sectors such as agriculture or raw materials or natural resources. But such a supply-side approach (establishing modern efficient technology without creating the mass market and the associated distribution system in the first place) can hardly generate the market conditions needed to render the mass production

---

[6]This may explain the puzzle of the "middle-income trap."

of heavy industrial goods profitable. The core of the heavy industry depends on the industrial trinity (energy/locomotive power/infrastructure). A nation cannot build a profitable heavy industry without building the industrial trinity first. However, the industrial trinity is not only essentially a public good but also an intermediate good, which is not profitable on its own without serving the final demand. So it must be financed publically by savings from the first industrial revolution.[7] Yet only after finishing the second industrial revolution is the mass production of the means of production (machineries and infrastructures) possible and can a nation enter the welfare state built on affluence with everything mass-produced, including the means of mass production itself.[8]

Incidentally, the previously described logic of the industrial revolution shed light on the current economic problems in Europe and the globe. The root cause of the European debt crisis since 2009 was not cheap credit or the lack of financial regulation *per se* in the Eurozone, but rather some (southern) European nations' decisions (since the 1980s) to enter the welfare state and financial capitalism immaturely before finishing their second industrial revolution. Hence, the consequent rising labor costs under various social welfare programs and generous public pension schemes made their labor-intensive light industries internationally uncompetitive when China and other emerging economies rose to

---

[7] After all, energy and locomotive devices, and infrastructure are merely the means of production instead of the goal of production. So the entire modern roundabout industrial structure is erected on the foundation of the final demand for consumption goods.

[8] Through international trade, an industrialized nation can afford to forgo a light industrial base at home, since it can export mass-produced heavy machinery goods in exchange for light consumer goods. But an agrarian developing country cannot get rich by importing manufactured consumer goods and exporting agricultural goods produced with primitive technologies. This is why the classical Ricardian theory of trade based on the so-called "comparative advantage" misses the point of industrialization.

dominate world trade in light consumer goods. This is especially true after China joined the WTO in late 2001. The collapse of these European countries' light industries caused a persistent rise in unemployment and a slowdown in GDP growth, which exposed and magnified their government deficits and international debts and reduced their ability to repay or refinance their debts. A debt crisis was thus doomed to happen in Europe.

However, European countries such as Germany did not suffer (directly) such problems because they had successfully finished their second industrial revolution after World War II and thus benefited from China's rise by exporting mass-produced machinery goods and high value-added durable consumer goods to meet China's rising demand. Resource-rich countries such as Australia and parts of Africa also benefited from China's rise. Hence, the ultimate solution to the European debt crisis is neither austerity nor Keynesian policies, but to find ways to pay their long overdue "debt" in industrialization and become competitive in the world market for heavy manufacturing or other high-tech areas such as pharmaceuticals and financial services. This, however, requires a powerful government and visionary state-led development and trade strategies.[9]

---

[9]The German reunification in 1990 was a far more painful process for all Germans than expected, precisely because the industrialized West Germany had forgotten List's theory of national system building and overlooked East Germany's backward stage of economic development and its associated comparative (dis)advantage. One of the West Germany's biggest mistakes after reunification, for example, was its attempt to immediately pull East Germany into the welfare state that West Germany had enjoyed; this made East Germany's manufacturing sector far less competitive than it could be, so it collapsed overnight. If even an industrial power like West Germany had such problems dealing with East Germany, how much can we expect from the other Eastern European nations after abandoning communism? These nations have been floundering in their attempts to rebuild their national economies, notwithstanding the misguided development policies recommended by the shock therapy, the Washington consensus, or the institutional theory.

Hence, the internal logic of the Industrial Revolution as well as the historical paths of all successfully industrialized nations (and the paths of unsuccessful nations as well) can help forecast China's continued development path and determined rise. China, since 1978, has followed the logical, successful path to industrialization, albeit unintentionally in the beginning. And this explains why China, since 1978, has not suffered from any stop-and-go development cycles or debt crises in financing its industrialization, unlike its earlier three attempts of industrialization and similar cases in some Latin American countries that took a top-down approach. China has relied entirely on its own domestic savings from its rural industrialization after 1978 to kick-start its first industrial revolution in the 1990s and it has also relied entirely on its consequent high saving rate from its first industrial revolution to kick-start and finance its coal/locomotive power/railroad booms and second industrial revolution. China's national saving rate today still remains the world's highest (about 50% of GDP), and China is thus fully (financially) capable of finishing its second industrial revolution in the next 10–15 years with its high saving rate and near 4 trillion dollars in foreign reserves. This unprecedented high saving rate also enables China to finance its global business investment in infrastructures in Africa, Latin America, Southeast Asia, Central Asia, and the entire European continent to build China's ambitious overseas supply chain of raw materials and energy and its global distribution network for "Made in China."[10]

Since China's population is larger than the United States' plus all of Europe combined, and since China is a resource-poor nation and does not rely on colonialism to extract free resources or savings

---

[10] China's geopolitical development strategy differs from the American approach and seems more acceptable to the developing nations than the Washington consensus approach. See, e.g., Kevin Gallagher (2011), "The End of the 'Washington Consensus'," available at http://www.theguardian.com/commentisfree/cifamerica/2011/mar/07/china-usa.

from other nations, it needs a much higher national saving rate, a much larger global market, and a farther reaching global infrastructure to accomplish its colossal industrialization.[11]

A popular misperception about China's rapid economic growth is the notion that it has relied primarily on investment or capital accumulation, instead of technological adoption and innovations. Hence, according to the neoclassical Solow growth model, China's high growth rate is not sustainable. Such a view is misleading. Technology is always embodied in tangible capital (equipment, machinery, and tools). Thus, the only way to improve technology is through fixed investment and capital accumulation, which requires savings to finance.[12] Therefore, China has been able to generate continuous hyper growth for the past 35 years precisely because of its exceptionally high investment rate, thanks to its phenomenal high saving rate (derived from its correct development strategies and industrial policies).

---

[11] For example, China is building railroads to connect China's east coast with Germany and Greece to the west and Singapore to the south. China is also investing massively in infrastructure projects in Africa and Latin America and gradually pushing the renminbi to become one of the world's major reserve currencies.

[12] The Solow growth model treats technology (A) and capital (K) as two separate physical entities in the production function for output: $Y = Af(K)$, where $f(\bullet)$ is a concave function. Thus, merely accumulating K through investment without improving A cannot generate long-run growth in output Y because (i) output is always less than doubled whenever K doubles (i.e., diminishing returns to capital) and (ii) the cost of investment increases proportionately with K. Consequently, the value added, $Af(K) - sK$, is always finite regardless of the level of K. Hence, the only way to continuously increase net output is to continuously increase technology A. However, the fundamental weakness of such arguments is that in reality technology A cannot exist without capital K as its embodiment. Hence, investment in technology necessarily entails investment in capital.

Despite the apparent institutional differences, the correct steps China has taken to industrialization are essentially no different from what the British went through in the 18th and 19th centuries and what other successfully industrialized nations (such as the United States, France, Germany, and Japan) went through at other times in history. The difference is that these older industrial powers all relied on colonialism, imperialism, and unfair trade with colonies and other weak nations to finance their industrialization. Without these tactics at their disposal, China must keep an unprecedentedly high national saving rate, significantly higher than any of the earlier industrialized powers, to propel its industrialization. And China does have the required national savings to achieve its peaceful rise.

ii. "Learning by Doing" — the Ultimate Source of Technology Innovation

The second explanation of China's unstoppable rise is a response to the institutional theorists and many commentators on China. They may question China's ability to innovate once it moves to the frontier, given its authoritarian government and "extractive" political institutions (see, e.g., Acemoglu and Robinson, 2012). They argue that China's one-party political system implies that it necessarily constrains (or lacks) the freedom and incentives of technological innovations. Hence, China's rapid development and miracle growth so far cannot have been propelled by innovations but instead by its backwardness and through duplicating technologies from advanced countries.[13] Such institutional views are misleading

---

[13] "[China's] growth was feasible partly because there was a lot of catching up to be done. Growth under extractive institutions is easier when creative destruction is not a necessity" (Acemoglu and Robinson, 2012, p. 440). Besides appealing to China's backwardness, Acemoglu and Robinson (2012) also attribute China's growth miracle to its authoritarian government's ability to mobilize and allocate resources. But such an argument raises several questions. (i) If the

and are not supported by economic history (e.g., Japan, Germany, and Russia before World War II and South Korea and Singapore after World War II).

For the sake of argument, consider the historical path traveled by the United States. A proto-industrial developmental stage took place in the United States before it detonated its first industrial revolution in the middle 19th century. Charles Morris (2012) noted that by 1812 (similar to China in the 1980s), the countryside of the northern states were thoroughly commercialized, the manufacturing activities were carried out in little hamlets around water falls, which provided the power to turn the mill wheel. This was an organic, bottom-up form of proto-industrialization during a natural market-fermentation period, originating in the increasing prosperity of ordinary farmers. Even during the late 18th century before 1812, American farmers had already become increasingly entrepreneurial and had engaged in market activities through commerce — exchanging homemade consumer goods. By the 1820s, such market exchanges were rapidly replaced by networks of organized commerce — built by rich merchants. Wage labor became a popular form of farm employment, and farm surpluses were often invested in mercantile and industrial undertakings instead of invested in land. Local merchants provided the impetus toward new enterprises.

However, this rapid proto-industrial development — which would soon set off the American industrial revolution and its economic takeoff — went completely unnoticed by the British. No, not even Karl Marx noticed. In the same way, China's proto-industrialization in the 1980s and its significance for detonating the 21st century industrial revolution went completely unnoticed by the West in the 1980s and 1990s and even until today. Through

---

government-directed resource allocation is against the market principle, why would it promote growth? (ii) If it is consistent with the market principle, what is wrong with it? And (iii) if it achieves something the market fails to achieve, should not it be praised instead of criticized?

a European lens, America at that time looked very backward because of its overwhelmingly rural demography. In the 1820s, more than 90% of Americans still lived in the countryside, a pattern that changed very little even by the middle of the 19th century. "[B]ut America's agrarian patina concealed a beehive of commercial and industrial activity" (Charles Morris, 2012, "The Dawn of Innovation," p. 76).

The well-known British man of letters Sidney Smith once wrote in 1820 that "Americans are a brave, industrious, and acute people; but they have hitherto given no indication of genius, and have made no approach to the heroic ... . Where are their Foxes, their Burkes, and their Sheridans? ... . Where their Arkwrights, their Watts, their Davys? ... . Who drinks from American Glasses? Or eats from their plates?" (Charles Morris, 2012, "The Dawn of Innovation," p. 76).

However, as Charles Morris (2012) also keenly noted, the secret of the American surge in the middle and later half of the 19th century to overtake Great Britain did not lie first in advanced technology. Not until the United States had overtaken the British to become the workshop of the world after the 1890s. Throughout the entire 19th century, Americans were students of the British in steelmaking and most other science-based industries.

Even by the 1880s, when America was about to surpass Britain for first place in manufacturing output and become the "workshop of the world," had already successfully finished its first industrial revolution, kick-started its second industrial revolution, and built up its most magnificent railroad network in the world,[14] pure scientific research was still very backward compared with that in Europe, especially in the United Kingdom, France, and Germany. Henry

---

[14] Railroad mileage in the U.S. more than tripled between 1860 and 1880. By 1869, the First Transcontinental Railroad was constructed, which linked formerly isolated areas with larger markets, leading to the rise of commercial farming, ranching, and mining. American steel production surpassed the combined total of Britain, Germany, and France in that period.

Augustus Rowland (1848–1901), the first president of the American Physical Society and one of the most brilliant American scientists and physicists of his day, complained openly about the backwardness of American higher education and scientific research and made an impassioned plea for pure scientific research in American universities:

"I have before me the report of the commissioner of education for 1880. According to that report, there were 389, or say, in round numbers, 400 institutions, calling themselves colleges or universities, in our country! ... About one-third aspire to the name of university; and I note one called by that name which has two professors and 18 students, and another having three teachers and 12 students! ... And these instances are not unique, for the number of small institutions and schools which call themselves universities is very great ... . Who can doubt that an institution with over 800 students, and a faculty of 70, is of a higher grade than those above cited having 10 or 20 students and two or three in the faculty? Yet this is not always true; for I note one institution with over 500 students which is known to me personally as of the grade of a high school ... . Each one of these institutions has so-called professors, but it is evident that they can be only of the grade of teachers ... . It is not those in this country who receive the largest salary, and have positions in the richest colleges, who have advanced their subject the most: Men receiving the highest salaries, and occupying the professor's chair, are to-day doing absolutely nothing in pure science, but are striving by the commercial applications of their science to increase their already large salary ... . But danger is also near, even in our societies. When the average tone of the society is low, when the highest honors are given to the mediocre, when third class men are held up as examples, and when trifling inventions are magnified into scientific discoveries, then the influence of such societies is prejudicial ... . The National academy of sciences contains eminent men from the whole country, but ... it has no building, it has no library; and it publishes nothing except the information which it freely gives to the government, which does nothing for it in return … . it in no way takes the place of the great Royal society, or the great academies of science at Paris, Berlin, Vienna, St. Petersburgh, Munich, and, indeed, all the European capitals and large cities … . [A]n institution calling itself a university, and not having the current scientific journals upon its table or the transactions of societies upon its library-shelves, is certainly not doing its best to cultivate all that is best in this world … . In our science, no books above elementary ones have ever been published, or are likely to be published, in this country" (H. A. Rowland, 1883, *A Plea for Pure Science*).

The same could be said about 1980s' and 1990s' and even today's China. To paraphrase Sidney Smith: "The Chinese are a brave, industrious, and acute people; but they have hitherto given no indication of genius, and have made no approach to the heroic … . Where are their Thomas Edisons, Andrew Carnegies, Henry Fords, J.P. Morgans, John D. Rockefellers, and Cornelius Vanderbilts? … . Who wears clothes made in China? Or builds homes with Chinese-made tools?"

But merely 10 years later in the 2000s after China joined the WTO, the Americans started to drink from Chinese glasses, wear clothes made in China, and build homes with Chinese-made tools. However, they could say this today: "Who rides in Chinese trains? Or drives in Chinese cars? Or flies in Chinese airplanes?" Perhaps in another 10–20 years these questions will be answered, firmly.[15]

---

[15] On October 23, 2014, Boston transport authorities awarded China CNR Corp. a $567 million contract to supply trains for the city's subway system, the first deal of its kind for a Chinese company in the U.S. As another example, see the case study on how one Chinese battery firm began making electric buses in America (Paulson Papers on Investment, Case Study Series, June 2015). Also see the documentary program about China's pace of urbanization and technological innovations: "How China Works?" available at the Discovery Channel: http://www. discoverychannelasia.com/shows/how-china-works/. As another example, it was reported on Nov. 18, 2014, that airplanes made in China will be flying U.S. skies

Similarly, despite its hyper speed of wealth accumulation, China's higher education and pure science today are still far behind those in the United States. But China has been catching up and shrinking the gap rapidly in recent years after finishing its first industrial revolution and kick-starting its second industrial revolution, just as H. A. Rowland (1883) predicted in the 1880s for America in *A Plea for Pure Science*:

"In conclusion, let me say once more, that I do not believe that our country is to remain long in its present position. The science of physics, in whose applications [in generating wealth] our country glories, is to arise among us, and make us respected by the nations of the world. Such a prophecy may seem rash with regard to a nation which does not yet do enough physical work to support a physical journal. But we know the speed with which we advance in this country: We see cities springing up in a night, and other wonders performed at an unprecedented rate. And now we see physical laboratories being built, we see a great demand for thoroughly trained physicists, who have not shirked their mathematics, both as professors and in so-called practical life; and perhaps we have the feeling, common to all true Americans, that our country is going forward to a glorious future, when we shall lead the world in the strife for intellectual prizes as we now do in the strife for wealth."

So, to return to the original question of this chapter: Why is China's rise unstoppable? It is because of the colossal national wealth China has created, based on proper development strategies and industrial policies, based on its vision for manufacturing and industrial system, and based on its state capacity to support scientific research. The entire nation has been mobilized and poised for technology adoption and innovation, thanks to its successful completion of a proto-industrialization and detonation of its first and

---

for the first time as a California-based company has agreed to purchase 20 Y-12 aircraft manufactured by a unit of Aviation Industry Corp of China (see http://usa.chinadaily.com.cn/us/2014-11/18/content_18935103.htm.)

second industrial revolutions. But more importantly, because major technological progress and industrial innovations throughout history and even today do not come from pure science or from a handful of geniuses, but from widespread manufacturing practices, from grassroots practitioners and their hands-on experiences in daily manufacturing processes. It is "personal contact that is most relevant in learning" to adopt and invent new technologies (Kenneth Arrow, 1969, quoted in McCloskey, 2010, p. 162).[16]

The English Industrial Revolution (e.g., the division of labor and the spinning jenny and the steam engine and the factory system) was not a revolution in scientific theory nor its applications, but rather a revolution in practical knowledge, in industrial organization, in manufacturing skills, in the art of making things, in organizing practical matters, and in the way people produce, distribute, travel, communicate, and consume. Such breakthroughs and discoveries and accumulations of manufacturing knowledge can only be based on and driven by the activities of manufacturing itself, by the hands-on learning process of producing and organizing things.[17] Any country can become the global leader of technology innovations as long as it can embark on the path of industrialization and become the workshop of the world (or dominate a segment in global manufacturing value chains), because technological knowledge and innovations are mostly tacit, come mainly from repeated

---

[16] In fact, despite Rowland's passionate plea and optimism for American pure science, the U.S. did not become dominant in world scientific research until post-World War II, decades after first becoming the world's industrial giant. American advancement in pure science was also greatly facilitated by its immigration policy. For example, American dominance in rocket science was propelled greatly by German scientists after World War II, see https://en.wikipedia.org/wiki/List_of_German_rocket_scientists_in_the_United_States.

[17] In my view, it is now a consensus among most economic historians that the British Industrial Revolution did not originate from the 17th century European Scientific Revolution (see, e.g., R. Allen (2009) and D. McCloskey (2010) and the references therein).

practice, from concrete industrial buildup, from competition for excellence, from incentives for satisfying market demand and grabbing market shares, from the manufacturing process itself.[18] By the same token, an already industrialized nation can completely lose its technological advantage and innovative power as soon as she gives up manufacturing.[19]

Tacit knowledge pervades the realms of industry. The many laws of nature and the expertise behind industrial technologies are primarily based on causal relations, which we experience directly. These causal relations cannot be deduced from pure logic based on a set of axioms; they can be obtained only through experiments and active participation in the processes involved.

This iron law of "learning by doing" or "innovating by practicing" has repeatedly been proven to be a powerful force in human history. The German philosopher Hegel formalized this law in his philosophical analysis of the master-slave (*Herrschaft und Knechtschaft*) dialectic relationship (Hegel, 1807, The Phenomenology of Spirit). True knowledge and source of innovation belong to the practitioners ("slaves" or "apprentices") instead of the masters or lords.

---

[18] An example of tacit knowledge is the Bessemer steel process — which was the first inexpensive industrial process for the mass production of steel from molten pig iron prior to the open hearth furnace. The key principle is removal of impurities from the iron by oxidation with air being blown through the molten iron. Related techniques had been used in China for hundreds of years, but not on an industrial scale. The knowledge has existed since at least the 11th century and was described first by the Chinese scholar Shen Kuo (Chinese: 沈括) in his famous science encyclopedia book. In the 17th century, accounts by European travelers detailed its possible use by the Japanese. The modern process is named after its inventor, the Englishman Henry Bessemer, who took out a patent on the advanced steelmaking process in 1856. Bessemer sold the patent but was sued by the purchasers who couldn't get it to work. In the end Bessemer set up his own steel company because he knew how to do it, even though he could not convey it to his patent users. Bessemer's company became one of the largest in the world and changed the face of steel making.

[19] "Technical knowledge is largely tacit, non-write-downable, and requires people quick on the uptake" (McCloskey, 2010, p. 162).

The same logic of industrial innovation has applied equally to China. Through an American lens, throughout the 1980s, 1990s, and 2000s or even up to today, China has been merely the "blue color worker" for her American boss, using 100 million t-shirts to exchange for one Boeing 737 airplane. China still may appear backward despite decades of hyper growth (now the world's second-largest economy) because of its enormous agrarian population and low levels of per capita income (again: Only $1/20^{th}$ of the U.S. in the 1990s and $1/8^{th}$ of the U.S. in 2014) and even still lower per capita consumption level (only $1/30^{th}$ of the U.S. in the 1990s and $1/12^{th}$ of the U.S. in 2014). China today still has more than 50% of its population living in rural areas. However, the Chinese are now the world's busiest manufacturing practitioners, they discover new practical knowledge daily by manufacturing and assembling and moving and shoveling things around.[20] For example, to build high-speed trains for travel and cargo across massive mountainous areas with dramatic day-night temperature fluctuations, Chinese engineers need to solve numerous practical and technical problems that German and Japanese engineers did not encounter. Moreover, Chinese engineers must conquer practical problems in all fields of manufacturing on a daily basis to compete with other manufacturing giants and remain the world's largest manufacturing powerhouse. Ten years ago, German high-tech companies might have allowed the Chinese engineers (but not Japanese engineers) to see their

---

[20] China established its patent law in 1985, and patent applications grew rather modestly during its proto-industrial and first industrial revolution period. However, after China entered the stage of a second industrial revolution around the end of 1990s, patent applications have surged dramatically. For example applications from domestic inventors surged at an annual rate of 30% from 1999 to 2009 (see Dang and Motohashi, 2015). By 2013, China submitted one-third of the world's patent applications, surpassing the U.S. and Japan (see http://www.industryweek.com/global-economy/china-drives-growth-patent-applications-worldwide). Also see Tian Zhu's commentary article on China's ability to innovate, http://www.ftchinese.com/story/001059724.

blueprints and not worry about their ideas being stolen, but no more.[21] The Chinese have already caught up to the frontier of key manufacturing technologies in electronics, information, telecommunication, satellite navigation, supercomputing, semiconductors, precision lathes, material science and nanotechnology, shipbuilding, bullet trains, tunnel and canal construction, power generation and transmission, space science and military technology, among many others, through "learning by doing."

Such advances through "learning by doing" and "inventing by practicing" may appear humble in the beginning, but from inches to miles and drops to waterfalls the Hegelian master-slave dialectic logic will propel China to the height of technological achievement in the not-so-remote future because it has the world's largest manufacturing center to practice and innovate and push the frontier.[22]

Once one learns how to build, one opens the door to knowledge for creation and innovation. Without understanding the tacit nature of technology knowledge, the history of the American Industrial Revolution, and the fact that the iron laws of "learning by doing" and "innovating by practicing" govern all nations' industrial revolutions, one's perceptions will be clouded. No wonder U.S. Vice President Joe Biden has repeatedly expressed in public critical views of China (similar to what Sidney Smith had said about America in the 1820s). He specifically responded in 2012 and 2014 to concerns that China was overtaking the U.S. to become the manufacturing superpower:

"We are the world's largest GDP. We have the most innovative companies and productive workers, the finest research universities in the

---

[21] For a fascinating history of technological espionage, see Charles Morris (2012), "The Dawn of Innovation."

[22] The Chinese workers and engineers started 20 years ago from the low point of using 100 million t-shirts to exchange for one Boeing 737 airplane, but they can now produce their own fifth-generation stealth fighter — equivalent in ability to Lockheed Martin's F-22 Raptor or F-35 Lighting II Joint Strike Fighter.

world, an entrepreneurial instinct that is unmatched by any country in the world. And within a decade North America will be the epicenter of energy in the world, not the Arabian Peninsula. China, by contrast, had not developed one innovative project, one innovative change, one innovative product. I challenge you, name me one innovative project, one innovative change, one innovative product that has come out of China."[23]

Of course, it is hard to separate political speeches from personal beliefs, but people resist change, whether a change to their status or a change in their own perceptions of how the world works. The irony here is that, just as Americans were the best students of the British in the 19th century and eventually surpassed them; just as American ingenuity and innovative powers were hidden behind their low-grade low-value-added but dynamic manufacturing that had yet to manifest itself in grand innovations and fundamental scientific breakthroughs; just as Americans were adept primarily in learning, copying, absorbing, and even "stealing" advanced technologies from Britain; and just as Americans were constantly inventing practical, small-step technologies in the industrial manufacturing process (such as in cotton harvesting/processing and turnpike building) that were often invisible to outsiders, so also have the Chinese been the best students of the Americans. What may be the most frightening thing about China is not how much China tries to "steal" from America just as the America "stole" from the British, but perhaps how much China resembles America. China is able to absorb and digest the most advanced frontier technologies in such a short time without the top universities in the world, such as Harvard and MIT, to train first-rate scientists.[24] China has, instead, the world's largest manufacturing "campus," where their practitioners

---

[23] See http://politicalticker.blogs.cnn.com/2014/05/28/biden-name-one-innovative-product-from-china/.

[24] China's Beijing University and Tsinghua University still lag far behind Harvard and MIT.

can learn, practice, discover, and train younger generations of engineers and innovators, just as America in the 19th century absorbed the frontier of British technology, despite its lack of Trinity College (where Isaac Newton graduated and taught) or Oxford or Cambridge.[25]

In the entire 19th century or even the 20th century, America produced no philosophers like Kant and Hegel, no scientists like Newton and Darwin, but America later on (after having finished its first industrial revolution and kick-started its second industrial revolution) produced the world's greatest inventors such as Thomas Edison and industrial giants such as Andrew Carnegie, Henry Ford, J. P. Morgan, John D. Rockefeller, and Cornelius Vanderbilt. The late 19th to early 20th century America was an epoch "which called for giants and produced giants — giants in power of thought, passion and character, in universality and learning" (Friedrich Engels, *Dialectics of Nature*, Moscow, 1974, p. 20).[26]

The British must therefore give the Americans credit for their ability to absorb technologies from Britain in the entire 19th century. In the 19th century, China and India did not have the capabilities of the U.S. to learn and innovate and mimic or even steal British textile and rail industrial technologies, let alone the ability to improve upon them and invent their own. China and India (unlike Japan after the 1860s) lacked a powerful business-orientated mercantilist government (or the state capacity) to mobilize their grassroots craftsmen through village industries to kick-start a proto-industrialization, and

---

[25] From 1860 to 1890, 500,000 patents were issued for new inventions in the United States. Companies like AT&T helped build a good communication network. Scientists like Nikola Tesla and Edison (who also co-founded General Electric) invented a number of electrical devices, providing a huge boost to power plants. Rockefeller founded the Standard Oil Company, consolidating the oil industry and producing mostly kerosene.

[26] Engels was referring to the Renaissance Italian giant Leonardo da Vinci.

thus lacked the powerful market demand to create the mass supply, the manufacturing base to "learn by doing" and "invent by practicing." However, in the 19th century, the United States had created the powerful market demand and detonated the chain of industrial revolutions and hence was in the position to become the next world superpower, thanks to one of its founding fathers, Alexander Hamilton (1755–1804), for his vision and advice of not to build America through its static comparative advantage of agriculture (at the time) but on its future strategic competitive advantage of (textile) manufacturing. Based on Hamilton's development strategy manifested in the "American System," it took America only 60 years (starting from the 1820s) to catch up with Great Britain and her technology supremacy. By the late 1880s and especially around the turn of the 20th century, America had become the world's manufacturing powerhouse and leader of industrial technology.

The ability to mass-produce capital (or mass-*reproduce* capital) was achieved in history through the second industrial revolution. The second industrial revolution took place in Britain after the 1830s and finished around the 1900s, started in the United States around the 1870s and finished around the 1930s, started in Japan around the 1920s and finished around the 1970s (interrupted by WWII for about 10 years). China has entered this stage after a decade of booming light-industrial activity and infrastructural buildup since the late 1990s. China just became a net capital (FDI) exporter by the end of 2014. Over the next decade, China is expected to export $1.25 trillion in fixed capital to finance global infrastructure buildup.

China's expansive industrial growth and progress have borne fruit on an international scale: The first direct China-to-Spain freight train arrived in Madrid on December 10, 2014, from China's Yiwu city on the east coast, after traveling 13,000 kilometers (8,000 miles) in a 21-day journey through Kazakhstan, Russia, Belarus, Poland, Germany, and France. The epic 13,000 kilometer journey cuts the traditional maritime shipping time by more than 50%.[27] This newly operational route is the longest railway route in the world and is reminiscent of the Silk Road connecting China's ancient capital city Xi'an and the Mediterranean Sea some 2,000 years ago.

Britain built the world's largest railroad system in the 19th century, driven by a demand for transportation and market expansion so as to mass distribute raw materials and manufacturing goods. China is now building the world's largest speed-rail system both domestically and internationally. It is always the capital suppliers who manage the production and distribution of mass-produced goods, not the goods-demand side. China is now the workshop and manufacturing powerhouse of the world and hence the supplier of goods and mass-produced capital. So China by nature needs a first-rate world distribution system to deliver its mass-produced goods/capital and intake raw materials from other corners of the world. Thus, building a new worldwide system of infrastructure to facilitate the delivery and distribution of its mass-produced goods is the natural manifestation of China's capitalism.

Since Columbus, the cheapest way to navigate through the globe was ocean travel, which paved the way for the British Industrial

---

[27] Currently, China has eight multi-customer cargo rail routes to Europe, in addition to the Yiwu-Madrid railway, there are China Chongqing-Germany Duisburg route (launched in 2011, 11,179 kilometers and 16 days for a single journey), China Chengdu-Poland Lodz route (launched in 2013, 9,965 kilometers and 14 days for a single journey), China Zhengzhou-Germany Hamburg route (launched in 2014, 10,214 kilometers and 15 days in a single journey), China Suzhou-Poland Warsaw route (launched in 2014, 11,200 kilometers and 14 days for a single journey), China Wuhan–Czech Pardubice route (launched in 2012, 10,700 kilometers and 15 days in a single journey), China Changsha-Germany Duisburg route (launched in 2014, 11,808 kilometers and 18 days for a single journey), and China Hefei-Euro route (launched in 2014, run through northern Chinese city Zhengzhou, west China's Xian, Lanzhou and Urumqi, Kazakhstan, Russia, Belarus, Poland, and Germany.) More routes are expected to operate in the near future. See, e.g., http://www.guancha.cn/economy/2015_04_19_316486_s.shtml.

Revolution. Hence, all the old industrial powers relied on the Atlantic, Pacific, and Indian oceans for trade and mass distribution. But times have changed, or at least China is bringing about this pivotal change. With its low manufacturing costs and know-how in mass producing roads, railways, ports, natural gas pipelines, high-speed trains, and other infrastructure, China is connecting and integrating South East Asia, the Middle East, Central Asia, Russia, and Europe by rail, including another new line stretching 15,000 kilometers from China's south coast city Shenzhen to Rotterdam. This is what the media called China's "New Global Marshall Plans."[28] Rail transportation is much faster and more punctual and predictable than ocean transportation, and thus meets the 21st century's needs for truly globalized industrialization. A new age of international trade based on land transportation is being created by China. There may not be a world economic event more significant than this new Silk Road — at least since the great voyage and the English Industrial Revolution. This reveals in just one particular angle the force of China's rise and its magnificent impact on the world economic and geopolitical structure in the 21st century.

This law of "learning by doing" or "innovating by practicing" also helps to explain the "resource curse" — a typical development-failure phenomenon that refers to the paradox that countries and regions with an abundance of natural resources, such as land, minerals, and oil, tend to have less economic growth and worse development outcomes than countries with fewer natural resources. Such resource-rich countries tend to rely on their comparative advantages (a la David Ricardo) in agriculture and non-reproducible resources to generate quick wealth and high wage incomes through trade, instead of taking the slower and more difficult path of promoting

---

[28] More accurately, this is called "One Road, One Belt" strategy in China. "One Road" refers to the land-based rail network system and "One Belt" refers to the ocean-based maritime route starting from China's eastern and southern coast lines all the way to Africa through the Indian Ocean.

manufacturing (first in the rural areas through proto-industrialization and costly market creation). Land-intensive production (such as agriculture and resource extraction) is subject to rapid diminishing returns to labor, but capital-based production (such as manufacturing) is not: Capital is reproducible through manufacturing, whereas land (natural resources) cannot be reproduced through farming (extraction). More importantly, industrial technologies and their discoveries originate only from manufacturing, and such technologies have tremendous productivity spillovers to agriculture and resource extraction. The reverse is not true: Resource extraction *per se* does not lead to deeper technological knowledge and productivity spillovers to other sectors of the economy. Yet a developing nation can learn and master developed nations' cutting-edge industrial technologies through learning by doing (manufacturing), a bottom-up approach that begins modestly but aims high, and a process of continuous state-led sequential market creation based on correct industrial policies.

iii. A Capable Mercantilist Government as Market Creator

The third reason China's rise is unstoppable is that China has a capable mercantilist government with both highly centralized command power and a highly decentralized administrative structure; a government that can mobilize and organize and manage its national economy through both central planning (e.g., in national development strategies and infrastructure buildup) and decentralized intranational competition among local administrative regions for economic growth and governance (akin to the 15th–19th century European state-competition); a government that is guided by both pragmatism (instead of dogmatic economic theories) and an iron will to develop and open itself up to international competition with the world's superpowers in commerce and manufacturing and management; a government that can self-correct major policy errors through controlled nationwide experiments and pragmatic institutional innovations at both the upper and lower administrative levels.[29] Such a government is what *state capacity* truly means.[30] Built on a politically stable one-party system that avoids some typical dilemmas of both democracy and dictatorship facing developing countries, the Chinese government can draw from its source of administrative talents and support from the majority of the grassroots population based on a merit-based leader-selection (meritocracy) system.[31] Such a system is not perfect but has been China's great political comparative advantage — despite the need of continuous learning and reform and transformation in accordance with the evolving economic structures. The government understands the nature (both virtues and vices) of capitalism and the developmental history of the West (thanks partly to the teachings of Karl Marx).[32]

---

[29] For documentation of China's political structure and gradualist approach to reform and institutional innovations since 1978, see Ronald Coase and Ning Wang (2013).

[30] The lack of such state capacity was precisely one of the major contributing factor to Russia's economic collapse since the early 1990s when the democratically elected Russian president Boris Yeltsin outlawed the Communist Party and torn it out of political power, which literally "broke the backbone of the new state" (Chrystia Freeland, 2000, p. 20). Such state capacity is also seriously missing in many developing nations, especially those adopting democracy immaturely before finishing industrialization, such as Afghanistan, Egypt, Iraq, Libya, Pakistan, Philippines, Tunisia, Ukraine, and even upper middle-income countries such as Argentina and Greece.

[31] For scholarly analyses of China's meritocracy system, see Zhang Weiwei (2012), *The China Wave: Rise of a Civilizational State*. World Century Publishing Corporation. Also see "A Tale of Two Systems" by Eric X. Li. Available at http://blog.ted.com/2013/06/13/a-tale-of-two-systems-eric-x-li-at-tedglobal-2013/, "*A Nation in Question: Understanding the Rise of China*" By Xiaopeng Li, and "*The China Model: Political Meritocracy and the Limit of Democracy*" by Daniel A. Bell.

[32] In the 1950s–1970s, the Chinese government used Marxism to reject capitalism and hoped to achieve industrialization through central planning by skipping the

In this way, China can take a much longer historical view of the evolution of human societies as it designs and implements its development strategies. (A much longer view than, say, those of democratically elected politicians, who are often incompetent in managing the economy, prone to the manipulation of powerful interest groups, and constrained by voters' short-sighted immediate self-interests.)[33]

The Chinese government understands (finally) that the wealth and power of nations lie in commerce-lubricated and market-supported mass production, which generates competitive "scale economies" and industrial affluence, and along with it the middle-income class and the "bourgeois dignity" (a la McCloskey) that comes with it.

"Whosoever commands the trade of the world, commands the riches of the world and consequently the world itself."
— Sir Walter Raleigh, c. 1600[34]

Trade creates mass market, and mass market supports mass production. The more the economy produces, the cheaper the output price gets, hence the larger market share it commands and further creates. So, capitalist economies are outward looking, aggressive, innovative, and expansionary in nature. Just look how open and outward looking China is today compared with China in

---

stage of capitalism (featuring primitive accumulations based on market competition and private property); today it uses Marxism to acknowledge and rationalize capitalism as a necessary stage of industrialization and social-economic development. The so-called "socialism with Chinese characters" is essentially socialism (central planning) with capitalistic characters (market competition), or capitalism (market competition) with socialistic characters (state-guided industrial policies).

[33] A particular view on the inefficient aspects of American democracy can be found in Francis Fukuyama (2014), *Political Order and Political Decay*. New York: Farrar, Straus, and Giroux.

[34] See Stephen R. Bown, 2010, p. 1.

the 18th and 19th centuries or even just 40 years ago under Mao (who was not against mass production but against commerce and profit-motivated trade). The mass supply of goods with ever increasing quantity and variety and declining prices means not only increasingly greater social welfare but also persistent destructive power on all the traditional production modes and culture in backward agrarian economies that trade (voluntarily or involuntarily) with capitalistic economies:

> "[Capitalism], by the rapid improvement of all instruments of production, by the immensely facilitated means of communication, draws all, even the most barbarian, nations into civilization. The cheap prices of commodities are the heavy artillery with which it batters down all Chinese walls, with which it forces the barbarians' intensely obstinate hatred of foreigners to capitulate. It compels all nations, on pain of extinction, to adopt the bourgeois mode of production; it compels them to introduce what it calls civilization into their midst, i.e., to become bourgeois themselves. In one word, it creates a world after its own image" (Karl Marx and Friedrich Engels (1848), Manifesto of the Communist Party, Chapter 1).

Qing Dynasty China refused to open trade and change its physiocratic ideology and feudalistic way of living when confronted by British industrial technologies and navy power. But today's China has enthusiastically embraced changes and engaged in international competition and trade. By embracing capitalism, China today enjoys (in a peaceful manner) the same power and pride Britain did during the First Opium War 175 years ago.[35]

---

[35] Three massive Chinese naval ships arrived in Portsmouth for a formal visit on January 12, 2015, which was the biggest visit by the Chinese Navy to Britain in history. Portsmouth Naval Base Commander Jeremy Rigby told news reporter: "China, like us, relies on trade at sea for its prosperity." Notice he did not mention the Glorious Revolution at all, not because he forgot, but because it was not really relevant. See news report at https://www.navynews.co.uk/archive/news/item/12225.

Capitalism cannot hide or protect its technology secrets. The ability to mass produce machinery and economies of scale will impel profit-driven capitalists to mass-export such means of production despite possible government bans on doing so (to keep technological advantages over other nations),[36] thus bringing the fruits of the Industrial Revolution to all corners of the world. The British did this to Europe, India, and the United States; other European countries did this to Africa, Latin America and Japan; the Japanese did this to Asia; and the Americans did this to the entire postwar world.

But despite this "leaking" and "spillover" of advanced technologies from industrial powers to developing countries, many developing countries remain underdeveloped and unable to absorb/adopt modern technologies despite the great efforts of world organizations (such as the IMF, the World Bank, and the United Nations) in eliminating global poverty in the postwar world. So, agricultural nations remain agrarian and resource-rich countries remain poor. What exactly has made these developing nations incapable of industrializing despite readily available modern technologies? Or how exactly has capitalism failed to create a world (such as in Sub-Saharan Africa) after its own image?

The institutional theory blames this failure of technological diffusion on developing nations' extractive institutions. The Washington Consensus (see Chapter 5) attributes this to developing countries' government distortions of the free market and obstacles for free capital flows. Thus, their prescription for development is democratization through a political revolution (such as the Arab Spring) or shock therapy through immediate and complete adoption of free

---

[36] For the history of British government acts of banning the export of technology, see Charles Morris (2012), *The Dawn of Innovation*. Also, since 1989, the United States government has banned exports of sensitive high-tech industrial technologies to China, which motivated China to develop many of its own frontier industrial technologies, including China's space and satellite programs.

markets, free capital flows, free exchange rates, and privatization of state-owned banks. But such well-intended reform policies have often ended up barking up the wrong trees or leading to chaos.

For many developing countries, the root obstacles of development are not a lack of freedom to print and find and purchase Shakespeare's books, nor that the free market is forbidden so that private enterprises cannot emerge; but rather that the freedom of speech fails to spread technology and that firms fail to flourish despite private property right. Many developing countries have opened their doors to foreign capital, lifted their regulations on banking and finance, and embraced democracy (such as the Republic era of China after the 1911 Xinhai revolution), yet they collapsed and corrupted and malfunctioned rather than civilized and industrialized and modernized. Why? Many ex-communist Eastern European countries decided to move to a market economy and their political leaders were enthusiastic in doing so, but they ended up with deep political crisis and economic stagnations. Democracy and massive privatization have failed to create in these economies the market for mass-produced consumer goods except perhaps most easily drugs and pornography and prostitution. In sharp contrast, China under "faulty" and "extractive" institutions, with its fierce refusal to subscribe to the neoliberal Washington Consensus and Shock Therapy tactics, has nonetheless succeeded in creating the world's largest market for commerce and global trade. How?[37]

History has already provided the answer. What has made the Industrial Revolution possible first in Great Britain, later in the United States, France, Germany, Japan, South Korea, Singapore, and many other late-developed countries was not democracy, but a powerful business-oriented government and government-engineered

---

[37] Eight of the world's 10 largest container ports are now in China. The world's largest and busiest port, the Port of Shanghai, set a historic world record by handling over 33.6 million TEUs in 2013. By 2017, this port alone will have shipping capacity larger than all U.S. ports combined.

nation-building through guided commerce and trade policies; nor was it free capital flows and flexible exchange rates based on static comparative advantages of trade but a mercantilist development strategy aiming at future strategic comparative advantages of manufacturing; nor was it a purely top-down approach with revolutionary institutional changes to accommodate modern efficient technologies and financial system but a bottom-up approach with evolutionary experimental policy changes to facilitate the sprout of proto-industries and light manufacturing in the beginning through "primitive accumulations," in conjunction with the government's centralized unifying power and iron will to facilitate the creation of unified commercial markets and competition with foreign powers on manufacturing exports (initially in labor-intensive textile industries).

With this development strategy of embedding the wealth of the nation in commerce and trade, in primitive accumulations, in political stability and social order, the British government engaged in a long process of nation building and wealth creation through gradual market creation and industrialization.[38] Democracy and universal suffrage were only the consequence and by-product of industrialization, not the cause of it.[39] Trying to kick-start the Industrial Revolution by mimicking the consequences rather than the causes of industrialization is a recipe for failure.

> "What has made England powerful is the fact that from the time of Elizabeth, all parties have agreed on the necessity of favoring

---

[38] Nation-state building also facilitates the formation of social trust and a spirit of community.

[39] Such is also the view of the modernization theory, see Seymour Martin Lipset (1959), Robert A. Dahl (1971), Samuel P. Huntington (1991), Dietrich Rueschemeyer, John D. Stephens, and Evelyn H. Stephens (1992), among many others.

commerce. The same parliament that had the King beheaded was busy with overseas trading posts as though nothing were happening. The blood of Charles I was still steaming when this parliament, composed almost entirely of fanatics, passed the Navigation Act of 1650" (cited in David Landes 1999, p. 234).

By the same token, what has made China's rise powerful and unstoppable is the fact that from the time of Deng Xiaoping, all communist party members agreed on the necessity of favoring commerce and manufacturing-led exports. The same political bureau that just had Liu Zhijun (the Minister of Transportation chiefly responsible for initiating and building China's high-speed train system), Bo Xilai (the ex-Minister of Commerce who helped negotiate China's WTO entry) and Zhou Yongkang (former security tsar) purged is busy with overseas trading posts as though nothing has happened.

Regardless of political institutional forms (monarchy or parliament) or the legal systems (common law vs. civil law) or religions (Protestantism or Confucianism), a powerful mercantilist government with interests aligned with peasants and the grassroots population (for all to become wealthy) is essential for economic development, because industrialization is first and foremost a task of nation-building that involves nationwide unification of anarchic and autarkic markets and the organization, orientation, mobilization, and coordination of national resources and the entire labor force on a grand scale. Adam Smith in 1776 thought that the mass market for the division of labor could automatically create itself and solve such organizational and coordinating problems through the interactions of self-interested individuals guided by the invisible hand. But in a backward agrarian society with anarchic peasants and autarkic artisans, the mass market would repeatedly fail to emerge because of the formidable social coordination costs to intermediate trade or large-scale exchange between specialized supply and demand based on the principle of the division of labor. Without a mass market and its associated social trust and trade infrastructure and commerce network and distribution system, there would be no division of labor and mass-production firms.

To recap: The institutional theories have overemphasized formal institutions and private property rights as the prerequisites of industrialization. But such views are inconsistent with economic history. First, the rule of law and private property rights are ancient institutions that have existed for millenniums before the Industrial Revolution.[40] Second, their specific forms evolve over time according to the constantly evolving social-economic structures and mode of production because the specific forms and definitions of "crimes" and "rights" or what is legal and illegal change continuously overtime. So, capitalistic rule of law and property rights were the endogenous outcome of capitalism instead of its cause. As the economic historian Mokyr (2008) points out, British society provided little "law and order" to protect industrial "properties" and human "rights" before the Industrial Revolution and it had a "surprising quantity of robbers … . Local rioting, either for economic or political grievances, was common." "Hanoverian Britain had no professional police force comparable to the constabulary that emerged after 1830, and the court system was unwieldy, expensive, and uncertain. Britain depended on the deterrent effect of draconian penalties because it had no official mechanism of law enforcement, prosecution was mostly private, and crime prevention was largely self-enforcing, with more than 80% of all prosecutions carried out by the victims" (Mokyr, 2008, p. 10).

Therefore, what was important for promoting the accumulation of capital and the "proper" conduct of commerce before and during the British Industrial Revolution was not the formal corporate rule of law

---

[40] In fact, private land property rights and markets were more developed and secure in both the Qing dynasty and Republican China than in pre-industrial Europe (see, e.g., K. Pomeranz, 2001; Taisu Zhang, 2011), yet China failed to kick-start heavy industrial buildup until communism.

and the modern notion of property rights, let alone democracy, but rather the government-controled military power, the government-nurtured market forces, the government-promoted mercantile social value (including social trust, fairness, business ethics, and religion), and the privately enforced order by merchants themselves.[41]

Adam Smith failed to acknowledge that much of the international commercial "laws" and trade order in his days were created by European merchants' monopoly power and military force backed by their state governments, as recorded by the famous Dutch merchant and warrior Jan Pieterszoon Coen to the Dutch Monarch:

> *"Your Honours should know by experience that trade in Asia must be driven and maintained under the protection and favour of Your Honours' own weapons, and that the weapons must be paid for by the profits from the trade; so that we cannot carry on trade without war, nor war without trade."*[42]

---

[41] Adam Smith in his *Lectures of Jurisprudence* noted that "Whenever commerce is introduced into any country, probity and punctuality always accompany it. These virtues in a rude and barbarous country are almost unknown ... Where people seldom deal with one another, we find that they are somewhat disposed to cheat, because they can gain more by a smart trick than they can lose by the injury which it does their character" (quoted by Mokyr, 2008, pp. 15–16).

[42] See Stephen R. Bown (2010, p. 7). According to Stephen Bown, "[f]rom the early 1600s to the late 1800s, monopoly trading companies were the unofficial agents of European colonial expansion. They seized control of vast territories and many peoples, acquiring a variety of governmental and military functions in the wake of their commercial success. For European nations, granting monopoly trading rights to these companies was a convenient way of bankrolling the astronomical cost of colonial expansion ... As each of these privileged enterprises grew, it first assumed civil right authority over all Europeans in its employment overseas and then expanded this authority by subjugating local peoples. In working towards their political objectives, the merchant trading companies maintained their own policy forces and, sometimes, standing armies, and either controlled the local governments or became the sole government of their territories" (Stephen R. Bown, *Merchant Kings: When Companies Ruled the World, 1600–1900*. Macmillan, 2010, pp. 1–2).

In addition to providing (directly or indirectly) social order and political stability and solving the problem of missing markets and market-coordination failures, the government has another critical role to play: Industries and trade generate and impose enormous positive externalities on the national economic system that only the state can fully internalize. This is especially true for energy, locomotive power, finance, and infrastructure industries that are pivotal to development and national security.[43]

Hence, the lack of state support and government-nurtured and financed mercantilist (manufacturing-export-oriented) development strategies in continuous creation of global (textile) markets, supply chains, and commercial distribution systems must be the key reason behind the failure of 18th century Flanders and Ireland to kick-start the Industrial Revolution, despite their fabulous and flourishing textile proto-industries competing side-by-side with the British textile firms at the time.[44]

---

[43] This is essentially the view of Friedrich List (1841) in *The Natural System of Political Economy*. Even in today's developed nations such as the United States we still observe important government agencies or institutions such as the U.S. Department of Energy and its tight connections with American foreign policies. In contrast, although 19th century India had the most advanced rail system in Asia, built by the British colonizers, it generated little economic gains and spillover effects on the Indian economy (see Pomeranz and Topik, 2013), precisely because the rail system and its spillover effects were impossible to be internalized without a strong Indian government at the time.

[44] For detailed history of the rise and fall of textile proto-industries in Flanders, see Franklin F. Mendels (1981). For the rise and fall of textile proto-industries in other European countries such as Ireland, see Clarkson (1985, 1996), Kriedte, Medick, and Schlumbohm (1977), Mokyr (1983), O'Malley (1981), and Sheilagh C. Ogilvie and Markus Cerman (1996). These historians, however, all failed to emphasize the important role of the British mercantilist government in helping create the needed global market conditions for British firms to successfully transform from small-scale labor-intensive peasant workshops to large-scale organization- and capital-intensive factories. No wonder textile proto-industries in Flanders and Ireland, instead of transforming into factories, were driven out of the international market by British firms.

No wonder, China's rapid jump-start of its second industrial revolution (started in the middle 1990s and spread out in the late 1990s and 2000s) has benefited tremendously from the large-scale state-owned heavy industries and scientific research institutions established during Mao's era.[45] Such heavy industries and expensive public research institutions used to be highly "inefficient" (unprofitable) and were large financial burdens for China, but gradually no longer so after China (i) finished its proto-industrialization and its first industrial revolution by the mid to late 1990s and (ii) adopted

---

[45] China waited until 1997–1998 to start its massive reform of SOEs, by then China had already finished its first industrial revolution in mass-producing light-industrial goods and commodities. Because China's SOEs were mostly located in urban areas and large cities, such a measured development strategy enabled the SOEs to perform at least two important functions in facilitating China's economic transition and industrialization: (i) to maintain and stabilize urban employment during the rural-based proto-industrialization and first industrial revolution; and (ii) to play a leadership role in promoting and transferring more advanced production technologies to rural industries (recall that China's rural industries received most of their technologies and engineers from SOEs in nearby cities). But once rural industries caught up with SOEs in technological frontiers and China broadly finished its first industrial revolution in mass-producing labor-intensive light consumer goods, the historical role of China's small to medium sized SOEs (which were based on mass production technology to begin with) was finished and should naturally yield to newly formed but more productive and better managed private or collective enterprises. During the first two years of SOE reform between 1998 and 2000, about 21.4 million SOE workers were laid off, mostly in the textile, mining, military defense, and machinery sectors. However, because of prohibitive costs in finance and technological barriers to form large-scale private heavy industries, China privatized only the small to medium sized SOEs, which could be easily absorbed or substituted by the private sector, but kept the large heavy-industrial SOEs under the so-called "grasping the large and letting go the small" nationwide SOE reform. This by no means implied lack of reform for the remaining large SOEs. The government forced the remaining large heavy-industrial SOEs to reform management structure, upgrade technologies, and confront domestic and international competition. China's high-speed rail companies are good examples of such a measured and targeted SOE reform strategy.

a profit/cost-driven (competitive) approach to manage all heavy industries and a reputation/merit-based reward system of research and innovation.[46] China (wisely) chose not to abandon and destroy (through marketization and privatization) its "inefficient" heavy industries in the 1980s and early 1990s, unlike what Russia had done during its initial reform period under the Shock Therapy. China instead kept state-owned enterprises (SOEs) via a dual-track system and postponed their reform until the late 1990s after China finished both proto-industrialization and its first industrial revolution.[47] By the late 1990s, these earlier two stages of industrialization in the 1980s and 1990s since the reform had made China the world's largest market for modern infrastructures and heavy industrial goods, such as chemicals, raw materials, rare earth, energy, coal, oil, electricity, steel, transportation, automobiles, trains, communication, and all types of machinery and precision instruments. Such a large market was then able to profitably support a large state-owned domestic sector of heavy industries and render it viable, making the market-oriented reform and restructuring of China's old state-owned heavy industries much easier to undertake than, say, in the late 1970s and 1980s or even early 1990s. Thus, while Russia's heavy industries were mostly abandoned and destroyed by the shock therapy and the so-called "market" forces in the 1990s, China's heavy industries have waited for the right moment and then

---

[46] The private patent system was never as important in the advancement of science and technologies as the institutional economists claimed, not even during the English Industrial Revolution (see, e.g., Boldrin and Levine, 2008; Mokyr, 2008). In fact, Boldrin and Levine (2008) use historical evidences (the inventor James Watt and his steam engine) to argue that intellectual property rights has hindered innovation rather than stimulated it throughout history.

[47] See, e.g., Lau, Qian, and Roland (2000), China's Dual-Track Approach to Transition. Also see the literature's discussions on China's "grasping the large, letting go of the small" reform strategy implemented since 1997 for its heavy industries (http://en.wikipedia.org/wiki/Grasping_the_large_letting_go_of_the_small).

magically transformed and resurrected[48] — thanks to the emergence of a large domestic market and commercial system for heavy industrial goods after the middle 1990s, which came into existence not because of a sudden increase in China's population but because China by then had successfully built a colossal light industrial base and purchasing power to afford and finance a large-scale heavy industry. This also explains China's nearly 45% aggregate investment rate and the explosive inflows of manufacturing FDI from industrial economies since the middle 1990s, as well as China's rapid advancement in heavy industrial technologies since then, such as its lightening takeoff in electronic and steel-making and shipbuilding technologies, high-speed rail systems, and space programs (most of which are state-owned).[49]

---

[48] For example, some of China's military defense companies turned from producing guns and tanks to manufacturing durable consumer goods such as motorcycles and autos. The world's largest speed-train producer in today's China used to be a loss-maker in producing steam engines back in the 1960s under Mao.

[49] Since the operation of China's first high-speed railroad in 2008, 28 Chinese provinces are now already covered by the world largest and longest high-speed rail network (more than 16,000 kilometers in length and 50% greater than current world capacity). The Beijing-to-Shanghai high-speed rail registered positive profits in 2014 after being in operation for only three years. As of February 2015, several additional high-speed rail lines registered positive profits after being in operation only for 1–2 years, including the Beijing-Tianjin line, Shanghai-Ningbo line, Shanghai Hangzhou line, Hangzhou-Shenzhen line and Guangzhou-Shenzhen line. In the meantime, privately owned and operated high-speed trains in other advanced economies such as that in Taiwan and France have been enduring heavy losses for many years. This proves again that it is the size of the market and management that matters, not the form of ownership. For the same reason, many American public schools or universities do not necessarily underperform the private ones. In sharp contrast, heavy industries in Africa and Latin America are highly inefficient despite private ownership. Massive privatization in Russia in the 1990s did not make its heavy industries more productive and profitable because shock therapy has shrunk rather than enlarged Russia's domestic and international markets. Russia paid dearly for its economic reform because of the

An important lesson learned from China's privatization experience is that a nation should be extremely cautious in privatizing its SOEs once established. Do not blindly and indiscriminately privatize all industries before market conditions are ready. The market conditions for privatizing a particular industry are ready if and only if (i) the market is large enough to support similar-type private firms; (ii) private firms in this industry are well-developed and sufficiently competitive domestically or internationally in finance, management, and technological innovations; and (iii) privatization does not put national security at risk, and key industries involving national security should permit only mergers or joint ventures instead of full-fledged privatization.[50]

---

collapse and virtually permanent loss of markets for its heavy industries, not because of vested interests as portrayed by the institutional economists.

[50] Judged by such criteria, China's privatization of small to medium sized firms such as labor-intensive textile firms was extremely successful and smooth because the market conditions were fully ready for privatization in the late 1990s. But China's profit-based educational and healthcare reforms were disastrous because such market conditions were seriously lacking when such reforms took place (such conditions are even still lacking today). In retrospect, China should have waited until private hospitals and clinics (or private schools) are well-developed and sufficiently competitive with each other and with their public counterparts before introducing profit-motivated reforms into these public sectors. Such a waiting period also allows the government to develop necessary regulations to prevent massive corporate fraud in such important welfare-sensitive areas. Hence, as China currently undergoes its second industrial revolution, it must be extremely careful and take measured, dual-track, and experimental approaches to financial-sector reforms and privatization of its heavy industries. The danger and risk of Russian-style collapse under shock therapy still exists in China today. Most importantly, there is no sound economic theory suggesting that SOEs are necessarily less efficient than private-owned enterprises. Using a contractual approach, Jiang and Wang (2015) prove theoretically that there exist no general conditions such that one type of ownership strictly dominates the other. They also provide the following empirical literature to support their findings. For example, Caves and Christensen (1980) study two major Canadian railroads under different ownership and they do not find state ownership to be less efficient than private

An important measure of the depth and size of a nation's market is not only the nation's population size, or the population's purchasing power *per se*, but also its infrastructure and distributional logistics network. China's public capital formation in urban water supply, electricity, transportation, and telecommunications has been growing at the fastest rate in the world. From 1978 to 2014, China's infrastructure capital stock (in constant prices) grew by more than 12% per year on average, two full percentage points faster than its real GDP growth. Vast improvements have been made during the past 35 years in irrigation systems, underground sewerage systems, streets and highway networks, air and rail transportation, electricity transmission grids, gas and oil pipelines, schools, hospitals, and so on. For example, the total length of public roads reached 4,230,000 kilometers (about 2,643,700 miles), including 111,950 kilometers (about 70,000 miles) express highways by the end of 2014, surpassing the United States to become the world's largest expressway system by length.[51] More than 95% of China's villages are now connected by asphalt roads. As a result, China now enjoys an exceptionally high ranking in the World Bank Logistics Performance Index (LPI). China is one of the few developing countries to achieve an LPI score comparable to that of high-income nations in

---

ownership. Vernon-Wortzel and Wortzel (1989) find in their data sample that SOEs perform better than private enterprises. Martin and Parker (1995) examine eleven U.K. firms that were privatized in the 1980s and they cannot find evidence that private ownership is unequivocally more efficient than nationalization. Chang and Singh (1997) argue that SOEs and large private firms both face the same unwieldy bureaucracies. Since private firms have no inherent advantages in corporate governance, there is no guarantee that they are more efficient than SOEs. Kole and Mulherin (1997) study a sample of U.S. companies; they find that the performance of the SOEs is not significantly different from that of private firms in the same industry. The above references can be found in Jiang and Wang (2015, p. 4).

[51] As of 2013, the United States had a total length of 47,856 miles of expressways.

international shipments, infrastructure, custom services, logistics competence, tracking and tracing, and timeliness, with an overall LPI score of 3.53 in 2014, ranked 28th in the world, next to Portugal but above richer countries such as Turkey, Poland and Hungary (see World Bank, "Connecting to Compete 2014: Trade Logistics in the Global Economy").[52] Moreover, China's infrastructure-construction boom is still continuing at unprecedented speed both domestically and internationally. Such remarkable catching-up in infrastructure has no doubt fed-back and made a significant contribution to China's rapid market formation/expansion and prepared China well for the next decade of growth in industrialization.

---

[52] In terms of infrastructure category, China ranked 22nd among the 160 listed nations, even higher than the United States (26th), Canada (23rd) and South Korea (28th). China's GDP per capita in 2013 was only $6,800, compared with $21,00 in Portugal, $13,400 in Poland, $12,600 in Hungary and $10,900 in Turkey. China is thus well poised to overtake Poland, Hungary, and Turkey over the next decade in per capita income and to become an upper middle-income country.

Chapter 5

What's Wrong with the Washington Consensus and the Institutional Theories?

i. A Little Bit of Theory: The Fundamental Theorems of Welfare Economics

The Washington consensus and its inherited neoliberalism ideology (the Chicago school) was based on the belief that the two fundamental theorems of welfare economics (which are the cornerstones of neoclassical economic theory) more or less hold in reality. Hence, any economic policies and analyses based on these theorems must also be more or less true, correct, and applicable to the real world. But such a belief is not only wrong but also dangerous, as argued below.

The first welfare theorem states that any competitive equilibrium or Walrasian equilibrium leads to a Pareto-efficient allocation of resources.[1] The second welfare theorem states the converse, that

---

[1] A Pareto-efficient allocation means that the resource allocation cannot be further improved without making someone in the economy worse off. However, there

any efficient allocation can be sustained in a competitive equilibrium.[2]

The theorems are often taken to be analytical proofs of Adam Smith's "invisible hand" hypothesis and support of the non-interventionism ideology: Let the markets do the work and the outcome will be efficient.[3]

The two fundamental theorems of welfare economics are derived (proved) analytically (mathematically) from several key assumptions about human behaviors and social-economic structures that are hardly met or true in the real world:

- Complete markets (i.e., all imaginable markets, such as markets to trade goods, services, assets, state-contingent financial contracts and futures, exist and are complete; agents trading in these markets are infinitely lived with perfect rationality and without financial frictions such as borrowing constraints, or in the case of finite lives their altruistic parents are capable of taking good care of their offspring's welfare; and there exists perfect enforceability of contract so that a full set of financial tools can perfectly insure agents against all types of idiosyncratic risks by making state-contingent plans against present and future uncertainties).
- Complete information (i.e., all market participants have perfect information about the market structures of the economy including household preferences and firm production technologies and asset market trading rules, the price signals, the quality of goods

---

may be multiple such allocations and none of them is universally "desirable" by all agents in the economy.

[2] For simple reference, see http://en.wikipedia.org/wiki/Fundamental_theorems_of_welfare_economics. For sophisticated readers, see Mas-Colell, Andreu, Michael Dennis Whinston, and Jerry R. Green. *Microeconomic Theory*. New Yourk: Oxford University Press, 1995.

[3] Notice that the welfare theorems can also be taken as confirmation or support of central planning economies, provided that the government is altruistic and has perfect information (as the agents do) on the economy.

and services, the statistical distribution of exogenous shocks, and each other's actions and trading strategies).
- Price-taking behavior (i.e., all market participants behave "nicely" as price takers, there is no cheating, collusion, robbery, stealing, price manipulation, monopoly power, and costs of entry and exit from market).
- No externalities (i.e., individuals' self-interested actions do not generate direct benefits or harm to other persons' productivity and happiness and ability to perform their market functions including information processing, and there are no public "goods" or "bads" that are essential or possibly destructive for production and market exchange, such as infrastructure provision or violence).
- No convexities in the utility functions, production technologies, and market structures (i.e., no increasing returns to scale in the division of labor, in the specialization of consumption and production, and no large fixed costs of organizing firms, creating goods and services or their production capacities, signing and enforcing contracts, and processing information or making decisions).

When any or some of these highly idealized conditions are not met, a pure *laissez faire* market economy not only does not achieve efficient allocation of resources, but can also lead to malfunction, stagnation, poverty traps, inequality, prolonged unemployment, speculative bubbles, financial crisis, self-fulfilling boom-bust cycles, coordination failures, market-full of fake or "lemon" goods, business fraud, monopoly, oligarchy, and even self-destruction.[4]

---

[4] For arguments of inefficient or undesirable outcomes of market systems, see the classical book of Karl Polanyi, *The Great Transformation: The Political and Economic Origins of Our Time*, and many of Joseph Stiglitz's works, including his classical analysis on imperfect information (available at http://scholar.google.com/scholar?q=stiglitz&hl=en&as_sdt=0&as_vis=1&oi=scholart&sa=X&ei=OFiEVe PLBdOCyQSSoa3QDg&sqi=2&ved=0CBsQgQMwAA.)   For   the   so-called

First, the welfare economic theorems ignore the social-political environment in which markets can properly function. Neoclassical economists overlook two of the most important cornerstones (pillars) of the free market: (i) political stability and (ii) social trust. Both pillars require state power to build and nurture and protect and reinforce, yet both are seriously lacking in agrarian nations. This fundamental connection between political stability and orderly market activities based on social trust explains why after democracy was immaturely adopted or *imposed* on developing nations, such as Afghanistan, Egypt, Iraq, Libya, Pakistan, Tunisia, Ukraine, and other parts of Eastern Europe, it failed to bring economic prosperity in ways the institutional theorists and Western politicians would have hoped or predicted. Instead, democracy brought anarchy, chaos, and even endless civil wars to these poor nations. Markets would never emerge without political stability and social trust. Yet a safe and unified national market is the absolute prerequisite of the division of labor and the existence of cooperatives, organized trade, and financial contracts.

Second, the welfare economic theorems ignore (or assume away) the prohibitive social-economic costs of creating markets. Markets, especially a mass market, are very costly to create even under long-term political stability:

"[S]o it is upon the sea-coast, and along the banks of navigable rivers, that industry of every kind naturally begins to subdivide and improve itself, and it is frequently not till a long time after that those improvements extend themselves to the inland parts of the country ... There

---

dynamic-stochastic-general-equilibrium analyses of various types of market failures and the consequent economic collapse and chaos and boom-bust cycles, see, e.g., Azariadis, Kaas, and Wen (2015), "Self-fulfilling Credit Cycles"; Benhabib, Wang, and Wen (2014), "Sentiments and Aggregate Demand Fluctuations"; Coury and Wen (2009), "Global Indeterminacy in Locally Determinate Real Business Cycle Models"; Pintus and Wen (2013), "Leveraged Borrowing and Boom-Bust Cycles"; and Wu and Wen (2014), "Withstanding the Great Recession like China"; among many others.

could be little or no commerce of any kind between the distant parts of the world ... Since such, therefore, are the advantages of water-carriage, it is natural that the first improvements of art and industry should be made where this conveniency opens the whole world for a market to the produce of every sort of labor, and that they should always be much later in extending themselves into the inland parts of the country. The inland parts of the country can for a long time have no other market for the greater part of their goods, but the country which lies round about them, and separates them from the sea-coast, and the great navigable rivers. The extent of the market, therefore, must for a long time be in proportion to the riches and populousness of that country, and consequently their improvement must always be posterior to the improvement of that country" (Adam Smith, *The Wealth of Nations*, 1776, Chapter III).[5]

Geographical isolation and distances are not the only obstacles to the formation of markets. Think of social distances and social isolations: For example, the 2.5 million people of Papua New Guinea in the early 1970s had about 700 regional indigenous languages. Some, like Abaga, were spoken by as few as five people.

Third, it is even more costly to create market regulations, or regulatory institutions, to prevent cheating and fraud. Human beings do not always behave "nicely." The quickest way to meet consumption needs or generate wealth is not through hard labor; it can be much simpler to steal or seize other people's goods and wealth. So market participants may cheat, collude, lie, and steal. The rule of law may apply to these actions, but the rule of law means little when it is not enforceable. Enforcement is itself extremely costly and often a fundamental breeding ground for corruption. Human beings possess both creative and destructive powers that they can impose

---

[5] Adam Smith also mentioned about the other types of costs of conducting market exchanges, such as the costs of preventing robbery and piracy. Indeed, one of the most important functions of the powerful British navy was to protect its maritime trade. Mass international trade was impossible without a strong state and its military projection capacity (even true in today's "peaceful" world).

on others, and in the worst cases the results can be fatally harmful. It can cost a person very little effort to save a life (business) or destroy a life (business). Market forces need not be exclusively creative or destructive. They can be creative only under proper regulations but destructive without such regulations.[6,7]

---

[6] Ironically, the Washington consensus in practice often indiscriminately emphasizes deregulations when sophisticated market regulations and regulatory governance are seriously lacking in developing countries. China's environmental problems and many fatal incidents, such as the spread of the AIDS virus in Henan province in the 1990s among farmers and peasants and the 2008 milk scandal, are all driven by naked self-interests in unregulated markets. This is why careless market-oriented reforms guided by rapid privatization and indiscriminate deregulation have often led to unsatisfactory and even disastrous results in many developing countries in Africa and Latin America and Eastern Europe yet without stimulating economic growth, in sharp contrast to China's overall incremental and experimental approach with measured bottom-up reforms and experimentations, such as the household-responsibility system and the dual-track system. Even in such a case China has made many mistakes due to adopting one-size-fits-all marketization and deregulation in certain areas, especially in the healthcare and education and mining sectors. Fortunately, China wisely avoided the rush into financial reforms and capital liberalization and indiscriminative privatization of large SOEs in its early stage of economic development, despite demand from the West and advice from the West-trained neoliberal economists and international organizations. The Washington-consensus-minded reformers often chose developing countries' banking, energy, mining, and telecommunication sectors as targets of deregulation because these are often the only sectors left with public ownership; yet they overlook the lack of rural industries or proto-industrialization in poor countries despite private land property rights and lack of government regulations in rural areas. But it is precisely the lack of a massive rural industrialization that is holding back economic growth and industrialization in many developing countries, as China has demonstrated. This key to jump-starting industrial revolution in developing countries has been seriously ignored by the Washington Consensus because it cannot find much public ownership in developing countries' rural areas and therefore assumes it is not the problem. It instead blames the few state-owned industries or lack of democracy for these nations' poverty.

[7] As a matter of fact, all states regulate, such as the United States. "From rules and laws governing trade, banking, and education to hazardous material,

Fourth, human beings are endowed with only finite physical and intellectual abilities. They have only two legs to paddle a water-wheel and two arms to spin yarn, and only a limited number of brain cells to learn and process information. So it is in their best interest to cooperate to accomplish tasks, conduct business, and be competitive in the market. Yet, collaboration is costly (extremely so in early stages of development), and market principles fail to apply to collective activities, such as activities within cooperatives, which are ruled by the usual hierarchical power structures that have existed even in ancient civilizations before any modern markets and organizations appeared. For example, for much of history, price mechanism and spot-market bargaining as well as democracy have not existed within these enterprises — much as they do not exist in the military today. No teamwork within any firm can be bargained on site with price tags. No CEOs or generals are democratically elected by employees or soldiers.

Last but not least, physical and intellectual abilities do not distribute equally among human beings. Hence, free markets with "winner-takes-all" can lead to dismal outcomes and excessive poverty instead of prosperity.

---

health standards and so on, the state rules on what will be produced, how it will be produced and often who will be the beneficiary of what ... For example, in the United States of America the costs of social regulation tripled from $80 billion in 1997 to $267 billion in 2000 ... of the total $542 billion in regulatory costs in the United States of America (9% of GDP in 1991 dollars), $189 billion were the costs associated with the paperwork and implementation of regulations" (Seema Hafeez, 2003, pp. 1–3). Economic historian Marc Law and Sukkoo Kim (2011, p. 113) also wrote: "Despite the United States being the world's largest free market economy, government regulation of economic activity is a pervasive feature of the American economy ... The foods Americans eat, the cars they drive, the medicines they take, and the financial institutions from which they borrow and to which they lend are all subject to some kind of regulation." But ironically, regulations do not appear in neoclassical growth models and institutional theories, or in the case they do, they appear as negative constraints and impediment to development and growth.

In light of these problems, the market is only part of the resource-allocation mechanism even in modern developed nations and always complemented by non-market forces.[8] Therefore, economic organizations, cooperatives, communal spirit, teamwork, ethics, trust, ideology, religion, culture, the state, and all types of coordinated and cooperative and collective actions are essential (in addition to markets) for achieving "efficient/effective" resource allocations and economic development.

What a market provides, among other things, is a form of impersonal competition and creative destruction, a discipline on management and technology adoption, and a mechanism of Darwinian "natural selection" of the "fittest." However, the fundamental limitations of human rationality, information-processing capacity, foresight and intellectual abilities dictate that the winners of market competition are not autarkic and anarchic individuals or artisan workshops, but rather well-organized corporations based on *non-market* principles such as the division of labor, specialization, collaboration, command, commitment, dignity, ethics, friendship, honor, ideology, loyalty, reputation, shame, and trust.

Hence, markets and organizations go hand in hand; invisible hand and visible hand go hand in hand; self-interests and collective interests go hand in hand; private property rights and public property rights go hand in hand; deregulations and re-regulations go hand in hand; freedom and discipline go hand in hand; and individuals and

---

[8] Market is an ancient form of institutions, not an invention of the Industrial Revolution or the Glorious Revolution. Yet even in industrial economies where the extent and scale of the market and its principle (ideology) has been enormously expanded and penetrated into all dimension of social life, the bulk of economic activities and exchanges and transactions and economic relationships still do not really take place in the market, but instead within firms and cooperatives where the market mechanism does not rule (Ronald Coase, 1937, The Nature of the Firm). Also see Alfred D. Chandler, Jr.'s (1977) bestselling book, *The Visible Hand: The Managerial Revolution in American Business*. Cambridge: Harvard University Press.

the state go hand in hand. By denouncing or undermining the pivotal role of the state and social collective spirit in both market creation and the formation of industrial organizations and trade networks, as well as the necessary market regulation in place, *laissez faire* approaches to economic development are doomed to fail.

ii. A Case in Point

Unfortunately, the social costs for individuals to form cooperatives and organizations to compete in the market are prohibitively high, especially for the anarchic, autarkic, poor, and uneducated peasants in agrarian societies. Hence, we observe through history across many nations the pervasive market failures in achieving industrialization or even proto-industrialization despite highly secured private land ownership and institutions that protect alienable land contracts, as described and studied by the developmental economists Michael Lipton (1977) and Joe Studwell (2013). In such a market-failure equilibrium, although land is privately owned with alienable contracts (such as in the Qing dynasty and the Republic era of China), powerful Darwinian forces often lead to high concentration of land in a few landlords while the majority of the farming population become tenants.[9] In such an equilibrium, as argued by Joe Studwell (2013), because of population growth, land becomes increasingly scarcer over time. So the landlords can easily lease out plots at higher and higher rents. They also act as money lenders at phenomenal interest rates (usury). Tenants have no incentives to make the investments to improve land productivity (e.g., through using fertilizers or building irrigation systems) when they have little security of tenure and must face stiff rents and carry expensive debts. Landlords also have no

---

[9] For example, "In the 1920s, when 85% of Chinese people lived in the countryside, life expectancy at birth for rural dwellers was 20–25 years. Three quarters of farming families had plots of less than one hectare, while perhaps one-tenth of the population owned seven-tenths of the cultivable land" (Joe Studwell, 2003, p. 17).

incentives to invest in fertilizer and irrigation systems or rural industries because they make money more easily through the skyrocketing rents and usury. When debts cannot be paid, landlords simply take over the plots along with collateral and lease out to others. Most importantly, the high rate of returns to land means that landlords have very little incentives or interests in developing manufacturing or proto-industries.

Nations in such a market-failure equilibrium cannot withstand the slightest natural shock such as drought or flood and thus constantly experience chronic famine. Évariste Régis Huc (1813–1860), who traveled through China from 1839 to 1851 as a French missionary Catholic priest, bears witness to such misery in his book, "*A Journey through the Chinese Empire*":

> "... unquestionably there can be found in no other country such a depth of disastrous poverty as in the Celestial Empire. Not a year passes in which a terrific number of persons do not parish of famine in some part or other of China; and the multitude of those who live merely from day-to-day is incalculable. Let a drought, a flood, or any accident whatever occur to injure the harvest in a single province, and two thirds of the population are immediately reduced to starvation. You see them forming up into numerous bands — perfect armies of beggars — and proceeding together, men, women, and children, to seek some little nourishment in the towns and villages ... Many faint by the wayside and die before they can reach the place where they had hoped find help. You see their bodies lying in the fields and by the roadside, and you pass without taking notice — so familiar is the horrible spectacle" (quoted in David S. Landes, *The Wealth and Poverty of Nations*, 1999, p. 346).

The 1911 Xinhai revolution did not change China's miserable rural landscape and agricultural market failure. The revolution introduced pluralistic political system at the top but inherited the Qing dynasty's private land ownership at the bottom. According to R. H. Tawney, the British economic historian who visited China in the late 1920s (more than 70 years after the French missionary Évariste Régis Huc), wrote about the devastating situation of Chinese peasant-farmers: "There are districts in which the position of the rural population is that of a man standing permanently up to the neck in water, so that even a ripple is sufficient to drown him... in Shanxi province at the beginning of 1931, 3 million persons had died of hunger in the last few years, and the misery had been such that 400,000 women and children had changed hands by sale" (Quoted in Joe Studwell, 2013, p. 17).

The American writer, William Hinton, who conducted research in China's Shanxi province in the 1940s, also wrote about "the mundane realities of death by starvation during the annual 'spring hunger' when food reserves ran out, and of the slavery (mostly of girls), landlord violence, domestic violence, usury, endemic mafia-style secret societies and other assorted brutalities that characterized everyday life" (see Joe Studwell, 2013, p. 18).

Such was the situation facing many pre-industrial agrarian societies. It served as the social-economic foundation for the rise of communism and radical land reform in China led by Mao's communist party.[10] Ironically, after being defeated by the communist army and fleeing to Taiwan, the Nationalist government conducted essentially the same type of land reform as the communists did in the mainland by taking the available land from landlords and dividing it up and distributing it equally among the farming population. Such a land reform in conjunction with *proper* mercantilist industrial policies triggered Taiwan's economic takeoff.[11] Deng Xiaoping's miracle success in generating agricultural growth since 1978 also hinged critically on the land reform conducted in Mao's era.[12]

---

[10] As Karl Polanyi (1944, p. 248) notes, "Fascism, like socialism, was rooted in a market society that refused to function."

[11] See, e.g., the analysis of Joe Studwell (2013).

[12] Do these facts suggest that institutional changes are the prerequisites of economic development? Not really. They merely suggest that institutions are built by the state to serve economic development strategies. Mao's government built public land ownership to facilitate the Great Leap Forward development strategy

iii. The Washington Consensus as Antithesis of ISI

In practice, the Washington Consensus (which arose in the 1980s) was a response to the failure of the Import Substitution Industrialization (ISI) program. ISI was popular in the 1950s to the 1970s and implemented to jump start industrialization in agrarian nations and the ex-colonies of the West after WWII. The ISI featured a strong government-led "Big Push" with an all-around buildup of a comprehensive industrial base, from modern agriculture to efficient capital-intensive heavy industries, based on the philosophy of self-reliance and self-sufficiency. China tried this approach during Mao's era and failed. The failure was not simply because of communist ideology, since many non-communist nations have also tried such an approach and failed just as miserably (e.g., India, Egypt, and many Latin American countries in the 1950s–1970s). The key to this failure is the lack of understanding of the conditions of mass production and on the Smithian (first) principle that the division of labor is limited by the extent of the market.

ISI as a form of mercantilism may work under a bottom-up approach (e.g., it worked in early to middle 19th century America and late 19th to early 20th century Japan and late 20th to early 21st century China), but can hardly work under a top-down approach (such as in Latin America and Asia in the 1950s–1980s). Under top-down approaches to ISI, developing nations, such as China in the 1950s and 1960s, built too many large-scale capital-intensive heavy manufacturing firms, including automobile and even aircraft industries and intermediate-goods production facilities (such as steel and chemicals) that belong to the developmental stage of the *second*

---

based on the utopian idea of large-scale farming. For the same reason, Deng's government built the household-responsibility system to facilitate the new incremental development strategy of Xiaokang society, which aims at enriching the farmers and grassroots population (as first priority) based on profit-driven small-scale farming without changing China's basic political institutions such as the one-party system and public ownership of land.

industrial revolution and thus require a colossal amount of capital (both financial and human) and sophisticated division of labor and advanced distribution systems and supply chains of parts and raw materials. Meanwhile, these nations paid insufficient attention to encourage rural industries or promote proto-industrialization in rural areas. Hence, such countries were unable to kick-start a first industrial revolution in mass-production-based light industries. Consequently, large-scale heavy-industrial enterprises were simply not supported by equally large domestic and international markets to render their operations profitable, given the large fixed costs of investment, capital, management, and daily operations and the requirement for efficient supply of parts and raw materials and distribution of final goods. In the end, although many developing countries around the world have managed to establish a "self-sufficient" industrial base under ISI, they did so in a highly unbalanced, unprofitable, unproductive, and internationally uncompetitive manner. Such a heavy-industry-oriented ISI strategy contradicts the historical logic (sequence) of industrialization and ends up creating a dichotomy of rural–urban economies with high income inequality and the majority of the nation's labor force stuck in the poor countryside or idle (unemployed) in the big cities.[13]

By being unwilling to embed into the international value-chain system through international trade and specialization, the self-reliance philosophy under ISI also means the loss of the international market to exert competitive pressure and support the developing nations' mass-production technologies, which further reduced the market size for the home industries. In the end, many industrial goods under ISI, including chemicals, steel, machinery, and machine parts, were not truly mass-produced, or else the production capacities were highly underutilized. As Justin Yifu Lin (1996, 2013) keenly noted, such an ISI approach completely goes against

---

[13] See, e.g., Joe Studwell's (2003) analyses of failed ISI programs in some South East Asian countries, such as Indonesia, Malaysia, and Thailand.

the developing nations' comparative advantage — their abundance of cheap labor.[14]

An economic consequence of the top-down approach to development under ISI has been the colossal amount of price distortions, government deficit, and public debt. A nation cannot pay for its debt if its economic structure is not profitable and internationally competitive, just as no firm or enterprise could.

The Washington Consensus thus emerged in the 1980s among the international loan institutions (such as the World Bank and the IMF) as an antithesis to the ISI development strategy. The Washington Consensus is based on neoliberalism and the Chicago School of economic thought and recommends the other Smithian doctrine (the Smithian second principle) of *laissez faire*, with no or little government intervention.

The core principles of the Washington Consensus can be summarized by deregulation, privatization, marketization, and liberalization.[15] The "Shock Therapy" version of this Consensus approach applied these principles to economic reforms in Russia and the Eastern European communist countries in the late 1980s and early 1990s, in an attempt to engineer an essentially overnight and

---

[14] ISI also advocated an overvalued currency to help manufacturers import capital goods (heavy machinery) and discouragement of foreign direct investment. Such policies thus killed the developing country's export markets for labor-intensive goods and inflows of foreign technologies embedded in foreign direct investment. Hence, ISI is not export friendly and is actually against the spirit of traditional mercantilism.

[15] More specifically, the Washington Consensus often entails development programs such as complete trade liberalization, complete privatization of state enterprises, complete removal of state subsidies on food and other types of government spending, and complete financial and exchange-rate liberalizations, which were proposed by the U.S.-led international lending institutions such as the IMF and the World Bank to developing countries as conditions for international loans. These programs are also known as Structural Adjustment Programs aimed to decrease the recipient nations' deficits and to trigger private sector growth, which is something that didn't happen (Harrigan 2011).

one-size-fits-all economic transformation to a market economy by getting rid of all or most existing government regulations, privatizing all or most existing state-owned firms and national resources, introducing market mechanisms immediately to all or most sectors of the economy, liberalizing price and capital controls and the exchange rate, and reducing government deficits and subsidies and public debts. This Consensus approach thus swung from one extreme to another without grasping the root cause of the failures of ISI.

The rationale behind such neoliberal development strategy is the misbelief in the fundamental theorems of welfare economics and the magic power of the invisible hand. The economists of the neoliberal Chicago school (led by Milton Friedman) did not understand that it is extremely costly to create the market for the invisible hand to function in the first place and that it had taken the European powers (such as the United Kingdom) centuries to ferment a colossal market and commercial distribution (navigation) network required for the Industrial Revolution, even with windfall profits and colossal wealth generated from the slave trade and colonialism.[16]

Not surprisingly, the new consensus is that the Washington Consensus has failed,[17] but why? It has failed in creating the market system because markets and the state go hand in hand, deregulation and re-regulation go hand in hand, liberalization and centralization go hand in hand, and freedom and control go hand in hand. *Laissez faire* was not how Great Britain created her colossal international textile market in the 17th–19th century, nor how China created her

---

[16] See, e.g., Sven Beckert's (2014) *Empire of Cotton: A Global History*, which provides a detailed and insightful historical analysis of the importance of slavery and the slave trade for the British cotton empire and the Industrial Revolution.

[17] See, e.g., Ha-Joon Chang (2003), *Kicking Away the Ladder*, Dani Rodrik (2006), *Goodbye Washington Consensus, Hello Washington Confusion?* and Joseph Stiglitz (2002), *Challenging the Washington Consensus — An Interview with Lindsey Schoenfelder*, New York: *The Brown Journal of World Affairs*, Winter/ Spring 2003, Vol IX, Issue 2, pp. 33–40.

massive global consumer goods market in the late 20th and early 21st centuries. In the case of Latin America, despite the positive side of more private capital influx into the region and an expansion of investment (mostly in real estate) and export volumes (mostly in raw materials), real per capita GDP growth amounted to only 1.5% per year for a decade, well below the rate of 5% per year registered during the 1960s or the 1970s under ISI (see, e.g., Luciana Díaz Frers, 2014). "After the [neoliberal] reforms unemployment rose, poverty remained widespread and there was generalized disappointment and sense of injustice. There was a sharp rise in crime and violence."[18]

This second wave of failures created by the Washington Consensus (following the first under the ISI) and the associated SAPs or the Shock Therapy may have motivated the new institutional view on "Why Nations Fail" (a la Acemoglu and Robinson): It was the politics, stupid! More specifically, the politicians (and powerful elites) and the institutions they built to protect their vested interests were the problem, instead of the *laissez faire* principle (or the Washington Consensus and shock therapy) *per se*. The institutional economists justified their theory by arguing that private property rights, the rule of law, and pluralistic political structures that restricted government power and expropriation were the prerequisites of the British Industrial Revolution, hence also the pre-conditions for developing countries to achieve rapid industrialization and growth envisioned by the Washington Consensus. The premise is simple: Who would accumulate capital if it could be confiscated arbitrarily by an extractive system and the powerful elite class running that system? Hence, instead of tackling the problems of poverty by economic means based on various policy tools, institutional economists endorse political solutions through democracy and revolution, such as the Arab Spring movement. "Fundamentally it is a

---

[18] Luciana Díaz Frers (2014), "Why did the Washington Consensus Policies Fail?" *Center for International Private Enterprise*.

political transformation of this sort that is required for a poor country to become rich" (Acemoglu and Robinson, 2012, p. 5).

But, the Arab Spring movement (even in Tunisia) so far has failed to generate economic prosperity; and it has failed just as miserably as (or even more than) the Washington Consensus.[19] Why? Again, because all top-down economic and political approaches to economic development (as the antithesis of ISI), whether the Washington Consensus, Shock Therapy, or the Jasmine Revolution and the democratization movement advocated by institutional theory, are ideological fallacies and the legacy of Say's law — which proposes that supply (either goods or institutions) automatically creates its own demand. But Say's law holds only in a world where the fundamental theorems of welfare economics are valid; and modern Western institutions can take root only in the soil of a reasonably industrialized nation. Hence, top-down approaches are either economically misleading (such as the ISI and Washington Consensus) or politically naïve (such as the Jasmine Revolution and institutional theories).

iv. Such Theories Are Economically Misleading

First, such supply-side policies are economically misleading because they ignore the colossal costs of creating markets. They do not adequately consider financial stability and national security (such as food security). They naively assume that the market can automatically flourish and function once the government stops intervening in the economy.[20] They also naively assume that speculative financial

---

[19] See, for example, *The Economist*'s article (July 5, 2014), "Tethered by History," availableathttp://www.economist.com/news/briefing/21606286-failures-arab-spring-were-long-time-making-tethered-history.

[20] A case in point is China's dramatic failure in healthcare reform and education reform, in sharp contrast to its successful agricultural and industrial reform. The marketization of healthcare and education since the 1990s have paralyzed China's ability to provide basic healthcare service to its citizens and destroyed its

capital mobility can achieve better resource allocation and that private property rights can provide better incentives to work (than an environment without such features). But they overlook that liquid financial capital chases after only short-run profit opportunities and ignores developing nations' long-term economic interests; they only assert that private property brings higher rents to private organizations but do not acknowledge that non-reproducible properties such as natural resources and land can achieve better and more equitable income distribution under public ownership than under private ownership.[21] They do not account for the fact that financial capitalism is built on mass production, especially the ability to mass reproduce tangible capital; hence, monetary wealth and gold and the stock market and securities and government bonds and all sorts of debt and financial assets have no real economic value or power on their own without the ability of mass producing tangible goods and assets — Financial capital is rootless without tangible reproducible capital,

---

capacity to offer basic education for the grassroots population at affordable costs. Commercialized profit-driven market behaviors of hospitals and schools have dramatically reduced the accessibility and equality of the healthcare and education systems and increased the costs of basic healthcare and elementary education to a level far beyond ordinary people's disposable income. When the market is not well-fermented and government regulation not in place, under rapid privatization and marketization the tremendous degree of asymmetric information and natural monopoly power in doctors and educators can put patients and students in the worst possible position in their bargaining power. The reason of the failure is this: Instead of following Deng Xiaoping's philosophy of "crossing the river by touching the stones" based on social experiments and the very successful dual-track system of SOE reform in the manufacturing sector, China adopted a shock-therapy approach to its healthcare and educational reforms and all levels of the governments shifted their responsibilities too quickly to the market. But because of asymmetric information and natural monopoly power and externalities, the healthcare and educational sectors are the ones that suffer the most from market failures and hence require the most of government intervention and public finance.
[21] For insightful discussions on China's land privatization debate, see Hua Sheng (2014), available (in Chinese) at http://www.360doc.com/content/14/1210/21/14561708_431886261.shtml.

and the oversupply of financial assets does not "complete" the financial-credit market but instead will ruin the market (as proved repeatedly in history and also by the 2007 global financial crisis triggered by the securitization of the subprime mortgage loans). These theories fail to appreciate the fact that non-reproducible capital (such as land) constitutes a big chunk of the fixed costs of doing business in developing countries; hence, bubbles and rising land prices in these countries caused by free capital inflows and international hot money can choke off the host nation's development. They also do not acknowledge that organizational efficiency is achieved mainly by management and not by ownership.[22] Private property rights are touted as essential but without an understanding that privatization of land and natural resources often leads to private monopolies and oligarchy, which can be worse than state ownership (for example in Mexico and Russia).[23] Financial liberation is also put forth as an automatic route to efficient resource allocation, without considering insider trading, corporate malfeasance, and asset bubbles with distorted asset prices; the same

---

[22] Western economists work very hard to achieve fame in their profession yet they do not at all own the universities and institutions they work for. Scientists working in modern cooperatives such as pharmaceutical companies do not even own the right of their intellectual property and discoveries. The Soviet Union under communism produced many 20th century world-ranked scientists in fields such as biology, chemistry, materials science, mathematics, and physics.

[23] Most advocates of private property rights fail to distinguish two types of fundamentally different capital: (i) capital endowed by nature and (ii) capital re-producible by people. Land and natural resources are the first type of capital and hence should be owned by all citizens (the state) to ensure fair rental income distribution, although their management can be delegated to private agents. Reproducible capital, on the other hand, is better owned and managed by its producers. The right to own and the right to operate (manage) are two fundamentally different concepts. Also, ownership and residual claim can be completely detached in corporate management. Countless examples of oligarchs created by mass privatization of state-owned natural resources can be found in Chrystia Freeland (2000)'s book, *Sale of the Century: Russia's Wild Ride from Communism to Capitalism.*

assertions are made for the benefits of the free market, that it will automatically lead to innovation and prosperity, without considering coordination failures, fraud, private monopolies, and economic stagnation (caused by market failures). Such radical policies undermine the host nation's ability to reform and manage its national economy and resources, and they make poor nations (especially their natural resources, land, and other assets) cheap prey for self-interested, short-sighted, profit-driven foreign capital or financial tycoons.

Financial instruments (such as bonds, credit default swaps, certificates, credits, debts, equities, futures, securities, stocks, etc.) and the associated ability and regulation and sophistication to enforce financial contracts and debt payments are the endogenous demands of, as well as responses to, large-scale trade and commerce. Financial deregulations and liberations imposed on developing countries help create risk and risk-taking behaviors more than stimulating the growth of trade and the size of their goods market. This is why the financially (immaturely) liberalized countries in Latin America, Asia, and Europe (such as Russia after its shock therapy) have been more prone to financial crisis and stagnation than financially "repressed" China. Again, supply does not automatically create its own demand.[24]

Even a nation as mighty and prosperous as the United States requires sophisticated and strong financial and banking regulations and supervision and auditing and is *still* deficient in such institutions.[25] So, how can a developing country with little administrative

---

[24]This is why the popular microfinance programs have not been as effective as expected in promoting rural industrialization in developing countries — because such microfinance programs solve only the supply-side problem of setting up small businesses without directly tackling the demand-side problem of creating markets. Even for small village firms a major fraction of their labor resources must be involved in making sales and the bulk of its credit resources must be invested in marketing unless there already exist well-developed local commercial networks and systems of trading posts with timely retail and wholesale services.

[25]See, e.g., the Dodd–Frank Wall Street Reform and Consumer Protection Act, which was signed into law by President Barack Obama on July 21, 2010, in Washington, DC.

capacity and informational infrastructure in supervising and regulating its banks and financial markets withstand the colossal risk of financial liberation and lack of capital controls?[26]

It is extremely costly to create markets, and even more costly to create the regulatory institutions to regulate market activities. Without proper market regulations, markets will malfunction and market forces will destroy social trust — the very foundation of the market itself. Yet the Washington Consensus and the institutional theory have offered no instructions to developing nations on how to build market-specific regulatory institutions to prevent or mitigate the destructive power of market forces and corporate freedom — which respect nothing but naked self-interests — when it comes to deregulation, liberalization, marketization, privatization, and democratization.[27]

v. Such Theories Are Politically Naïve

Top-down development theories are also politically naïve (especially the new institutional theories advocated by Acemoglu and Robinson in *Why Nations Fail?* 2012).[28] They underappreciate political stability

---

[26] For examples of corporate and financial scandals in the United States and other developed nations in history, see https://en.wikipedia.org/wiki/List_of_corporate_collapses_and_scandals, and http://list25.com/25-biggest-corporate-scandals-ever/ as well as http://www.accounting-degree.org/scandals/, where each of these scandals may be powerful enough to destroy a developing country's national economy and financial system under the slogan of financial liberation and deregulation.

[27] "Truly free markets for labor or goods have never existed. The irony is that today few even advocate the free flow of labor, and while the advanced industrial countries lecture the less developed countries on the vices of protectionism and government subsidies, they have been more adamant in opening up markets in developing countries than in opening their own markets to the goods and services that represent the developing world's comparative advantage." (Joseph E. Stiglitz, Forward to *The Great Transformation: The Political and Economic Origins of Our Time,* Karl Ponanyi, 2001).

[28] These authors, however, do acknowledge the role of *state capacity* in economic development. But it is not a core concept in their institutional theory and is in

and social order and confuse what reforms are most appropriate in different environments. They take reforms that are potentially beneficial for advanced nations that have already industrialized and apply them to developing countries that have not finished or even started industrializing.[29] Specifically, the need for smaller government and more

---

many ways inconsistent with their dichotomy of *extractive vs. inclusive* political institutions. More importantly, their notion of state capacity is over-simplified. For example, Acemoglu (2005) views state capacity simply as the ability to raise taxes. Such a view faces the danger of mixing the notion of a modern state in industrialized nations with that of a traditional state without finishing industrialization. The extent of state capacity required to achieve industrialization goes far beyond the ability to collect taxes. Even the sheer ability to raise taxes implies far greater state power than tax collection itself, as this subsection shows.

[29] The new institutional theories (e.g., Acemoglu and Robinson, 2005 and 2012) have not yet provided clear and precise definitions for "institutions" and for what they mean exactly by "extractive" and "inclusive" institutions. Are China's collectively-owned village industries a form of "extractive" or "inclusive" institutions toward better or worse political rights compared with the artisan workshops and private land ownership in the Qing dynasty? Is a 30% tax rate in current China more extractive than a 4% tax rate in Qing dynasty China? If so, then the Qing dynasty government was much less extractive even than the 19th century British government since the tax rate of the former was less than one fifth of the latter. Unlike the Arab Spring, which is portrayed by Acemoglu and Robinson (2012, pp. 1–5) as a movement toward political inclusion, the Glorious Revolution did not make British government more "inclusive," but simply more authoritarian and powerful in levying taxes and imposing mercantilist trade restrictions (see data provided in Acemoglu and Robinson, 2012, pp. 191–202). As another case in point, Acemoglu and Robinson would call the 19th century U.S. political system with slavery "inclusive" but the 20th century Chinese communist institutions "exclusive" despite women's equal political and economic rights. Such institutional theories thus appear to indiscriminately mix many characteristics and layers of institutions with one another based on an over-simplified notion of political power and vested interests, so much so that they call the same type of mercantilist business restrictions "extractive" if practiced in modern China and "inclusive" if practiced in 18th century England after the Glorious Revolution (see Acemoglu and Robinson, 2012, pp. 200, 437).

deregulation in advanced nations does not apply in the same way to developing countries, which may need more (instead of less) regulations, political concentration, and state-building based on good governance.[30] These theorists apply a narrow understanding of human nature by assuming that absolute freedom must lead to absolute creativity and prosperity but ignore the potential for absolute anarchy and violence. The theories neglect the economic foundations of democracy in modern capitalistic civilization. Democracy, if established immaturely in unindustrialized nations, is doomed to collapse or tarnish.

Universal suffrage and open access to political power were the fruits of the Industrial Revolution, not its causes. Political power in all 19th century capitalist nations, and even today, has always been based mainly on corporate wealth and has concentrated disproportionately in the hands of the wealthy class (merchants and capitalists), not ordinary workers and the grassroots, despite democratization and significantly increased social mobility.[31] In 1830, near the end of Britain's first industrial revolution, only 2% of the U.K. population could vote. In 1832, the Reform Act extended

---

[30] Major economic transformations in human history have always relied on consolidated political power and will, seldom on democracy. Great politicians (like great scholars) care more about their impact and influence on the society and their legacy in history than about their personal consumption. Even ordinary people can opt to die for belief and honor, rather than just for food and present material wealth. It is capitalism that has trained ordinary people to equate material wealth with glory and social status — such a trained materialistic population then became the ideal subject of the neoclassical economic theory and the institutional theory. But, these economic theories fail to acknowledge that the utility functions in their models are shaped by ideology — the meta-utility functions. It is in this sense that capitalism is not only a new mode of production but also a new form of ideology.

[31] Even for the industrialized nations, democracy has not completely fulfilled its promise of "of the people, by the people, and for the people." The so called "one person one vote" system in practice has often been a "one dollar one vote" system. The rule of law has often meant the rule of lawyers (whom only the rich can afford).

this number to 3.5%. In 1867, long after finishing the first industrial revolution and well into the Second Industrial Revolution, this number became 7.7%. It was not until 1928, *long after* becoming the greatest industrial power and richest nation on earth, did Great Britain establish universal suffrage for all male and female citizens. But still, even in modern democratic societies (let alone unindustrialized ones) votes can be bought, government positions can be purchased, and news media can be manipulated by money and wealth.

The freedom to act, contract, cooperate, exchange, and organize parallels with the freedom of bribing, cheating, despoiling, lawbreaking, looting, monopolizing, plundering, raping, robbing, stealing, and violence. So the extent of freedom and democracy can only grow proportionately with the state's ability to enforce the rule of law and its capacity to govern and manage the governed.

Modern Western democracy is built on the modern industrial state — which is far more powerful and superbly organized and managed than any agrarian natural state. But the modern industrial state is itself the byproduct and invention of mercantilism, the fruit of the Industrial Revolution. Its mighty military power and unprecedented administrative power of surveillance and potential intrusion into society are unmatchable by any agrarian or unindustrialized nations. The modern industrial state is a gigantic and unified organization based on mass specialization and mass coordination of all social classes. Every citizen as well as his monetary value has to either embrace and be governed by this industrial system; or reject and be abandoned by it. This is why large-scale organized crime and underground rebellion and military coups are the norm of unindustrialized societies (especially those that adopt democracy before finishing the industrialization, such as Egypt, Mexico, Pakistan, Philippines, Thailand, and many African and Latin American countries) but absent or under control in industrialized nations (such as in most OECD countries).

Industrialization equips the state with unprecedented ability and capacity to govern its population; to collect, sort, and retrieve information from its citizens; to react to violence and insurgence through the speed of information transmission, transportation, and delivery of (at least a semi) militarized police force; and to intrude on the privacy of the governed population whenever needed. People are free to move about in industrial societies within and across country boundaries only because of the state's power and capacity to register and track them down through a sophisticated social security system and tax system and immigration system. "Surveillance is a necessary condition of the administration of states, whatever end this power be turned to ... The provision of welfare cannot be organized or funded unless there is a close and detailed monitoring of the lives of the population, regardless of whether they are actually welfare recipients or not" (S. E. Finer, 1999, p. 1624, "The History of Government III: Empires, Monarchies, and the Modern State").

The rule of law and the ability to collect taxes and punish tax evasion depends on such capacities. The 19th century political economist and philosopher Proudhon vividly described and characterized in 1851 this hyper-capacity of the industrialized state government powered by the resources and technologies that arose from the Industrial Revolution: "To be governed is to be watched, inspected, spied upon, directed, law-driven, numbered, regulated, enrolled, indoctrinated, preached at, controlled, checked, valued, censured, commended, ... To be governed is to be at every operation, at every transaction noted, registered, counted, taxed, stamped, measured, numbered, assessed, licensed, authorized, admonished, prevented, forbidden, reformed, corrected, punished ..." "... then [when encountered by the police] at the slightest resistance, the first word of complaint, to be repressed, fined, vilified, harassed, hunted down, abused, clubbed, disarmed, bound, choked, imprisoned, judged, condemned, shot ..." (S. E. Finer, 1999, pp. 1610–1611, "The History of Government III: Empires, Monarchies, and the Modern State").[32]

---

[32] Compare the shooting of Michael Brown which occurred on August 9, 2014, in the city of Ferguson, Missouri.

But managing and running such a powerful state surveillance system and enforcing the rule of law are extremely costly. Take the growth of bureaucracy as an example. In 1821, the number of bureaucrats or public servants in the United States was 8,000 (0.083% of the population). In 1881, after finishing its industrial revolution, the number increased to 107,000 (0.21% of the population). In 1985, it increased to 3,797,000 (1.6% of the population). The average growth rate was more than 3.8% per year, higher than the country's real GDP growth in that golden period of growth. Similarly in Britain, the number increased from 27,000 in 1821 (0.26% of the population) to 1,056,000 in 1985 (2.25% of the population). In sharp contrast, this number was merely 30,000 (0.015% of the population) in the late Qing Dynasty of China despite a much, much larger population (200 million) than 19th century U.K. and U.S.[33] In other words, the number of bureaucrats as a share of population in the late 19th century China was merely 6% of the U.K. level in 1821 and 8% of the U.S. level in 1881, even though China in that time period was well known for its "gigantic bureaucratic system": Truly, China's system paled in comparison with the freshly industrialized U.K. and U.S. Nowadays, it costs the United States more than $400 billion each year for law enforcement and legal services, amounting to about $1,500 per person per year. In addition, the United States spends $800 billion in total (or $2,500 per person) on national defense. These numbers are unmatchable in poor developing countries even if these countries could spend all their GDP on police and national defense.

It is under this comprehensive capacity of police force and law enforcement that the freedom of speech and expression (including the freedom of spreading rumors and creating false information) is tolerated. It is under this capacity of state power and control that democracy with universal suffrage is meaningfully exercised. It is

---

[33] See S. E. Finer (1999, p. 1613 and pp. 1623–1624), *The History of Government III: Empires, Monarchies, and the Modern State.*

under this capacity of surveillance and monitoring that human rights (including the right to assemble, the right to organize, gun rights, and the rights of criminals and prisoners) are meaningfully respected. It is also under this capacity of registration, recording, information tracking, and tax collection that absolute labor mobility is encouraged, protected, and productive.[34]

This dialectic contradiction between "freedom" and "control" means that advising developing countries to adopt modern forms of Western democracy, freedom, and full-fledged financial liberalization as the prerequisite of economic development is politically naïve if not downright destructive. It could also be described as malicious, a recipe for anarchy, turmoil, violence, and instability.[35] Regardless of the motivations behind such advice and encouragement, it amounts to a Pandora's box for corruption and administrative inefficiency. Rampant corruption exists in developing countries not because of the *lack* of the rule of law but because of the *lack of resources to enforce it.* Unenforceable laws are a major breeding

---

[34] The U.S. government's massive "global surveillance program" run by its National Security Agency (NSA) with the cooperation of private telecommunication companies, as revealed by Edward Snowden, should not be surprising to anyone because it is precisely the accumulation and advancement of such technological capabilities of the state government since the American Industrial Revolution that has made the United States far more tolerant than any developing nations of the freedom of speech, human rights, democracy, and any chaotic or negative social outcomes they may bring about.

[35] A former director of home affairs in the colonial government of Hong Kong, John Walden, called Britain's push for democracy in Hong Kong a "grand illusion." In a speech in 1985, Mr. Walden said: "If I personally find it difficult to believe in the sincerity of this sudden and unexpected official enthusiasm for democratic politics it is because throughout the 30 years I was an official myself, from 1951 to 1981, 'democracy' was a dirty word. Officials were convinced that the introduction of democratic politics into Hong Kong would be the quickest and surest way to ruin Hong Kong's economy and create social and political instability" (See "Hong Kong Democracy and Independence," *Financial Times*, October 14, 2014, ft.com > Comment).

ground for corruption in developing countries. It should not be taken by the institutional economists as a surprise to find that the degree of freedom and democracy is perfectly correlated and matched by a nation's regulatory capacity, security forces, and military power.[36]

---

[36] The fact that industrialization implies (that is, it gives rise to) state power manifests not only in the colonial 19th century but also in the postwar world order. Even in the 21st century democracy and human rights are still built on and subject to nationalism. The only country that can openly claim in any foreign or international forums that its own self-national interest is the guide and only guide of its foreign policies, is the mighty United States. No other nation, except maybe the former Soviet Union, is able to use self-national interest as the only argument to justify their foreign policies and actions against other sovereign nations. "Every nation has to either be with us, or against us," said Hillary Clinton and similarly said ex-president George W Bush. So, "a weak nation has no diplomacy," as the foreign minister Li Hongzhang of the late Qing Dynasty monarchy sadly expressed in front of the 19th century Western colonial powers. It can be said that the strongest motive of industrialization ever since the Great Voyage and especially the British Industrial Revolution has always been driven by the interest of nation-building and nationalism. Improved welfare for the grassroots is only a by-product of industrialization. Ironically, it turned out that industrialization can only be accomplished through nation-building because it involves nationwide coordination and collaboration of all social classes and it has tremendous positive externalities and spillover welfare effects upon all citizens that only the state can fully and effectively internalize. Thirty years ago China was completely incapable of evacuating or protecting its citizens in foreign soil during crisis, but that is no longer the case today. When the wars in Libya and Syria broke out in 2011, for example, China was the first country to send in military planes and ships to achieve long-distance evacuation (about 36,000 Chinese citizens were safely evacuated, see the report at NBC News: http://worldblog.nbcnews.com/_news/2011/03/03/6181345-china-organizes-hasty-retreat-from-libya). Hence, not only is mercantilism a form of economic nationalism, but industrialization itself is as well. Throughout history, no nation that tried to industrialize or maintain the fruit of industrialization has not appealed to nationalism in one way or another. A good example is illustrated by "The Strenuous Life," the famous speech given by one of America's greatest presidents, Theodore Roosevelt, on April 10, 1899, as the United States was rising to global power and supremacy. In that speech, Roosevelt claims that the strenuous life can benefit not just the individual but also the entire country.

Therefore, freedom is not free. Freedom is not always meaningful, either. Setting up traffic laws in open farmland with little traffic is meaningless, as well. Traffic laws and speed limits mean nothing to drivers unless such laws are strictly enforced.[37] Yet, enforcement is not only costly but also itself a source of corruption and hence requires large-scale and expensive social coordination.

Corruption happens in any society, including the industrial nations, precisely at the junction of enforcement and regulation, but not because the rule of law or the rhetoric against corruption is lacking. If we do not want people in backward societies to have the freedom to kill, loot, rob, riot, and terrorize in the name of freedom, semi-militarized policy force, as exists in the modern United States, may be a necessary step. If we want people in developing countries to receive fair trials in court under the rhetoric of human rights, we may need to spend a colossal amount of resources to build a complicated and sophisticated legal system and prison system with a multitude of lawyers, as is the case in the United States.

Nonetheless, he advocates imperialism as an extension of the strenuous life. Another good example is John F. Kennedy's Inaugural Address on January 20, 1961: "[M]y fellow Americans: ask not what your country can do for you, ask what you can do for your country." For insightful analyses of the relationship between nationalism and industrialization or capitalism, see Liah Greenfeld, *"Nationalism: Five Roads to Modernity"* (Harvard University Press, 1992) and *"The Spirit of Capitalism: Nationalism and Economic Growth"* (Harvard University Press, 2009). However, nationalism is a double-edged sword: excessive nationalism can backfire if it implies discrimination against foreign investment and trade. A healthy form of nationalism encourages open-trade policies and active participation of the government in international competition.

[37] As an example, although the Declaration of Independence stated "We hold these truths to be self-evident: That all men are created equal," the United States did not stand by or enforce this conviction for almost 200 years after the document was signed. The Civil Rights Act of 1966 was the first civil rights legislation proposed in U.S. history. Martin Luther King Jr., the most famous leader in the African-American Civil Rights Movement, was assassinated on April 4, 1968, nearly 200 years after the Declaration of Independence was adopted by the U.S. Continental Congress on July 4, 1776.

Democracy is a political-welfare concept. But people must eat before they can vote. So the right to survive (live) trumps the right to vote. The world's first industrial power, the United Kingdom, did not establish universal suffrage until 1928, long after Britain finished her first and second Industrial Revolutions and became affluent. African-Americans were still fighting for their human rights in the 1960s, long after the United States became the world's largest manufacturing power and richest nation. The Violence against Women Act was signed into law in the United States only 20 years ago in 1994, not 225 years ago in 1789 when the U.S. Constitution was born. Why? The capitalistic industrial powers managed to reach a long-lasting peace among themselves only after the two most bloody and immense world wars in the first half of the 20th century — merely a minute ago compared with the 8,000 years of human civilization. Therefore, it is naïve for modern industrial powers and the institutional theorists to advise poor agrarian countries that democracy is the prerequisite of economic development, without asking themselves what democracy or universal suffrage can offer to a developing nation (and their large number of uneducated poor) when people can only grow crops with their bare hands and know little about the division of labor and have no toilets and TV sets in their mud straw houses. Will it offer the agrarian society state capacity and capable government with a sophisticated administrative apparatus that can organize anarchic and autarkic and illiterate peasants to form community and cooperatives for joint production and to combat fraud, looting, riots, and violence?[38]

Democracy cannot function without industrialization. Industrialization is impossible without a strong state. First things first.[39]

---

[38] If even a well-developed Greece in Europe cannot elect a capable government to resolve its debt crisis and stagnation problems through referendums, how could underdeveloped nations in Africa?

[39] The Arab Spring movement and the chaotic political-economic consequences unfolded thereafter serve as recent evidence. It is unimaginable that China could

As North and Thomas (1973) admitted in *The Rise of the Western World*, institutions all have costs in their creation and enforcement. These institutions emerge only when their benefits exceed their costs.[40] The logic applies to both political and economic institutions. "In a world where trade volumes were limited by small population sizes, low incomes and high transport costs trade will be anarchic and unstructured. But when trade volumes rise, there is more incentive to create institutions which facilitate it" (Gregory Clark, 2007). Great Britain fully embraced the "free trade" rhetoric and institutions only when the benefits of free trade exceeded their costs, *after* 1860 when it had fully finished the Industrial Revolution and established mass production with excess production capacity in both light and heavy industries and had become the manufacturing power of the world.[41] China today, more than ever before, has become an active advocator of free trade precisely for the same reason.

----

have built the world's largest high-speed rail system in less than 10 years without a strong state. However, a strong state is not sufficient for successful industrialization, which also requires correct development strategies and industrial policies. Moreover, democracy does not automatically follow industrialization, but its proper functioning requires industrialization.

[40] It may be precisely the shift of balance between costs and benefits of government regulations that gave rise to the regulatory state in the late 19th to early 20th century United States during the take-off stage of the American second industrial revolution.

[41] The Navigation Act of 1651 prohibited foreign vessels from engaging in coastal trade in England and required that all goods imported from the continent of Europe be carried on either an English vessel or a vessel registered in the country of origin of the goods. All trade between England and its colonies had to be carried in either English or colonial vessels. The Staple Act of 1663 extended the Navigation Act by requiring that all colonial exports to Europe be landed through an English port before being re-exported to Europe. It was not until 1860, when England removed the last vestiges of the mercantilism era and industrial regulations, that monopolies and tariffs were abolished and emigration and machinery exports were freed.

The more fundamental the institutions, the more costly are they to create, reform, and reinforce, so the longer have they to wait until sufficient economic development. Only industrialized societies where labor, instead of land and capital, has become the scarcest resource in production are more likely and capable of developing democracy with universal suffrage and to have the ability to benefit from it and the resources to enforce it. The market value of a nation's average life insurance measures the extent of its human rights. The gap of life insurance between industrial nations and agrarian nations is several hundred fold, the same as the gap in human rights. But the causation goes from the former to the latter, not the other way around. Hence, political institutions imposed or transplanted from industrialized nations upon developing countries are not only NOT the prerequisites of their economic development, but may also become themselves a new source of anarchy, political disorder, and development failures.[42,43]

---

[42] Again, think of Egypt and Ukraine where democracy advances only to collapse, precisely because of the lack of economic foundations and reinforcement mechanism.

[43] Institutions of course matter for shaping economic incentives. But the key point is this: First, there is a gigantic difference between macro institutions and micro institutions. And it is impossible and erroneous to forge a black-white dichotomy of "extractive" vs. "inclusive" institutions. All institutions have both an "extractive" aspect and an "inclusive" aspect in them. Second, even if such a dichotomy may exist, correct economic policies crucial for economic growth can often be designed and implemented under either "extractive" or "inclusive" macro institutions. Third and perhaps more importantly, institutions are often built endogenously to facilitate a nation's long-term development strategies. Nations fail or succeed mostly because of their ill- or correctly designed economic policies and development strategies, not because of the associated institutions built to facilitate the implementation of such strategies, *per se*. In other words, institutions do not cause development strategies, but development strategies do explain or call for corresponding institutions. This order of causal relationship between development strategies and economic institutions does not deny institutional inertia and the challenge of institutional reforms when national development strategy

Democracy *does not* produce the invisible hand, and the invisible hand *does not* provide the free market. Without a mass market to support mass production, who will feed the hundreds of millions of impoverished and unemployed people in Afghanistan, Egypt, Iraq, Libya, and Syria?

Deng Xiaoping seemed to understand this political-economic logic in the 1980s, and so do the current Chinese political leaders. This means that the world cannot expect China to build democratic political institutions in the way and at the pace wished by the West so long as the costs of building them, running them, and enforcing them exceed their benefits. This, however, does not imply that China would not establish the rule of law and property rights (without democracy). The successful development experiences of Japan, South Korea, Taiwan, Hong Kong, and Singapore offer ample examples of the rule of law and protection of property rights as well as government officials' accountability before achieving genuine democracy. These economies all enjoyed political stability and the colossal benefits of political order and social trust during industrialization.

More importantly, democracy at the national level is fundamentally different from administrative democracy at the micro level or within organizations. The way enterprises and firms manage production and human resources can be fundamentally different and detached from the way the nation runs its political system. And it is precisely the micro level administrative capability and management capital that matter for productivity, wealth accumulation, nation building, and economic development — that is, for the formation of

---

changes. China's successful development experience shows how exactly new institutions are built gradually to facilitate China's gradualist bottom-up development strategies after the 1978 economic reform. China's previous failure under Mao also showed how central planning institutions were built to facilitate China's leapfrog development strategies.

mass-production firms and the mass market with mass distribution networks. Many developing countries that chose democratic political institutions immaturely at the macro level before industrialization at the micro level often failed to run them effectively and paid dear prices for the consequent political and social disorder, caused by the lack of organizational infrastructures and resources to enforce and benefit from such institutions. Democracy with universal suffrage belongs to a welfare state. But how can an agrarian nation incapable of feeding its population enjoy the benefits of a welfare state?[44]

Economic development and industrialization require political stability and social order as the absolute prerequisite because risk and trust (more than expropriation risk) are fundamental characteristics of the market. Nothing can happen in the market without social-political order, safety, stability, and trust. But imposing modern political democracy in agrarian societies through revolution or wars is unlikely to offer such stability and social order.

---

[44] When being interviewed by *The Financial Times* to comment on China's new loans to Uganda to finance two hydropower plants — the 600 MW Karuma and the 188 MW Isimba dams — and a railway line connecting Kampala, the Ugandan capital, to Kenya, South Sudan and the oil-rich West Nile region that borders the Democratic Republic of Congo, Uganda's President Yoweri Museveni said "I was a bit embarrassed when I was talking to (representatives from) the World Bank. They talked about a lot of things like structural adjustment, but they don't understand the basics. How can you have structural adjustment without electricity?" According to Mr. Museveni, the Chinese understand the basics, China is a desirable partner in Uganda's infrastructure buildups not only because of its funding capabilities but also because it desists from interfering in the internal political affairs of other countries. He condemned those in the West for imposing legislation focused on gay rights on Uganda. "They are not serious ... They are jokers. They are mistake makers. You can't impose middle class values on a pre-industrial society. How can you make peasants have middle class values? They are peasants. Many of them are pre-capitalists. How can you make them have values such as liberalism?" (*Financial Times*, October 21, 2014 6:43 pm).

Such immaturely implanted democracy tends to generate rhetoric without substance. Because of the lack of resources and administrative capacity to enforce democracy, free elections often turn out as vote buying and corruption. China's industrialization is not based on political democracy, but on proper governance, on the correct development strategy and political decisions to maintain China's status quo political institutions while adjusting its core economic policies and building efficient microeconomic organizations. The correct strategy of reform is not to overthrow status quo political institutions with bloody revolutions. China tried such revolutionary top-down development strategies repeatedly over the past 120 years before 1978 but each time was quickly trapped into ferocious power struggles, assassinations, civil wars, military coups, and endless internal partisan fighting with ideological rhetoric. During the turmoil, China became easy prey of imperialistic industrial powers under the name of free trade and the tactics of "divide and conquer."

People must be organized (united) in order to compete. This is true not only for firms, but also for nations. The ex-communist Eastern European countries and Russia collapsed economically after introducing democracy and the shock therapy because such reforms destroyed their social-political fabrics and organizational (social) capital, which are pivotal for industrialization and market creation. China kept its status-quo social-political organizations erected under Mao and took great advantage of them in creating a unified national market with social trust and in mobilizing the grassroots labor force.[45]

---

[45] The situations of postwar Japan and Germany were fundamentally different from that of China in 1978. These two nations were not only fully (or nearly fully) industrialized under an advanced market system before World War II, but their entrepreneurs were fully experienced with self-organization and market creation in a private-property environment before the war. The war destroyed only their

The institutional theories (e.g., Acemoglu and Robinson, 2005 and 2012) have attempted to construct and solidify a world view that democracy, private property rights, the rule of law, and open access to political power have been the prerequisites (or even the fundamental causes) of Western economic development from the 16th through the 19th century in general and the British Industrial Revolution in particular. Once these institutions are in place, so the theory goes, free markets through the invisible hand can then work wonders to produce an industrial revolution out of backward and impoverished economies. This is a myth. In fact, the institutional theories are built atop another myth created by neoliberalism: That *laissez faire* policies and free trade were the secrets to Britain's success in detonating the Industrial Revolution in the late 18th and early 19th centuries. The fact of the matter is that private property rights and free trade existed in ancient civilizations, yet they did not lead to an industrial revolution in, for example, Egypt, Greece, China, or India. Democracy and the rule of law are the outcomes, not the causes, of industrialization. Moreover, capitalist mass production has historically been achieved only with strong involvement by the state and the enforcement of mercantilist policies to create markets

---

tangible capital but not their intangible organizational capital. In sharp contrast, after nearly half a century of central planning, the ex-communist countries completely lost their market-organizational capital. Their highly specialized and centrally planned industrial complex was virtually irreplaceable once erected, because it may take many decades or even centuries to ferment the market of mass production without strong government involvement and development strategies. The best alternative development strategy for Eastern European countries and Russia in the late 1980s and early 1990s was perhaps a dual-track approach like what China adopted in the 1980s and 1990s for its market liberalization (see, e.g., Lau, Qian, and Roland, 2000, China's Dual-Track Approach to Transition). But such an approach is implementable only under a patient authoritarian government with vision and centralized power and administrative efficiency that can resist the enticement of the Washington Consensus and shock therapy.

and succeed in an environment of fierce international competition for wealth, power, control, dignity, and pride.[46]

---

[46]According to the economic historian D. McCloskey, "Acemoglu in short has gotten the history embarrassingly wrong in every important detail, and his larger theme is wholly mistaken" (D. McCloskey, 2010, p. 322). Consider the following facts. First, truly inclusive political institutions were not achieved historically in the now-developed countries until the 20th century when most of them had long finished their industrialization: e.g., universal suffrage was attained in Australia in 1962, Belgium in 1948, Canada in 1970, France in 1946, Germany in 1946, Italy in 1946, Japan in 1952, Portugal in 1970, Switzerland in 1971, U.K. in 1928, and USA in 1965. After achieving democracy, vote buying and electoral fraud were very common in these nations. Second, property rights were no better protected in these now-developed countries right before and during their industrialization period than earlier periods, or compared with many late-developing countries today. For example, land enclosure in England violated the then-existing communal property rights by enclosing common land. The recognition of squatter rights was crucial in developing the American West but violated the rights of existing property owners. In 1868 the Pennsylvanian Supreme Court overrode the existing right of landowners to claim access to clean water in favor of the booming coal industry. Similarly, land reforms in Japan, Korea, and Taiwan after WWII all violated the existing property rights of the landlords. "What matters for economic development is not simply the protection of all property rights regardless of their nature, but which property rights are protected under which conditions" (Ha-Joon Chang, 2003, p. 83). Precisely for this reason, the French industrial revolution was delayed for decades because property was too secure in France: "[P]rofitable irrigation projects were not undertaken in Provence because France had no counterpart to the private acts of the British parliament that overrode property owners opposed to the enclosure of their land or the construction of canals or turnpikes across it" (Robert Allen, 2009, p. 5). Third, the rule of law (such as contract law, company law, bankruptcy law, competition law, inheritance law, tax law, land regulation law, intellectual property law, financial auditing and disclosure, and so on) was either non-existent, or poorly practiced and highly deficient in many of the now-developed countries before and during their industrial revolution. For many of these countries law enforcement was of poor quality well into the early 20th century after or near the end of their respective second industrial revolution. (See Ha-Joon Chang, 2003, pp. 71–123)

Chapter 6

Case Study of Yong Lian:
A Poor Village's Path to Becoming
a Modern Steel Town

This chapter provides a case study of a particular village to illustrate China's economic transformation. Before providing details, it is worth reemphasizing some general theoretical points.[1]

First, the significance of China's rural proto-industrialization is identical to the significance of Great Britain's proto-industrialization. Specifically, this initial industrialization process (in either China or Great Britain or other countries) is an activation of the subsequent industrial revolution and a critical transitional step from an agrarian economy to a mass-production economy; this step is absolutely necessary to overcome two fundamental challenges: (i) the curse of food security and the Malthusian trap and (ii) the otherwise prohibitive costs of creating a mass market to support the division of labor, specialization, and mass production.

---

[1]Yong Lian village's successful story has long caught the attention of Chinese national news media and been reported and written about in many books. The materials presented here draw heavily from Xin (2004).

In other words, despite the apparent differences in the political institutions of modern China and 18th century Great Britain, both economies needed this proto-industrialization stage to serve several important functions: (i) It improves agricultural productivity by stimulating commercial-based/oriented agricultural production and agricultural diversification, increases the specialization and utilization rate of agricultural labor (e.g., by taking advantage of evenings and idle seasons and allowing women and children to move out of farming and into workshops), and more importantly raises farmer income without jeopardizing food security; (ii) It trains and transforms the peasant population into a proto-industrial labor force, preparing the "reserve army" (called *"non min gong"* or migrant workers in China) for the coming industrial revolution; (iii) It creates and deepens the mass market (purchasing power of the grassroots population) for the coming adoption of the factory system nationwide; (iv) It helps reduce financial and technological barriers of entry into the manufactured-goods market (i.e., setting up firms) and lowers the prohibitive costs of investment by acquiring cheap land and avoiding labor relocation costs, thus facilitating primitive capital accumulation; (v) It stimulates regional specialization and intra-national and international trade based on each village's local comparative advantage, helps expand domestic and foreign markets, and accumulates valuable savings (or foreign reserves) needed for inventing or importing advanced technologies; (vi) It generates government revenue (or merchant capital, as in the case of Great Britain) for local infrastructural development; (vii) It nurtures entrepreneurs and engineers and other skilled labor based on "learning by doing" and "creative destruction"; (viii) And overall, it serves to create conditions for the formation of nationwide markets and commercial distribution systems, supply chains, and industrial clusters to prepare the economy for the era of mass production — the industrial revolution itself.

Second, China's proto-industrialization occurred with unprecedented speed and scale across China because Mao's regime had already built up a significant level of communal spirit, cooperative social capital, collective self-governance, and agricultural infrastructure into China's vastly impoverished rural areas before Deng's economic reform. So, by 1978, farmers were already familiar with self-organization and cooperative activities beyond their small-scale family-based activities. China's nationwide proto-industrialization would not have occurred without this enormous amount of social capital, including social trust, built-in collective institutions through land reform, collective land ownership, the provision of public services such as basic healthcare and schooling, the buildup of local irrigation systems and road networks, and the formation of centralized yet highly autonomous village-level and township-level government networks (or *local state capacity*) to maintain social stability and encourage social collaboration. The same is true for credit lending and joint production based on the division of labor that expanded beyond the family circle and other close village kinships. In fact, the lack of sufficient social trust and communal spirit (as well as the lack of any government-led market creation) was one of the key reasons behind the failure of the Qing and Republican China regimes to enact a proto-industrialization in the rural areas despite well-established private property rights in land ownership and alienable contract in those periods.

Third, both central and local governments under Deng's strong leadership have played pivotal roles in facilitating such transformations. Industrialization in China has specifically hinged on the government's ability (the so-called *state capacity*) to create both a unified domestic market and access to international markets (in both finished goods and raw materials) without losing control of China's financial stability. China's government has been especially important in overcoming challenges related to China's vast size, poverty, international isolation, lack of political stability, and the absence of a powerful and massive merchant class. In fact, many first-generation entrepreneurs after 1978 came from the ranks of local government (even at the village level) after the 1978 economic reform.

This progression from government official to entrepreneur features prominently in our case study.

This case study describes the village of Yong Lian, which had been one of the poorest villages on the east coast of China. We choose this village for several reasons: (i) It has gone through the same developmental stages as we describe for China as a whole, although Yong Lian progressed at an above-average pace. This village completed its entire sequence of industrialization in about 20 years, between 1978 and 2000. It moved from proto-industrialization, to a first industrial revolution, to a second industrial revolution, and as of 2000 entered the "welfare state." (ii) The entire village is itself a large cooperative enterprise with continuity of development. Because of vigorous creative destruction in China, many firms did not experience that same continuity; they came and went at an extremely rapid turnover rate. In particular, enterprises that emerged during China's first and second industrial revolution stages were mostly not the same firms that emerged during the proto-industrialization stage. Villages that prospered during the 1980s may have stagnated during the 1990s, and the peasant workers who supported the early village firms may have become migrant workers in other big cities supporting newer mass-production firms. But Yong Lian is an exception. Although its key industry is not textiles, but steel, Yong Lian's transformation is still relevant and instructive. (iii) Because this village's development has outpaced China's overall development, it provides a good indicator of where China may be heading in the next couple of decades.

Yong Lian, in English, literally means "permanent unification." The village is located in Suzhou County of Jiangsu province on the east coast of China near the mouth of the Yangtze River.[2] It was

---

[2] Jiangsu is a small but densely populated province that borders Shandong in the north, Anhui to the west, and Zhejiang and Shanghai to the south, with a 620-mile coastline along the Yellow Sea. Yong Lian is in the southern part of the province, where the Yangtze River passes through.

created in 1970 during the middle of the Cultural Revolution under a nationwide land reclamation movement. Under the supervision of the local township government, thousands of farmers helped build Yong Lian village with basic straw-mud housing and primitive irrigation systems after the draining of swampy or seasonally submerged wetlands to convert them to farmland. Once the land reclamation was completed, 255 families from nearby villages migrated and settled here to form this new village with an initial population of 692 in 1971.

Land reclamation is a complex investment project and engineering challenge, but it was made even more difficult in 1970s China because of the lack of modern technologies. Only primitive handmade tools were available, and the project required the large-scale coordinated efforts of thousands of village families. After a year of intensive manual labor (mostly during the winter, when crop fields were idle), the farmers reclaimed 1,022 Mu (about 168 acres or 67 hectares) of farmland.[3]

Poor natural conditions and frequent flooding had plagued Yong Lian over its short seven-year history before the 1978 economic reform. The villagers lived in extreme poverty. Arable land in Yong Lian village was about 1 Mu or 0.0667 hectare per person, compared with 0.08 hectare per person in the rest of China and 0.83 hectare per person in the United States in 1980. No family had a brick house; as mentioned, house walls were made of dried mud and roofs were made of straw. In certain especially dire periods, the villagers could afford only two meals per day and even those were simply rice soup without any fresh vegetables or meat. In good years, there might have been pork once per year during the Chinese Spring festival. As a result, Yong Lian village remained one of the poorest and smallest villages in the county, with per capita disposable annual income between 60 and 70 yuan (about $10 U.S. per current exchange rates) between 1971 and 1978. Although crop

---

[3] 1 Mu is 0.165 acres, and one acre is about 0.4 hectares.

production in Yong Lian increased steadily over that time, the population also grew at similar pace (about 2.6% per year), from 692 in 1971 to 809 in 1977. As a result, per capita income barely changed.

Ultimately, eliminating poverty was the promise of communism and the primary goal of Mao's "new agricultural co-operation" movement. What did change significantly in China's rural areas since 1949, however, were population size, life expectancy, and the rapid buildup of low-tech irrigation systems and local road networks connecting villages to towns across the countryside. Each year during the idle seasons, the local village governments organized the farmers to build roads, dams, canals, and other infrastructure deemed beneficial for improving agricultural productivity, albeit through primitive and low-quality structures.

But despite these coordinated efforts, farmers' living standards across China barely increased between 1949 and 1978. What had gone wrong? What was missing from the government's efforts to raise the population out of the Malthusian trap? Was it simply corruption and government's vested interests? Was it heavy government "extraction" that prevented farmers from escaping poverty no matter how hard they worked? Or was it the lack of private property rights and the rule of law, as the institutional theorists would suggest?

Based on detailed historical records, documents, and extensive interviews with the villagers of Yong Lian conducted by researchers in the 1990s (see, e.g., Xin, 2004), none of the above hypotheses seems to be the case. First, the families that voluntarily decided to relocate to Yong Lian in 1970 were subsidized by the government: The migrants received about half a year's worth of income compensation to cover their moving costs and a full year's worth of income in terms of other types of social benefits.

Second, during the entire period between 1970 and 1978, Yong Lian received more-favorable loans from the local county bank for various public construction projects than other villages did and nearly all villagers received food coupons (rebates) and other subsidies because of the well-known low productivity and low yields of their farmland. As a result, the village accumulated 60,000 yuan of public debt by 1978, roughly one thousand times the average villager's annual income or 200% of Yong Lian's aggregate annual product. Hence, Yong Lian village was heavily subsidized by the government instead of heavily taxed or "extracted."

Third, local village leaders were mostly democratically elected and were highly regarded and considered role models by the villagers throughout those difficult years and up to the present day. The village records and interviews show that most of Yong Lian's village leaders since 1970 possessed charisma, were perceived as holding the high moral ground, and were skilled communicators. They also worked harder and longer hours than others despite receiving the same income as others.

Fourth, the cause of the poverty trap in Yong Lian was not lack of private land ownership either. Instead, as this chapter will show in detail, Yong Lian's poverty trap was caused by the central government's ill-designed economic policies and the consequent lack of market and market creators (i.e., market-based commerce, production, and trade). In a centrally planned economic environment, the village as a whole and the individual households lacked the necessary freedom and responsibility in making daily economic decisions to pursue profits or to use profits as the correct measure of productivity and efficiency.

The only way to measure the productivity of a firm or cooperative effort (albeit imperfectly) is through market profits, even though profits can be contaminated by price fluctuations and speculation. Profits reveal productivity. If a production process is unprofitable, it is then deemed unproductive because the costs of inputs exceed the value of outputs. Even in the case of public goods, production is unproductive if its (properly) measured social costs exceed its social benefits. Therefore, if production decisions are never based on proper measures of profitability or market rates of return, then it is impossible to tell whether such activities are productive or not.

When markets and, hence, market prices are missing, economic organizations and investment projects, which both involve large fixed costs, will likely be misguided and economic growth will be unsustainable. This was why the industrial empire of the Soviet Union eventually collapsed in the 1980s because central planning completely ignored profitability in the absence of markets. The whole Soviet-style national system of industrial organization had been unprofitable for decades, which also explains why China was on the verge of collapse in 1977 (before the reform) even though China had managed to establish a broad industrial base since its independence in 1949.

Hence, Mao failed to industrialize China, his Great Leap Forward was an economic disaster, and most importantly his noble goals did not justify his means. Nonetheless, Mao's radical social experiments in China between 1949 and 1976 proved repeatedly that without market mechanisms and individual freedom, large-scale rural organization and cooperation are not profitable.

After the tragedy of the Great Leap Forward in 1959–1962, in the middle 1960s and especially in early 1970s, Mao started to emphasize the importance of village factories again with the following policies: (i) they must be collectively owned by all villagers; (ii) their purpose must be to improve agriculture and not generate profits; (iii) they must reflect local comparative advantage and natural endowment conditions — to "locally obtain raw material supply, locally produce, and locally sell or distribute" commodities (Xin, 2004, p. 100).

Hence, starting from 1970 and continuing toward the end of the Cultural Revolution around 1976, the number of village factories started to grow again in China's rural areas, from 474,000 in 1970 to 1,392,000 in 1977, growing at 17% per year on average. During the same period, the gross output (unfortunately, with no record of value added) of village factories rose from 6.76 billion yuan to 23.4 billion yuan, growing at 28% per year on average in the absence of any inflation.

Despite this phenomenal growth, as noted earlier, farmers' living standards in terms of the quantity and quality of food, clothing, and living space remained essentially unchanged. Hence, such growth in gross output must have been driven mainly by input growth instead of value-added growth or productivity changes.

Had profitability (value added) been used in the 1970s as the goal and criterion of production (which would have required market prices), many of the village factories perhaps would not have been established in the first place — or their choices of types of output and factory sizes would have been very different. This would have also applied to large-scale organized farming.

Not surprisingly, early factories were impeded by shirking and lack of individual creativity and initiative; these became the most severe problems undermining team-based large-scale farming methods. Farmers' spare time during growing seasons and the entire time during idle seasons were completely devoted to building public irrigation systems, which had reached the point of severe diminishing returns after 20 years of intensive buildup since 1950. Therefore, farmers' time was not spent (even partially) on commercialized agricultural production and wealth creation. Put simply, farmers pursued only collective goals to produce collective goods and not individual goals to produce private goods.

Was private land ownership the answer to overcoming these obstacles? Private property rights may seem on the surface to be the remedy, to provide the incentives for the land owners to innovate, increase production, and become more productive. But as we will see, these rights were not part of Yong Lian's experience and success.[4]

---

[4]The Qing dynasty (1644–1911) and the Republic era (1911–1949) both had private property rights (including private land ownership and alienable land contracts) and yet the farmers were poor. For one thing, as autarkic individuals, peasant-farmers in the Qing dynasty and Republic era were unable to organize to build large-scale irrigation systems and fight off natural disasters; hence, their labor

In fact, before Deng's 1978 economic reform, Yong Lian tried to increase farmers' income and mitigate poverty in many ways: The creation of village factories and agricultural diversification, for example. But none of the strategies targeted the market for profit. That is, none of them focused on how to facilitate and engage in making money through the buying and selling of goods outside of the village. For example, since 1973, Yong Lian village had established numerous types of village factories to produce a variety of light consumer goods to meet *local* village demand, such as linen, cotton, and wool textiles and clothing, gloves, nails, pins, containers, straw hats, among other things. But none of these factories were sufficiently profitable and all went bankrupt in the end.

In late 1978, the nationwide economic reform reached Yong Lian village. The township-level government recruited Wu Dongcai, a 42-year-old highly spirited and entrepreneurial former soldier in the Korean War, to serve as Yong Lian village's new village leader and communist party secretary. The regional officials hoped he could improve the conditions for this poorest village in the county. Wu turned out to be an excellent choice for this task. Under Wu's leadership, Yong Lian began its historical transformation into one of the most economically successful locations not only in the province but also in the nation.

Yong Lian's historical transformation is characterized by the following key steps: (i) Agricultural diversification and commercialization; (ii) Proto-industrialization through township-village enterprises (TVEs); (iii) Evolution into modern industries.

---

was not as productive as it could be and they relied completely on the mercy of mother nature: They could only pray for rain when there was a draught, for the dry season when there was flooding, for merciful gods when there was earthquake and disease. For thousands of years Chinese peasants had been unable to find a solution to escape from flood and draught and the curse of food security despite private property rights.

i. Agricultural Diversification and Commercialization

As noted, the scarce land around Yong Lian village was poor quality and susceptible to natural disasters such as frequent flooding, given its geographic location. However, because the village is located by a big river, the villagers decided to turn some of the reclaimed land into fish ponds, to exploit that specific local comparative advantage. Fish sold well in the local market because of high demand, but it could also serve as a food source to supplement the village's simple diet. In addition, the breeding cycle of the fish (maturation in one year) is quick, unlike that of pigs and cows, so that business risk was heavily reduced. Although this undertaking required a substantial degree of collective decision making among the 255 immigrant families and a huge amount of organized labor (during non-planting time), Wu managed to convince the entire village to take on the risk and initially covert about 80 Mu (about 13 acres or 0.5 hectares) of the low-lying area into fish ponds.

According to the accounts recorded in Xin (2004), Wu led about 300 men of the village and personally participated throughout this project: 60 full days during the winter of 1979, working in the deep mud, with mostly primitive tools and no modern machinery. Despite these hardships, the villagers were inspired and motivated by Wu's participation in the manual labor (despite a war-related injury) and that he received the same wages as other villagers. The villagers labeled this altruistic work ethic "Mao Zedong spirit" or "*Dazhai* morale."[5]

---

[5] In communist China, both before and after 1949, the rule was that only individuals deemed to possess such morale and spirit could be elected or promoted to leadership positions. Moreover, most local government officials and village leaders were selected from among the demobilized soldiers from the Red Army, the People's Liberation Army, or other soldiers who participated in the Korean War. These men were very well trained in organization and coordinated team action, with a sense of both leadership and individual courage.

This fishery investment turned out to be very successful. The initial investment was a 5,000 yuan loan from the local community bank to purchase juvenile fish and each village family's contribution of labor. By the end of the first year, in 1979, the initial fish sales had already fully paid off the initial loan and made a small profit of 600 yuan. In 1980, they added three more fish ponds and harvested 10,000 kilograms of fish, which they sold for more than 20,000 yuan with net profits of 8,000 yuan. More than 6,000 yuan was distributed as dividends to village "shareholders" in that year. On top of that, each family in Yong Lian village received 2.5 kilograms of fresh fish as a supplement to their low-protein diet. Soon, the fishery industry became a big business in Yong Lian and a critical source of financing for other types of investments. Yong Lian villagers finally had the hope of escaping from the Malthusian trap and the curse of food security and saw their living standards soar. The per capita cash income increased from 68 yuan in 1978 to 98 yuan in 1979, 119 yuan in 1980, and 126 yuan in 1981, growing at 16% per year on average over the initial four year period. Total village profits rose from merely 700 yuan in 1977, to 1,800 yuan in 1978, 5,600 yuan in 1979, 35,800 yuan in 1980, and 42,300 yuan in 1981, an average growth rate of 57% per year. Most of the profits were reinvested rather than consumed.

Even more growth and revolutionary changes came to Yong Lian soon after. But before we continue the story, it is worth noting a few points: Such a seemingly natural market-based decision to specialize in fishery production (according to the village's specific comparative advantage of natural resources such as access to rivers and canals) nonetheless required a deep-seated community-minded cooperative spirit and government leadership and financial support. As the case study shows, these factors have been vital components in overcoming the historic obstacles and promoting the recent economic success in China.

No individual peasant family in 1970s China could have ever achieved such dramatic progress alone. Limited financial and labor resources for building and managing the fish pond and financing the purchase of the juvenile fish would have been insurmountable unless financed and organized by some external source of wealth and expertise. In 16th–18th century Great Britain and other parts of Europe such as the Netherlands, the merchant class and bankers provided that wealth and expertise, basing their investments on sound credit and labor contracts under the putting-out system. In this case, Wu and other village leaders took on the substantial task of coordinating the work of hundreds of individual farmers; the local state-owned community bank provided the loan. Hence, financing and entrepreneurial expertise played the same pivotal role in Yong Lian as they did in Great Britain and the Netherlands, but the source of that financing and expertise was very different. Government officials and funding encouraged by the local government enabled the village to achieve this economic transformation.

Of course, the enterprise carried risk, for both the village and the community bank: This product specialization (i.e., the fishery) may have failed and wasted the investment of both time and money, but more importantly it could have jeopardized the food security of the village if the market for the fish turned out to be insufficient. Fish is not a perfect substitute for the villagers' diet; the main purpose of the investment was for market exchange, not for consumption. If the business had failed, many families would have gone hungry because a significant fraction of the village's labor force and arable land had been reallocated away from farming and toward the fishery, thus relying on the sales of fishery products in the market to make up for the reduction (i.e., opportunity cost) in farming and crop production. In addition, Yong Lian village alone could not have achieved its initial business success without a nationwide (or at least regional) movement toward commerce and trade in the late 1970s.

As noted, the local community bank supplied the critical 5,000 yuan of initial credit that would have been impossible to accumulate by pooling the village's individual family savings. Also, the loan was risky because it was uncollateralized, given that Yong

Lian village had nothing to offer as collateral. That loan was obtained entirely on the community bank's good faith in Wu's personal reputation and the government policy of supporting the poor. A business-minded commercial bank likely would not have originated the loan.

The government's efforts to create the village in the first place under the system of collective land ownership also contributed to the likelihood of success by significantly reducing the sunk cost of investment; the village families did not need to privately purchase land or sign land contracts with multiple individual land owners. Hence, private ownership was not only unnecessary but might have hindered Yong Lian's economic development.

And lastly a reminder that the essential ingredient (even more so than direct government-sponsored support of the enterprise) was the market to first buy fish eggs or juvenile fish as an investment and the market in which to sell the harvested fish. The isolated village, left to its own devices, would have been unable to make such connections.

In addition to these entrepreneurial efforts, Yong Lian had been actively engaged in crop diversification and establishing small rural factories. Agricultural diversification based on local comparative advantages and market-based crop planting and commercial exchanges dramatically increased the village's labor productivity and crop yields. Such revolutionary processes spreading across rural China greatly increased agricultural productivity and put an end to food shortages in China by the mid-1980s, creating conditions for China's subsequent industrial revolution in the next decade.

Similar revolutionary changes in agricultural productivity took place in 16th–18th century Great Britain (e.g., crop diversification, commercialized farming, switching from subsistence farming to wool production, conversion of land into fenced sheep pastures, land conversion, land drainage and reclamation, primitive infrastructure formation, and development of a primitive national market for woolen textiles).[6] But this British agricultural revolution took centuries to accomplish. It greatly facilitated (made possible) the movement of forced land enclosures that restricted access to the most productive land (at one time common land) to a selected few and drove landless peasants into the cities for wage-labor. That land transformation was primarily driven by the rapidly rising nation-wide demand for wool as the prime raw material for textile production and financed by wealthy merchants or landlords (instead of the local village governments) so those merchants and landlords were the primary beneficiaries of that agricultural revolution and land transformation. It is worth emphasizing that such revolutionary processes took place regardless of the 1688 Glorious Revolution.

ii. Proto-Industrialization through TVEs

The primitive agricultural revolution began to solve Yong Lian's poverty and enrich farmer income. In particular, improved agricultural productivity also created a substantial amount of "surplus" labor throughout rural China, including Yong Lian. However, China's cities and urban areas were not prepared to absorb this surplus labor in the early 1980s, which would require first establishing labor-intensive mass-production factories to engage in mass distribution to a mass market. Hence, the next critical step for Yong Lian was to fully engage locally available surplus labor by creating its own proto-industries, even if these industries had access only to limited rudimentary technologies.

As mentioned earlier, villagers in Yong Lian had tried to operate several types of rural factories since the early 1970s, during Mao's era, to produce linen and woolen textiles, gloves, household

---

[6] Long distance commerce was aided by the expansion of roads and inland waterways. Road transport capacity in England grew from three-fold to four-fold from 1500 to 1700. See, e.g., https://en.wikipedia.org/wiki/British_Agricultural_Revolution.

containers, nails, pins, and so on. But all of them were unprofitable financial burdens because of the lack of a market and profit incentives, and most went bankrupt. When Wu arrived in Yong Lian in 1978, there were only three proto-industrial firms left: a food-processing factory, a textile-weaving factory, and a grocery store, all collectively owned and serving only the consumption needs of the local villagers.

After initial successes in both the fishery business and other commercial agricultural ventures, Wu reassessed the conditions of the village and realized that several hundred farmers each year were idle and could contribute their "surplus" labor to other efforts. In some cases, these farmers were also skilled craftsmen. Wu organized them and sent them out of the village to work in nearby city factories, including a large cement factory. After these workers gained experience and knowledge of cement production, Wu organized these workers in their own cement factory based in Yong Lian, which became profitable. At one point, the factory employed 300 villagers from Yong Lian. In 1983, they sold this factory and used the profit to establish other more-profitable factories, producing containers, farming household items, and fans and selling them to nearby urban markets. Around 1985, there were so many village factories in Yong Lian that raw materials, tools, and other equipment cluttered the streets and villagers could hear the sounds of machinery and production noises like "an industrial symphony" from most parts of the village. They were very happy and content about the noise because it signified and symbolized industrialization and prosperity. Some of the products the factories produced were rattan handcrafts, wicker-weaved containers, cement floors, granite stones, bathtubs, jade, industrial paper, bricks, sofas, leather chairs, pillows, motor vehicle seats, simple automobile parts, optic lenses, industrial fans, as well as electrochemical painting and galvanization. These were small-scale labor-intensive rural factories and produced for known markets in the nearby large towns and cities, such as Wuxi, Suzhou, and Shanghai. Such factories were actually risky endeavors because sales were not guaranteed and competition was becoming intense. Hence, Wu's strategy was to remain flexible and responsive to market needs, with an ability to start up quickly to gain an advantage in a new market and shut down just as quickly to resume production for the next profitable opportunity. Wu tried to ensure a minimum amount of inventory and machinery, so that shutting down would not generate waste and place a financial burden on the village's finances. Between 1979 and 1984, Yong Lian experimented with about 20 different types of factories that produced about 50 varieties of goods.

Through these village factories, Yong Lian's public capital fund accumulated rapidly, from several thousand to tens of millions of yuan in just a few years, a spectacular growth of several hundred-fold in four years. Even by 1983, villagers' standard of living had improved dramatically, with enough surplus food (including meat), that families could make nonessential purchases: watches, radios, sewing machines, more-expensive cloth, and so on.[7] They could also afford to construct brick houses. These changes and enrichments were unimaginable before the 1978 economic reform. This economic prosperity across China's countryside and urban areas echoed the conditions that arose from the 16th to early 19th century in Europe preceding the Industrial Revolution. Yet China, and Yong Lian village in particular, achieved this commercial revolution in just a few years. The speed of this revolution was unprecedented, and made all the more remarkable because China accomplished it without colonialism, imperialism, or the slave trade.

Moreover, in the middle to late 1980s, Yong Lian under Wu's leadership managed to establish some modern infrastructure: Yong Lian (i) overcame its flooding problems during high tides through the construction of a modern irrigation and canal system, (ii)

---

[7] Note that these consumer goods were also simultaneously produced by other village firms or state-owned factories in the cities and such goods were rarely available or affordable during Mao's era.

established a power grid network to make electricity available to all households, (iii) constructed deep wells and a water purification system to supply potable water, (iv) paved new roads connecting to other villages and cities, and (v) established health clinics for all villagers and public schools. In 1985, Yong Lian was on the top 10 list of local county villages that had reached total GDP of 10 million yuan. Yong Lian was cited as a role model in the efforts to confront poverty by local news media and the local government.[8]

iii. Evolution into Modern Industries

By the early 1980s, the village had accumulated capital and gained market experience through their small-scale proto-industries. Wu decided to take advantage of these initial successes and take on a more ambitious project: In 1984, he began the process of establishing a modern steel rolling mill. The village engaged into a partnership with the township retailing and goods-distribution center (also called supply-and-retailing cooperative). This project was the boldest and riskiest the village had taken on, and many challenges had to be addressed: How would they select, purchase, and operate the necessary technology? Where would the experienced steel technicians and management come from? Who would their customers be? How would they ensure viable markets, supply chains, and distribution networks?

In fact, Wu had started to address some of these challenges from the beginning: Wu realized early on that proto-industries themselves would not be the only major source of income and economic advancement for Yong Lian. He also focused on technological upgrading and development of managers and workers and allocated resources (funds, human capital, land ...) to achieve future success. Wu initiated a social movement in Yong Lian village that promoted learning, especially as a

---

[8] In 1985, China had 12.22 million village firms and a significant fraction of the villages in Jiangsu province had achievements in income growth similar to that of Yong Lian.

requirement for members of the village leadership and administration. This effort involved business training in general, but also specifically learning to market and sell village-made products outside the village, to create new business, to absorb new knowledge and production technologies, to identify new industrial projects and sources of raw material, to establish supply chains and sales networks, to attract outside investment, and so on. He asked all village officials to develop keen business instincts and act quickly to grasp business opportunities. For his part, Wu ensured that funds, personnel, and equipment would be quickly available for new business projects. He selected the most capable villagers to be salesmen and had them travel to other regions to market and sell Yong Lian products, obtain commercial information, and establish customer relations and sales networks.

Although Wu was not given a corporate title, he had acted as the CEO of the village and imposed a strict set of rules and operational discipline on the villagers. He understood that the local population would be the main labor force that he would draw upon, and he developed that labor force. He also led by example: Wu himself worked 14–16 hours a day, seven days a week, which limited the time he could spend with his wife and children, despite a relatively minimal salary. In fact, his initial salary was the same as any other village leader's salary. Wu served as a role model for the villagers, although he had no entrepreneurial role models of his own. He instead relied on a strong work ethic and organizational skills he gained during his military service. He had never heard of Andrew Carnegie, Henry Ford, J. P. Morgan, John D. Rockefeller, or Cornelius Vanderbilt. In many ways, Wu's efforts and success in Yong Lian mirror those of China's overall industrialization, which occurred after some amount of trial and error but without reliance on any one economic formula or model. Wu invested his efforts in pragmatic projects that could leverage the available financing, local government support, and the village's comparative advantages. Equally important was Wu's insight into how to meet the growing demands that were emerging from the nation's industrialization. At the time, one of those new demands was for steel.

Yong Lian village's experience differed from that of many other parts of China, specifically in their stages of industrialization. Other rural areas progressed from a primitive agricultural revolution, to a proto-industrialization, to a first-stage industrialization (first industrial revolution), before reaching a second-stage industrialization (second industrial revolution). Yong Lian village did not go through the distinct phases of a first industrial revolution, typically involving mass-producing light consumer goods (such as textiles), before reaching a second industrial revolution, involving heavy industrial goods production. Yong Lian combined these two phases into one and progressed from the proto-industrial stage into heavy industries: Specifically, a steel-making enterprise. However, the development of Yong Lian's steel mill still features a gradual industrialization that is very similar to China's overall industrialization: from labor-intensive to capital-intensive industries, from low-tech to high-tech processes, from small to big, and from domestic to international markets.

In 1984, China's nationwide primitive agricultural revolution and ongoing rural proto-industrialization were in full force. Farmers' incomes were rising rapidly. Wu sensed that the demand for better housing, offices, and various types of small industrial buildings would also rise rapidly, in both rural and urban areas. Because the chief intermediate goods for small buildings in China were cement and rebar (a steel reinforcing bar used to strengthen concrete structures), increased demand for buildings would mean increased demand for rebar. Yet, large state-owned steel enterprises were not likely to supply a great amount of these small-scale intermediate goods. So Wu persuaded the other village officials to establish a small steel mill to produce rebar. To ensure enough of a potential market for their rebar, Wu and his colleagues spent several months traveling to nearby cities to personally conduct market research and collect technical information about how to establish and operate a rebar factory and sell and distribute the product.

Once the final decisions had been made to establish a rebar factory, the first problem encountered was how to finance the initial investment in equipment and structures. The total costs of investment for this rebar factory in 1984 were estimated to be around 600,000 yuan. But Yong Lian village could put up only half of that initial investment, even after selling two of its existing factories. Wu needed to find outside funds, and he approached the local township supply-and-retailing cooperative, Gong Xiao She (GXS).

GXS is a state-owned and operated nationwide distribution network of cooperative entities, responsible for coordinating the supply and distribution of goods and raw materials across China under the central planning system. Its local branches often also served as local community banks to provide credit to local villages for public projects. In 1983, local GXS branches changed from state ownership to local collective ownership and were encouraged to provide financial and commercial support to facilitate local rural industrial development. In conjunction with village-level governments, GXS entities at the township level in China played a role similar to that of 18th–19th century English merchants during the first industrial revolution.

Yong Lian village and the Nanfeng Township GXS office signed a contract to jointly finance, own, and operate the proposed rebar factory. Each party agreed to provide 300,000 yuan as the initial investment for this joint venture. Yong Lian's 300,000 yuan acquired the land and factory structures, and Nanfeng GXS's investment mainly purchased the equipment and provided initial working capital.

The original contract between Yong Lian village and the Nanfeng Township GXS office:

Partner A (party A): Nanfeng town Yong Lian village.
Partner B (party B): Nanfeng town GXS.

Based on mutual interests and the principle of voluntary participation, sharing of investment costs and profits and business risk, the
two parties decide to set up a joint steel cooperation according to the
following specifications:

1. Name. The cooperation is tentatively named "Yong Lian Steel
   Factory." The factory has an independent account separated from
   Yong Lian village's other business.
2. Scale of operation. The factory will have three workshops with
   the estimated production capacity of 2,500 tons of rebar per year.
3. Source of funds. The factory's production capacity needs to be
   matched with 360V electricity generation system and other necessary equipment, which costs approximately 600,000 yuan. Each
   party will share this total investment cost equally (300,000 yuan
   each). The main source of working capital comes from Nanfeng
   GXS's bank loans. Yong Lian village will supply the required
   land and factory buildings, which can be counted as part of party
   A's investment funds.
4. Profit sharing. Party A receives 60% of total profits and party B
   receives 40%. However, both parties share any business losses
   and risks equally.
5. Leadership. (i) Set up a six-person board of directors; each party
   contributes three people. Party A has Wu Dongcai, Wang
   Deming, Chen Jinrong; party B has Lu Yangtao, Wang Wenlong,
   and Chen Longda. The board of directors is in full charge of
   main decision making for this business, including finance,
   equipment, factory operation scale, business relations with outside business, choices of its administration. (ii) Set up a six-
   person administration to be in charge of daily business operations
   including accounting.
6. Party B has 10% right to decide sales of the products.
7. Party B covers the basic salaries and medical insurance of party
   B's personnel, but Yong Lian Steel Factory is responsible for all
   of their bonus income and business costs reimbursement.

8. The time frame of collaboration is tentatively set for one year, from April 1, 1984, to March 31, 1985. The board of directors will decide whether the relationship continues or not in the future.

The contract was approved by the Shazhou county government, which was responsible for addressing any legal disputes or business-related problems through a special county-level government administration called the Industry and Commerce Administration Bureau (工商管理局). This contract by no means matched the sophistication or legal rigor of contracts in developed nations, but it served well in China's early stages of industrialization because of the enormous amount of social trust and reliance on government authority that existed at the time.

Wu emerged as the chairman of the board of the firm, which in 1980s China was also effectively the CEO. One of his first directives was to send several skilled and intelligent village craftsmen to nearby steel firms to learn production technologies. He also learned the basics of steel production. Wu hired a senior engineer from a state-owned steel mill in Suzhou City to be a part-time technical advisor: He was called the "Sunday engineer" because he could travel to Yong Lian only on Sundays.[9]

The rebar factory took less than four months to build and become operational. Yong Lian villagers served as the factory workers, and the machinery was a used rolling machine purchased from a nearby state-owned steel factory.

The factory was immediately profitable, amassing 100,000 yuan in profits by the end of the first year of operation. Its total sales reached 10 million yuan the following year, with net profits of 1.56 million yuan — which is 156% annual growth. This initial success shocked the villagers and soon became known throughout the county. In 1985, Yong Lian was listed as one of the top ten richest villages in the entire Suzhou county area, which included several

---

[9] It was actually illegal for him to have a second job due to conflict of interests.

thousand villages. Recall that in 1978, Yong Lian was one of the poorest villages in the area.

Another Big Step

Because of the steel mill's success and rapid growth in sales, it expanded from one production line to three over three years: 1984–1985, 1985–1986, and 1986–1987. However, even this pace of growth in production could not satisfy market demand. In 1987, Wu further expanded and upgraded the factory to compete in the national steel market with large state-owned steel companies in China. Wu believed that China had entered a long period of economic expansion and prosperity, so the demand for steel would continue to grow. He saw Chinese prosperity and hyper growth for at least many decades. So he decided to take the next big step.

His development strategy was to move beyond the smaller projects and target major enterprises. This was the same strategy that China's ex-premier Zhu Rongji adopted in the 1990s when trying to reform and restructure China's state-owned enterprises.[10] Wu convinced the other village leaders and factory management team to shut down operations of all other village firms (nearly 20 of them) and allocate all resources (both financial and human) on steel making. The idea met huge resistance from the villagers, who argued that consolidating into a single enterprise was a risky idea, especially when the other firms were continuing to be profitable and the diversity of factories provided solid risk management. Wu persevered in his forward-looking strategy: His vision was for the strictly rural industries in the village to take the "next great leap forward" and evolve into modern mass-production enterprises with cutting-edge technologies. The market structure was changing so rapidly and *industrial* demand for high-quality steel was growing. Ultimately, the villagers agreed and put their trust in Wu's business sense and

---

[10] The late 1990s' SOE reform was called "grasp the large and let go the small."

leadership, which they recognized as the pivotal force behind the village's exceptional success to date.

In 1987, Yong Lian village sold or shut down all of its other existing factories, including a very profitable jade and jewelry factory, and invested 1.2 million yuan to set up a new production line for high-quality rebar. One year later, after Wu's management team successfully implemented the expansion and continued to meet the rising demand, the factory's net profits soared to 6.5 million yuan. In 1992, net profits reached 25 million yuan, another fourfold expansion in just four years. As the scale of the operation expanded, the variety of rebar products also increased. Between 1994 and 1995, Yong Lian Steel Cooperation invested 100 million yuan in new production lines and rebar products. Hence, from 1992 to 1995, total cumulative profits reached 150 million yuan. In 1996, the firm invested another 35 million yuan to upgrade old production lines, which increased Yong Lian Steel Co.'s national rebar market share to 1/15; by 1998, its national share reached 1/8. The firm became one of the largest rebar producers in China and owned several industrial patents.

In 1995, Wu was named one of the top 10 village leaders in China by China's national broadcasting network, CCTV. In 1997, Yong Lian Steel Co. was ranked as the 39th largest village firm in China. In 1998, one of its own name brand products, "Lian Feng" Rebar, was named as Jiangsu province's best brand and received a gold medal from China's Ministry of Metallurgical Industry. In 2001, due to its excellent reputation in high-quality rebar products, Yong Lian Steel Co. received a waiver from the annual quality inspection requirements of the central government.

By the end of 2002, Yong Lian Steel Co. had 2,900 employees, a production capacity of over two million tons, and 5.34 billion yuan in sales revenue. It also owned a shipping port on the Yangzi River with a shipping capacity of 30,000 tons. The company's fixed assets increased from 300,000 yuan in 1984 to 2.1 billion yuan in 2002, more than a 7,000-fold expansion in 18 years with an average growth rate of 64% per year. In 2007, its sales reached 24.5 billion yuan.

During the spectacular expansion and growth, Yong Lian village also merged with several nearby (relatively poorer) villages, so its total population increased from 808 in 1979 to 9,261 in 2006.

Because Yong Lian Steel Co. has remained collectively owned by the villagers of Yong Lian, it has provided significant social economic returns to the village's welfare programs and public facilities. By 2002, Yong Lian village already had its own K-12 school system, a nursing home, public parks, clinics and hospitals, a movie theater, hotels, gardened community residential areas (subsidized housing), and much more. All villagers and factory workers were enrolled in a generous pension system, with subsidized property and healthcare insurance. Also, the village implemented an education subsidy system from elementary school through university.

Competition for Market Share Drove Technological Adoption and Product Upgrading

Yong Lian Steel Co.'s transformation and rise from proto-industries to modern enterprises was stimulated by the soaring demand for rebar as a primary construction material in China. High demand enticed a massive number of firms to enter the market, which resulted in extreme competition. Yong Lian was not the first village to engage in steel production in the same area. In the same city area of Zhang Jia Xiang, there emerged by the mid-1980s 30 village steel firms, two of them located in Nanfeng township, which Yong Lian belongs to. The township consisted of 24 villages, 13,000 families, 44,000 farmers, and about 40 types of village firms in 1988. But all of the 30 other steel factories went bankrupt over time.

What was Yong Lian's secret for winning the fierce market competition? The factors include (1) good market research. As mentioned earlier, when deciding to build the rebar factory, Wu and his colleagues spent months traveling in cities to evaluate and sense the market demand for rebar. Wu's market sense was brilliantly correct because as an economy transforms from an agrarian society to an industrial one, there is going to be a long wave of construction boom. Hence, demand for basic construction materials such as rebar will be huge and long-lasting. (2) Talent recruiting. Wu himself was brought up as an iron maker in a craftsman workshop as a child, so he had the instinct and interest in steel making. He personally interviewed and recruited all the rebar engineers and treated them well and with deep respects. Most importantly, he self-taught himself about rebar making and constantly upgraded his knowledge through learning by doing, although as a CEO he was not expected to be working at the front of the production line. He always personally participated in confronting technical problems that emerged during production and solved them together with other engineers and workers. (3) Worker discipline. Wu has been very strict on worker discipline. Although the factory belongs to the village, it is an independent entity in terms of management and financial accounting. Villagers must apply and be screened to become workers. Any workers violating factory rules are fired instantly without any questions asked, including Wu's relatives. In fact, Wu fired several of his relatives. All workers must follow the factory rules strictly and receive training in their respective work duties. (4) Self-amended technology. Most of the rebar-making technologies are self-designed and self-built under the assistance of experts and engineers from big steel corporations. This not only avoided spending millions of dollars purchasing imported equipment and not knowing how to operate it and relying on foreign companies to supply the necessary parts and future services. Wu took a strategy of self-design and self-build so that the equipment is fully adoptive to local market environment and easy for self-repairing and self-improvement in the future. This strategy saved a great amount of money for Yong Lian village and provided the advantage and base of technological innovations in the future. Most of the industrial technology innovations are based on small changes and improvements in the beginning. But such small changes and improvements become especially easy when the equipment is self-designed and self-built. Hence, through learning by doing, Yong Lian Steel Co. later on mastered the production technology and was able to fully design its own rebar production line and equipment and produce brand-name products with high quality and market reputation (e.g., in 1998 one of its own brand products, "Lian Feng" Rebar, was named as Jiangsu province's best brand and received the Gold Metal from China's Ministry of Metallurgical Industry). The factory also established its own R&D institute. (5) Management. Wu reformed the factory's management system many times and experimented with several different pay schedules and contractual forms with its workers and management personnel. Such schedules directly connected performance with salary and bonus and specified clear rules for promotion and punishment. (6) Sustainable and stable raw material supply chain. Yong Lian Steel Co. utilized its good reputation in market sales and in timely credit repayments to establish several important relationships with raw material suppliers, and even merged one of the largest state-owned raw material suppliers in east coast China as a shareholder and joint business partner. (7) Reputation-based sales and commercial distribution networks. Wu selected the most talented personnel from the village and in the company to be sales representatives and send them out nationwide to create market and nurture market reputation. Yong Lian Steel Co. initiated refund policies for customers and relied on the local, province-level, and national governments to advertise its products. The central and local governments in China hold many exhibitions and product contests each year to help advertising firms with good reputations.

Chapter 7

Conclusion: A New Stage Theory of Economic Development

Poverty or backwardness or the lack of industrialization is always and everywhere a social coordination-failure problem.

The problem arises because creating markets and the corresponding economic organizations (based on the principle of the division of labor) are extremely costly and require gigantic coordination efforts and social trust from all market participants. In a most fundamental sense, the "free" market is a public good, and the most fundamental one, whereas its pillar is social trust.[1] All market transactions, such as those involving transportation, information, communication, exchange, management, negotiation, organization, payment, and contract enforcement involve cost and trust and coexist with fraud. These costs and trusts all depend on political stability

---

[1] In the absence of social trust, seemingly obvious opportunities for mutually beneficial collective action are squandered. Without basic trust, not only are credit and contract impossible, but even barter exchange is impossible. This is why even in well-developed industrialized nations most loans (especially large ones) are collateralized. But the base of collateralizable assets grows only with industrialization.

and social order. Because of the colossal costs in providing this most basic public good, what is fundamentally missing in agrarian countries is not democracy, but rather the basic market creators.[2] So, poverty is first and foremost a problem rooted in both missing markets and missing market-creators, in both market-coordination failures and government failures.[3]

The benefits of the market are largely social while its costs (in creation and participation) are largely private. Hence, historically, a natural process of mass-market formation/fermentation has been a lengthy evolutionary process. It was initially accomplished mainly by a powerful and colossal merchant class that acted *collectively* and monopolistically under a nationalistic mercantilist spirit and backed fiercely by their state government.[4] It took England and Europe several hundreds of years to accomplish this historical task

---

[2] Even in modern societies, the creation of new markets requires huge investment and the help of the government. The emergence of the internet as the market for e-commerce is a good example.

[3] Precisely because of the colossal costs and gigantic coordination failures in providing this critical public good, we still observe today massive poverty across the globe in so many developing countries despite 200 years passing after the English Industrial Revolution.

[4] During the period of European global exploration in the Age of Discovery, "indeed it was much easier to raise funds for overseas ventures if the investment prospectus mentioned plunder, glory, and national pride than if it kept to a discussion of commercial opportunities alone" (Pomeranz and Topic, 2013, p. 156). The European oversea explorations and trade were extremely capital-intensive because of the colossal costs and risks involved. Most long-distance trade carried out by European merchants was armed trade and endorsed and supported militarily by their governments. "[I]t was precisely the unique challenges of carrying out long distance armed trading to Asia — challenges roughly similar to those involved in conquering, settling, and carrying out armed trade with New World colonies — that caused the Dutch East India Company to become a more 'modern' kind of enterprise than anything that had previously existed" (Pomeranz, *The Great Divergence*, 2000, p. 192).

of mass-market creation in the 15th to late 18th century since the Great Voyage and the discovery of America.[5]

The 1688 English Glorious Revolution, as unique as it may be in Western history, was in many ways a consequence of this lengthy market creation and state-led wealth accumulation process. It concentrated the political power of the merchant class in the parliament. It ensured that all commercial and international trade policies of the monarch truly reflected and protected the interests of the merchant class who were the pivotal force of wealth creation and the main taxpayers who financed the monarch's repeated wars against other European powers. It meant that "despotic power was only available intermittently before 1688, but was always available thereafter."[6] It showed "how a state can become powerful by reliably paying its debts to citizens and to foreigners, as Venice, Genoa, Lubeck, Hamburg, and the Dutch Republic had long shown ... A parliamen-

---

[5] Even with the mass-market fermentation in Europe and the fierce competition for global dominance in trade and military power, different European nations tried different industrial policies to build-up their national wealth. The Netherlands tried shipbuilding and the mechanization of its fishery industry; Spain tried the spice trade and the mechanization of sugar production; Italy and especially Flanders tried woolen and linen textiles; and France tried to mechanize the printing industry. But none of these proto-industrial processes and industrial policies led to the Industrial Revolution. England was "lucky" because it first tried woolen textiles but then switched successfully to cotton textiles, and it was precisely the colossal textile market created by different European countries (including England itself) but thoroughly grabbed by British merchants and government, and the nature of cotton textile production (which made wood-framed and water-powered mechanization possible through multi-staged elastic input–output production chains) and its associated colossal world market and global supply chains of cotton materials (which made mechanization feasible, profitable, and sustainable) that triggered the English Industrial Revolution.

[6] Julian Hoppit, "Patterns of Parliamentary Legislation, 1660–1800", *History Journal*, vol. 39, pp. 109–131; cited in Robert Allen (2009, p. 5), *The British Industrial Revolution in Global Perspective*.

tary monarchy that could borrow reliably was one that could intervene in the balance of power on the Continent" (D. McCloskey, 2010, p. 314).[7]

---

[7] In other words, the Glorious Revolution did little to change Britain's long cherished tradition of mercantilism, did not make the British government more "inclusive" (in the sense of sharing political power with the working class and the grassroots, as portrayed by Acemoglu and Robinson, 2012); if anything, it made the government simply more authoritarian and powerful in intervening in the national economy. For example, after the Glorious Revolution the Parliament began to raise taxes and impose more strict regulations and bans on imports so as to protect British domestic textile market and manufacturing. Tax revenue of the "inclusive" British central government (in grams of silver per capita) increased sharply after the Glorious Revolution, from 31 in the decade of 1650–1659 to 92 in 1700–1709, and reached a peak of 300 in the decade of 1820–1829 during the heyday of the first industrial revolution. This extraordinary capacity of revenue collection was more than 200% times that in the Dutch Republic and 600% times that in Spain during the same period. Taxes amounted to 9% of British gross national product in the beginning of the 18th century and reached 23% in 1810. In comparison, taxes of the "extractive" Qing dynasty China were merely around 4% throughout the 18th and 19th centuries (see Peer Vries, 2015, p. 71, 100, 102). Also, right after the Glorious Revolution, a ban was imposed in 1700 on the imports of superior India cotton products (calicoes). In 1701 the British Parliament passed an Act that declared it illegal to wear Asian silks and calicoes in England: "All wrought silks, bengals and stuffs, mixed with silk or herba, of the manufacture of Persia, China, or East India, all Calicoes painted, dyed, printed, or stained there, which are or shall be imported into this kingdom, shall not be worn." The Calico Act of 1721 stated that "After December 25, 1722, it shall not be lawful for any person or persons whatsoever to use or wear in Great Britain, in any garment or apparel whatsoever, any printed, painted, stained or dyed Calico" (See, e.g., Acemoglu and Robinson, 2012, pp. 197–202). In addition, a series of Navigation Acts that were passed before the Glorious Revolution remained in force for the next 200 years regardless of the Glorious Revolution and Adam Smith's "free trade" rhetoric. The aim of the Acts was to facilitate England's monopolization of international trade and made it illegal for foreign ships to transport goods from anywhere to England or its colonies. Property rights did not become more "secure and efficient" (a la Acemoglu and Robinson, 2012; and North and Weingast, 1989) after the Glorious revolution; but England did

As economic historian Sven Beckert aptly put: "The first industrial nation, Great Britain, was hardly a liberal, lean state with dependable but impartial institutions as it is often portrayed. Instead it was an imperial nation characterized by enormous military expenditures, a nearly constant state of war, a powerful and interventionist bureaucracy, high taxes, skyrocketing government debt, and protectionist tariffs — and it was certainly not democratic" (Sven Beckert, 2014, p. xv).

What China's development experience showed to the world is that the centuries-long Western-style "natural" and lengthy market-fermentation process can be dramatically accelerated and re-engineered by the government, by its acting as the market creators in place of the missing merchant class, yet without repeating the Western powers' old development path of barbaric primitive accumulations based on colonialism and imperialism and slave trade.

Proto-industrialization in early European history is a well-documented phenomenon and well-researched topic by economic historians. It is regarded by many as the necessary step for subsequent industrialization based on mass production and mass distribution. Yet historians have long been puzzled by the fact that in some nations, proto-industrialization led to industrialization but in some others it failed to trigger industrialization.[8] China's development experience sheds considerable light on this puzzle: The transition from proto-industrialization to mass production (or the first industrial revolution) requires continuous market creation and mercantilist state-support. *Laissez faire* and democracy is the recipe for failure.

China's development experience thus suggests a new model (theory) of economic development, which can be labeled as the

---

become richer and more powerful through its continued proto-industrialization and global market creation under mercantilist policies regardless of the Glorious Revolution.

[8]See, e.g., Sheilagh C. Ogilvie and Markus Cerman (1996), *European Proto-Industrialization*, and the references therein.

New Stage Theory (NST), or "Embryonic" Development Theory (EDT). NST is closely related to the old stage theory of List (1841), Marx (1867), Gerschenkron (1962), and Rostow (1960) and the other schools of development theory, such as the Structuralism and New Structuralism, as well as the ISI and the "Big Push" theory of development (as advocated by Paul Rosenstein-Rodan in 1943, and Kevin M. Murphy, Andrei Schleifer, and Robert W. Vishny in 1989).[9]

The NST suggests that measured economic policies and development strategies operating in a politically stable environment matter the most in determining whether nations fail or succeed in

---

[9] NST is also closely related to the development pattern identified by Joe Studwell (2003) in his very interesting book, *How Asia Works — Success and Failures in the World's Most Dynamic Region*. The book identifies three critical interventions that the government can use to speed up economic development. They are: (i) a full-fledged land reform that redistributes land from landlords to a large farming population based on a small-scale family-farming system, which can maximize agricultural yields; (ii) promoting manufacturing and technological upgrading in manufacturing through subsidies that are conditioned on export performance, which can help utilize the unskilled labor force released from the agricultural sector and provide "export discipline" to foster competition and Darwinian "creative destruction"; and (iii) intervention in the financial sector to focus capital on "intensive, small-scale agriculture and on manufacturing development," which allows the economy to focus on long-term high future profits rather than on short-term returns and individual consumption. The NST complements Studwell's important findings and offers a conceptual framework to explain why such government interventions work while the top-down approaches to economic development such as the ISI, the neoliberal Washington consensus, and the institutional theory do not work. NST also complements another insightful analysis on China's growth miracle, by Xiaopeng Li (2012), *A Nation in Question: Understanding the Rise of China*. Li's analysis focuses on the creative as well as destructive power of entrepreneurs and emphasizes the importance of government regulations in the market. Different from this China-related literature, the NST also provides a conceptual framework to shed light on the long-standing puzzle of the Industrial Revolution itself and help explain why it took place first in 18th–19th century England instead of China or India or other parts of Europe.

creating wealth and technologies. Institutions are endogenous and are often created to facilitate the execution or implementations of a nation's development policies and strategies. This general point is in line with the arguments of Justin Yifu Lin (1996).[10]

The NST identifies missing markets and missing *market creators* as the key problems of development (as already understood in one way or another by many existing theories), and emphasizes the important role of government in overcoming the coordination failures and *colossal costs* in market creation and industrial organization.[11] Similar to the old stage theory and structuralism, NST emphasizes that, even for later developed or developing countries, industrialization must always go through several major and distinctive stages *sequentially*, with each stage facing its own problem of missing markets and market creators. Hence, the development

---

[10]Also see Lin (2009, 2011, 2012, and 2013) for his detailed analyses on how China's central planning institutions and price control system were built to implement China's leapfrog development strategies in the 1950s through 1970s. The importance of economic policies and the state government in economic development are also stressed clearly by many others, such as Dani Rodrik (2008). Jinglian Wu (2005) provides detailed studies of institutional changes in China from 1949 to present. For other China-related books with rich empirical data analysis, see Gregory Chow (2015), Loren Brandt and Thomas G. Rawski (2008), and Barry J. Naughton (2007), among others.

[11]Justin Yifu Lin (1996, 2009, 2011, 2012, and 2013) emphasizes development strategy based on a country's "comparative advantage." The NST complements Lin's theory by emphasizing the costs of market creation. For example, India has the same comparative advantage in cheap labor as China does, but its development lags behind China by decades, precisely because its local and central governments have failed to create the same-sized domestic and international markets for India as the Chinese government has done for China. Consequently, India is unable to produce as many labor-intensive goods as China does even though its labor cost is actually lower than that of China. Indian farmers simply cannot build such mass markets on their own no matter how cheap their labor is. International merchants and foreign firms have no incentives to do so either. This responsibility falls upon the shoulders of the Indian government.

problem cannot be solved by just one big push through a one-time colossal national investment boom facilitated by foreign aid or a top-down approach. Successful economic development requires many rounds of step-by-step *sequential* "big pushes" from the bottom up by both the local and central governments.

Hence, industrialization is an organic "embryonic" development process of *sequential* market creations, with each stage financed through "primitive" accumulations in earlier stages. Put alternatively, this sequential embryonic development process goes through distinctive stages of organizational evolution and structural transformations and each stage is associated with newer and deeper market creation and involves newer and larger and more roundabout industrial structures, which are financed by savings accumulated from earlier stages and supported by the purchasing power (demand) created in earlier stages.

The essence of this developmental process is to gradually build up the required size of market to support mass production with the capacity of mass distribution and mass supply chains and industrial clusters to exploit the economies of scale (in multiple steps through the push-and-pull interactions and feedbacks between demand and supply). This process sequentially overcomes the problems associated with the curse of food security, the Malthusian trap, the missing Industrial Trinity, the infant industry, the middle-income trap, and the lack of competitiveness, and so on encountered by so many developing countries at various developmental stages in various forms. Through this developmental process, the industrial structure becomes more and more specialized and roundabout, more and more competitive and open for trade, and more and more capital intensive.[12]

---

[12]This development pattern applies also to small economies without an agriculture sector, such as Hong Kong. With proper industrial policies and development strategies, Hong Kong's economy started as a fishery village with small craftsmen workshops in the 1950s, gradually upgraded to export-oriented labor-intensive

In particular, to catch up with and evolve into a modern industrial economy similar to Great Britain, France, Germany, Japan and the United States, an agrarian nation (even in the 21st century facing the third industrial revolution) must go through three main stages to fully industrialize: (i) the proto-industrialization stage,[13] (ii) the first industrial-revolution (IR) stage, and (iii) the second IR stage. Modern financial capitalism is built on the second IR stage and is powerful because of the ability to mass supply tangible reproducible capital, not because of the capacity to print money or issue debts (which, after all, are backed by real reproducible assets; otherwise the nations run into debt crisis such as in Argentina and Greece). Each stage requires a "big push" since successfully embarking on each higher stage requires collective actions and public finance that are beyond the financial capacity of the individual industries and

---

manufacturing in textiles and toys and electronics in the 1960s–1970s, and then through heavy investment in infrastructures eventually evolved into a modern capital-intensive trade and financial center in Asia. In fact, one of Hong Kong's first successful industries was wig-making, a labor-intensive operation that required workers to attach individual strands of hair.

[13] As emphasized by L. A. Clarkson (1985, 1996), proto-industrialization hinges on rural industries that are distinctively different from urban craftsmen workshops. The latter produces to satisfy local and restricted markets whereas the former produces to satisfy national and international markets. Urban craftsmen existed long before the stage of proto-industrialization in any agrarian societies, such as ancient Rome and medieval Europe. Proto-industrialization took place much later in 17th–18th century Europe because the dramatically enlarged national and international markets and commercial networks after the Great Voyage induced the enriched merchants and the early capitalists to seek cheaper and more abundant source of labor supply residing in the countryside to satisfy the ever increasing national and global demand. At the proto-industrialization phase, however, the size of market was still not yet large enough and the supply chains and commercial distribution networks not yet sophisticated enough to render the factory system and mass production profitable and financially (and organizationally) feasible. Hence, further market creation (fermentation) is needed to kick-start the first industrial revolution.

firms; but the initial first stage is the most critical and fundamental because the economic and industrial structures at higher stages are all based and built on those of the proceeding earlier stages. Using mathematics as a metaphor: one cannot hope to understand calculus without learning algebra first, which in turn is impossible without knowing arithmetic first.[14]

For example, China in 1980 had about 800 million people living in rural areas with 300 million rural "surplus" labor. This means that even if the entire stock of modern American firms in all industries were relocated to China in 1980, they would absorb at most one third of Chinese rural surplus labor, even if assuming that Chinese peasant-farmers were as skilled as American manufacturing work-ers.[15] Hence, China's industrialization simply cannot start in the cities by directly relocating rural labor into urban factories as suggested by the Lewis (1954) model or Gerschenkron's (1962) leapfrog strategy. It must start in the countryside through proto-industrialization — repeating the same process that Great Britain went through before the Industrial Revolution.

Within each stage of industrialization, there can be three phases: the activation phase, the takeoff phase, and the completion phase. The last phase of each stage also constitutes the initial activation phase of the next higher stage. For example, the three phases of the first IR are characterized respectively by (i) the proto-industrializa-tion featuring primitive commercialized agriculture production, the division of labor, regional economic specialization, and primitive capital accumulations through regional and long-distance trade in labor-intensive and low value-added goods, (ii) the formation of large-scale factories and the mass production of light consumer

---

[14] In a deep sense, this learning process essentially repeats the key stages of the evolution of mathematics in human history. For example, how children learn and develop the concept of numbers is very similar to the origins of numbers in early human civilization.

[15] Total American civilian employment was about 100 million in 1980.

goods through mechanization (e.g., the stage of using 100 million t-shirts to exchange for a Boeing airplane as China did in the 1990s), and (iii) the demand-driven boom in the industrial trinity of energy, locomotive power, and transportation/communication infrastructure. The flagship industry in the second phase (the takeoff phase) of the first IR stage is the super income-elastic textile industry, and that for the third phase (the completion phase) is the coal/oil and railroad/highway and steam/combustion engine industries.[16]

This last phase of the first IR stage also constitutes the initial activation phase of the second IR stage. Driven by the increasing demand for the industrial trinity and machine tools used in light industries naturally leads to the mass production of machinery, electricity, minerals, cement, steel, chemicals, trucks, ships, and motive engines. Hence, the high point of the second IR stage (its takeoff phase) is the ability to reach the point of mechanized production of engines and heavy machineries (including fine precision lathes and instruments) that once enabled and powered the mechanization of the first industrial revolution featuring the mass production of light consumer goods. The flagship industry in the second IR stage is the steel industry (for the activation phase), the automobile and shipbuilding industry (the takeoff phase, where China is now), and the information technology (IT) and financial industry (the completion phase).[17]

---

[16]The concrete forms of the industrial trinity evolve over time. In terms of energy, it was coal in the 19th century but oil in the 20th century and solar power in the 21st century. In terms of communication, it was the telegraph in the 19th century but the telephone in the 20th century and electronic mail in the 21st century.

[17]The finishing phase of the second IR thus signifies a historical shift from manufacturing to information-intensive high-tech services such as finance and healthcare. The intensive reliance on information technologies will trigger demand for the third IR featuring breakthroughs in information technology and artifical intelligence. The third IR will feed back to the fruits of the first IR and second IR by making all manufacturing process and their products dependent on (controlled by) information technologies and artifical intelligence.

The full mechanization of agriculture can be achieved only during the second and third phases of the second IR stage when mass production of machinery (and mass crop storage technology) becomes possible or profitable. So only the second IR can fundamentally solve the curse of the food security problem that has haunted human societies throughout the age of agricultural civilization.[18]

Unlike the old stage theories, the NST does not suggest single once-for-all "Big Push" and determinism. Every development phase or stage requires substantial amount of public investment led by the government, or relies on the state to play a critical role of strategic leadership, intermediation, market creation, regulatory institutional building, and social coordination.[19]

Great Britain went through the initial phase of the first IR stage during 1600s–1760s, the takeoff phase of the first IR stage during 1760s–1830s, and the finishing phase during 1830s–1860s.[20] It

---

[18] The curse of food security, and the problems associated with it (such as food price inflation), has been the single most important trigger of social unrest and revolution in developing countries. This was true in China's 5,000-year history, also true in today's world, such as the Arab Spring of 2010–2011 (see, e.g., Jane Harrigan, 2011, "Did Food prices Plant the Seeds of the Arab Spring?" and Natali Fytrou, 2014, "World food crisis and the Arab Spring." Available at http://www. academia.edu/5743155/World_food_crisis_and_the_Arab_Spring).

[19] This lack of strong government support in industrial policies and technological upgrading explains why so many proto-industrialization processes in 18th century Europe (such as those in Flanders, France, Germany, Spain, Switzerland, Sweden, and Ireland, except England) failed to kick-start the Industrial Revolution. As a matter of fact, many European countries even experienced deindustrialization after their proto-industrial booms in the 17th–19th century. See Franklin F. Mendels (1981) and Sheilagh C. Ogilvie and Markus Cerman (1996), *European Proto-Industrialization*. This also explains China and India's failure in kick-starting an industrial revolution in the 17th and 18th centuries.

[20] During the first 30 years of the 19th century (the heyday of the first industrial revolution), Great Britain built less than 300 miles of railways, which was limited to small-scale localized railroads, most of them attached to a mine or iron

entered the initial (activation) phase of the second IR stage during 1830s–1860s, the second (takeoff) phase during 1860s–1890s (the time Karl Marx wrote Das Kapital), and the third (completion) phase during 1890s–1920s.

The United States went through these stages, respectively, during 1700s–1820s (proto-industrialization), 1820s–1850s (first IR takeoff), 1850s–1880s (railroad and steel industrial boom and activating second IR, caught Europe's attention as a rising world power),[21] 1880s–1910s (second IR takeoff, automobile industrial boom, took over England and became the global manufacturing powerhouse and superpower, activating financial industrial boom), 1910s–1940s (finishing second IR and agricultural mechanization and financial industrial takeoff, activating the welfare stage or post-industrial stage), 1940s–1970s (welfare stage takeoff and activating information-technology stage of the third IR), 1970s–2000s (finishing welfare stage and the information stage takeoff), 2000s–2030s (information stage completion and finishing the third Industrial Revolution).[22]

China has partially gone through these stages during 1978–1988 (full-fledged proto-industrialization, activating first IR), 1988–1998 (first IR takeoff, becoming a global giant in textiles and other light consumer goods, and activating industrial-trinity boom in coal,

---

works and dependent on the draught power of horses or stationary engines. The British industrial trinity boom took off in the following three decades, with the peak of railroad building activity reached in 1847 when nearly 6,500 miles of railway were under construction. By the 1850s the railroad construction boom was over and the main framework of the British railway network had been laid down. At this point, the railway mania had generated excessive mass-production capacity in the iron-making industry, so Great Britain was able to supply enormous amount of the railroad iron for foreign railways (see Phyllis Deane, 1979, p. 117).

[21] The total miles of railroad track in the U.S. increased from just over 20 miles in 1830 to over 52,000 miles in 1870 and in excess of 166,000 miles by 1890.

[22] Events beyond 2014 are based on pure conjecture. The same applies to China.

steel, and infrastructure), 1998–2008 (continuing industrial-trinity boom in energy, steel, infrastructure, communication, chemicals and activating second IR), 2008–2018 (second IR takeoff, becoming the "factory of the World" in heavy manufacturing such as automobiles, ships, and speed trains, and taking over the United States to become the largest exporter of machinery and capital goods and the largest economy in PPP-based GDP, and activating the financial industrial boom and RMB internationalization), 2018–2028 (finishing second IR, completing urbanization and agricultural modernization/ mechanization, achieving RMB dominance in global trade and capital flows, entering the age of financial capitalism and becoming the financial center of the world,[23] formally entering the welfare stage with mature medical and healthcare industries, activating the third industrial revolution in automation and information technology and green technology), 2028–2038 (full-fledged information-stage takeoff and becoming a world leader in heavy and computational industrial technologies and catching up with the U.S. in automation and informational technologies), and 2038–2048 (finishing the third industrial revolution and surpassing the U.S. to become the global full-fledged leader of technology innovations).

According to this NST chronology, China's overall degree of industrialization in 2014, from a historical perspective, is equivalent only to that of the United States around 1910s–1920s, despite the fact that some Chinese frontier technologies are only 20–30 years behind those of the United States. This estimation of China's overall degree of industrialization is also consistent with two independent

---

[23] As a major government-led agency providing low-interest loans to foreign countries to buy American goods, the Export-Import Bank of the United States has issued $590 billion loans over the past 80 years. Yet China has issued $670 billion similar loans over the past two years. The successful establishment of the Asian Infrastructure Investment Bank (AIIB) , as well as recent inclusion of RMB into IMF's SDR, is another example of China's increasing influence in global finance.

estimations based on (i) the rural/urban population share and (ii) per capita income growth. China's urban population share reached around 52% in 2014, whereas the U.S. urban population share reached about 51% in 1920. Also, real U.S. per capita GDP in the 1910s (1920s) was about one tenth (one eighth) of its current level, which is about the same gap as current per capita GDP between China and the United States.

However, the most important similarity between today's China and early 20th century United States is not the level of income or urban population share, but rather the momentum (force and dynamism) of transformation and growth. The United States burst forth onto the world stage with a spectacular run of industrial growth in its manufacturing capability around the 1910s–1920s, so did China in the 2010s. Assuming that China's per capita GDP can maintain a growth rate of 7% per year while the U.S. can maintain a growth rate of 2% per year for the next few decades, in only 40 more years (or 30 more years based on PPP) China will catch up with the United States in per capita income, which is again roughly consistent with the prediction based on the NST chronology.[24] By then China's economy will be four times larger than the U.S. economy, assuming similar population growth in both countries.

But China must overcome a series of key challenges before reaching this point. First, across the developmental stages, the mode of production (hard core technology) experiences revolutionary changes, and so too does the method of management. Management is the soft power of industrial revolutions. For example, around the turn of the 19th century during the takeoff period of the first industrial revolution (1760–1830), the British industries experienced a management revolution as represented by the factory system. Around the turn of the 20th century during its takeoff period in the

---

[24] Due to regional inequalities, China's east coast area such as Jiangsu, Zhejiang, and Guangdong provinces can catchup with the U.S. living standard in a significantly shorter period of time.

Second Industrial Revolution (1880–1920), the United States experienced a management revolution (as represented by the Taylor System). China today is at the juncture of its second IR takeoff period, so it also faces the bottleneck of product-quality and service-quality upgrading, and thus badly needs a management revolution, not only inside firms and enterprises but also across all public administrative institutions and local government offices.

Hence, China's second industrial revolution cannot be accomplished without a management revolution in industrial manufacturing, consumer service provision (including financial and medical and retail services), and government administration (including public service and facility provision and school system regulation). A rapidly growing market for large corporations and rising market demand for managerial human capital — skilled managers and administrators in all sectors at all levels — will trigger China's management revolution.

Second, China needs to institutionalize its anticorruption movement and eventually establish a transparent, rule-based government administrative system and bureaucracy. With more than three decades of rapid industrialization and hyper growth, China now has the state capacity and informational infrastructure to establish a more efficient and rule-based political administration system.

Third, China needs to create a modern financial system that is both prudent and also more efficient in channeling funds from unproductive agents (savers) in the society to productive ones (entrepreneurs). For this, China has much to learn from the long historical experiences (bad and good) of Western capitalism since at least the Dutch Republic (e.g., the tulip bubble).

Fourth, China needs to invent a modern education system (from elementary to college) that combines both its traditional oriental conservative virtues that emphasize within-family and school learning and Western liberal education that encourages creativity and critical thinking.

Last but not the least, China needs to develop a public health-care system and drug-and-food administration system that can strike a balance between equality (mass access) and quality and can balance the costs and benefits of such systems. Healthcare-pharmaceutical and food processing sectors are two of the key industries where the market mechanism can fail dramatically and miserably because of the severe degree of asymmetric information in the high-tech knowledge involved and the tremendous spatial-natural monopoly power of doctors over patients and companies over consumers. In such industries the classical demand-and-supply analysis and price mechanisms simply go astray. However, despite these and other formidable challenges, China's fundamentals look good and future looks bright.

The fundamental reason the Great Britain, instead of the Netherlands, kick-started the Industrial Revolution was because of Great Britain's successful creation of the world's largest textile market and commercial distribution system in the 17th and 18th centuries. The fundamental reason the United States, instead of France and Germany, overtook the Great Britain to become the next world superpower was its much larger unified domestic market (several times the size of the Great Britain's domestic market), which enabled the United States to emulate the British Industrial Revolution at a significantly larger scale and adopt mass production and mass distribution not only in the textile industry but also in almost any other industry, including the home-construction industry, the auto-mobile industry, and even the food-processing industry. This far more thorough adoption of the mode of mass production has generated for the United States far larger demand for energy, motive power, and infrastructures (e.g., the rail and highway system), which in turn has generated for the United States far more colossal productive force and capital supply and financial depth. And it thus dominates the global trade and world capital flows.

By the same token, the fundamental reason that China, instead of India, is well-positioned to overtake the United States to become the next superpower in the 21st century, despite the fact that China's current per capita income is only about one tenth or one seventh of the U.S. level, is not because of its later-comer advantage, but rather because of its correct state-led development strategy and its much larger unified domestic market than the United States. China has a population four times that of the United States and a unified domestic market with a continuously upgrading world-rank network of infrastructure. On top of that, it has a 2,000-year cultural tradition that emphasizes national unity and education and a capable mercantilist government that embraces pragmatism (John Dewey's philosophy rather than dogmatic ideology), thus making China highly adaptive to business-oriented social-political-institutional changes. This fourfold larger unified domestic market and a business- and education-oriented open society (fully open to international competition and trade and student exchanges) will make it profitable to adopt mass production in China in aspects and at levels never seen in the United States, as has already been manifested in China's rapid buildup of a full-fledged domestic speed-train network (as noted previously, stretching all the way south to Singapore and north to Russia and east to Europe) and its gigantic international "One Belt, One Road" plan for building the new "Silk Road" across both the Eurasian continent and the Indian and Atlantic oceans. Behind this ambitious and unprecedented infrastructure and market-creation program is China's 50% national saving rate (equivalent to 25% of U.S. GDP or 50% of U.S. GDP based on PPP) and nearly $4 trillion dollar foreign reserves accumulated through proto-industrialization in the 1980s and its first industrial revolution in the 1990s and its second industrial revolution in the 2000s.

A gigantic market creates a gigantic demand for manufacturing innovations and engineering wonders. This was how the United Kingdom surpassed the Netherlands to become the first industrial superpower by inventing the spinning jenny and the steam engine in the 18th century. This was also how the United States surpassed the United Kingdom to become the next superpower by inventing the Ford assembly line and the internet in the 20th century. This is also why China will likely surpass the United States to become the new superpower in the 21st century by inventing technologies that can shrink and flatten the earth once again by many more hundreds of percent than what Columbus's great voyage had once achieved.

The rise of the West, despite its spectacular scale and thundering impact on humanity, still has not been able to lift Africa (human's common birthplace and land of origin) out of the Malthusian poverty trap for several hundred years, because of the legacy of Western colonialism and misguided development policies designed by international organizations such as the IMF and the World Bank.

But China offers the developing world a "new" model of development based on the "old" iron logic of the Industrial Revolution and capitalism. It is reasonable to hope that with China's rapid rise, with its domestic market larger than North America and Europe and Russia and Japan all combined and its non-interventionist pragmatism in international and geopolitical relations, may mean one step closer to reaching the "goal" or "historical end" set (implicitly) by the English Industrial Revolution — the goal of capitalism to (re) create the whole world according its own image (affluence based on mass production), the goal of empowering every impoverished human being on earth with "bourgeois dignity" and material wealth, and the goal of realizing the communist ideal of "from each according to his ability; to each according to his need."[25]

The prospects of China's rise, based on the iron logic of the Industrial Revolution and capitalism, explains why the legendary investor and capitalist Jim Rogers stated repeatedly that "just as the

---

[25] But China cannot get the job done alone. China needs to change the old-fashioned nationalistic America-centric and Eurocentric capitalism (which has resulted in two bloody world wars and has lacked genuine international coordination even after establishing the United Nations and ending the cold war). China needs to use its colossal manufacturing power and rising productive force and capital leverage to unite the industrial world with South East Asia, Central Asia, Latin America, the Middle East, and Africa into a single market, based not on culture, religion, dogmatic ideology, or moral superiority, but on speed-train railroads, commerce, and down-to-earth common business interests — the very essence of capitalism that transcends culture, religion, and ideology.

future belonged to the British in the 19th century and the Americans in the 20th century, so the Chinese will own the 21st century ... People worry about Chinese economic growth and whether it can be sustained. It is worth remembering that in the U.S. in the 19th century, we had 15 depressions, a horrid civil war, few human rights, little rule of law, periodic massacres, you could buy and sell congressmen (you can still buy and sell congressmen, but in those days they were cheap) and in 1907 the whole system was bankrupt. This was just as the United States was on the verge of becoming the most powerful country in the world."[26] Mr. Rogers may not have economic theory to back up his bold claims and bullish assessments about China, but he has made these claims based on his basic business instincts, common sense of history, and lifetime global investment experiences.

Institutions are endogenous.[27] They are built to serve and created to implement long-term development goals and to protect the fruits of development. Different development strategies call for different institutions. The rule of law and the notion of private property are ancient, but their specific forms and content have evolved over time according to the mode of production, the structure of the economy, and the goals of development. The Law of Moses specified only a dozen rules, but modern civil and corporate laws specify millions of rules (as endogenous responses to business practices and social-economic changes).

---

[26] See, e.g., https://www.youtube.com/watch?v=doMXl89Lur8.

[27] Based on cross country data and instrument variables widely used in the existing literature, Luo and Wen (2015) in a recent working paper, "Institutions Do Not Rule: Reassessing the Driving Forces of Economic Development" show that institutions or institutional qualities (such as property rights and the rule of law or the strength of protection against expropriation risk) do not explain economic development and the degree of industrialization, but are instead explained by economic development, in sharp contrast to the conclusions reached by Acemoglu, Johnson, and Robinson (2001) and their other empirical analyses elsewhere.

Anticorruption is the endogenous demand of any society at any stage of development, because corruption (i) undermines the government's (or the ruling class's) legitimacy, (ii) distorts the fundamental notion of fairness — one of the key elements to organize a civilization and society, (iii) goes against social norms and the rule of law regardless of autocracy or democracy,[28] (iv) endangers social-political order, and (v) makes the state and national interests prone to foreign (economic, political, or military) intrusions or invasions.

However, anticorruption (enforcing the rule of law) is extremely costly. This is why, historically, only industrial capitalism at the critical juncture of finishing the second industrial revolution — with its mighty financial and informational technological capabilities in surveillance and with both the middle-income working class and the government becoming critical stakeholders of the fruits of industrialization based on increasingly intertwined vested interests in a highly organic and organized society based on nationwide division of labor and specialization — has been able to seriously combat and contain corruption to a level that is no longer endemic and does not pose a serious threat to further economic growth and prosperity.[29]

---

[28] For example, Mao's communist China in the 1950s and 1960s was significantly less corrupt than Deng's capitalist China in the 1990s and 2000s.

[29] "The 'spoils' system, where public officers were allocated to the loyalists of the ruling party, became a key component in American politics from the emergence of the two party system in 1828 with the election of President Jackson. This got much worse for a few decades after the Civil War. There was a loud cry for civil services reform throughout the 19th century to create a professional and non-partisan bureaucracy, but no progress was made until the Pendleton Act of 1883," (Ha-Joon Chang, 2003, pp. 78–79) when America was already in the middle of its second industrial revolution. Research shows that corruption in the U.S. in the early 1870s, when it had just finished its first industrial revolution with real income per capita about $2,800 (in 2005 dollars), was seven to nine times higher than China's corruption level in 1996, the corresponding year in terms of income per capita when China reached similar development stage. By the time the U.S. was about to finish its second industrial revolution and reached per capita income

Hence, if rampant corruption throughout the 19th and the early 20th centuries did not stop the United States from finishing its second industrial revolution and rising to global economic and political power, why would it stop today's China given that China is already in the middle of finishing its second industrial revolution and has already become a highly specialized society with every part of its industrial apparatus interdependent, so much so that every social class's self-interest hinges critically on the continuous prosperity of the nation?

The time always comes to call for the industrial-age rule of law and new forms of accountability of the government in any nation as the industrial revolution unfolds and escalates.[30] Modern Western

---

level of $7,500 in 1928, approximately equivalent to China's current development stage in 2014, corruption levels were significantly reduced and similar in both countries (see Carlos Ramirez, 2014). Starting from 2014, China has launched an unprecedented new wave of anti-graft campaigns to ensure that it can succeed in finishing its industrialization and modernization by the middle of this century. Yet, this has been viewed by the Western news media simply as a new round of internal political power struggle among the vested interest groups within the communist party. How could it be viewed as anything else if the Westerners can only see things through the ideological glasses of the institutional theory?

[30] The current Chinese president Xi Jinping's fierce anticorruption movement is a good example of such a Hegelian historical necessity. It is a sign of China's success in rapidly climbing up the ladder of industrialization. Most of the Western media portray China's current anticorruption movement merely as a show of internal power struggle in Xi's government among the vested interest groups. This narrow view is just another manifestation of the Western misunderstanding and underestimation of China under the bad influence of the institutional theories. The truth is that, after more than three decades of rapid industrialization, China has accumulated enough social-political demand as well as the financial resources, administrative capital, and information technologies to support more thorough institutional reforms and law reinforcement. China has arrived at a critical juncture of finishing its second industrial revolution and the necessary institutional building to protect the fruits of the second industrial revolution, a juncture where the benefit of institutional reform outweighs its cost. This is a China-centric epoch that calls for great politicians and produces great

institutions were set to protect the fruits of the Industrial Revolution, which made all social classes' vested interests intertwined and mutually indispensable. Such institutions became desirable and affordable *because of* the Industrial Revolution. Universal suffrage, the rule of law, protection against expropriation, the accountability of the government, the capacity to provide social order and other public goods, the redistribution of political power and mobility of social classes, the decay of religion in its power of organizing societies and reining over the meaning of life and family structures, the ability to defend equality and the modern notion of human rights (including minority and children and women's rights) and reinforce distributional fairness across sexes and races ... these have all been the *consequence* of the Industrial Revolution, the *effects* of unified impersonal market exchanges, the *outcomes* of the rise of the middle-income class as stakeholders of the economy and the hundreds-fold appreciation of the value of labor relative to capital, and the *social-political response* to capitalistic mass production and mass distribution.

Genuine social equality is achieved and based ultimately on the ability to participate in an impersonal mass consumeristic culture sustained by mass production, not on the rhetoric or mere declarations that "all men are created equal."

Capitalistic mass production is the greatest invention of mankind since the discovery of agriculture, because it is rooted in the principle of the division of labor (impersonal and interpersonal cooperation) and the economies of scale, thus with tremendous productive externalities and spillover effects coming from and feeding back on all individuals' actions. It is only through

---

politicians — politicians with powerful leadership, passion, and character, with the strategic planning and vision to build an economic superpower for the 21st century. Great politicians, like great scholars, care more about their impact on societies and legacy in history than about their personal consumption beyond a subsistence level.

capitalistic production based on the division of labor (including mental labor) and the economies of scale that human societies can achieve affluence in goods and services and knowledge and information and enter the stage of a welfare state. Hence, capitalistic production is not and has never been a zero-sum game, not even during the age of colonialism and imperialism. Therefore, just as the rise of the United States has greatly benefited (instead of diminished, in absolute terms) the United Kingdom and the welfare of the English working class, the rise of China has also and will continue to benefit (instead of diminish) the United States and the welfare of the American people. For example, total American exports to China since 1983 have increased by a stunning 50-fold in merely 30 years, yet its domestic inflation rate remained exceptionally low for decades, thanks to China's rise.[31]

By the same token, the possible rise of India and Sub-Saharan Africa will be even more spectacular in due time. But to make that happen, *correct procedures* of development, *right sequences* of development, and *proper strategies* of development, based on the historical logic of the Industrial Revolution (outlined in the NST), matter.

The last shall be first,
The slow shall be fast,
Inches will be miles,
Provided the road taken is right.

---

[31] But how these two giant countries can deal with each other peacefully to realize the tremendous non-zero-sum gains remains the greatest challenge in the 21st century.

References

Acemoglu, Daron. Politics and Economics in Weak and Strong States. *Journal of Monetary Economics*, 2005, 52(7), pp. 1199–1226.

Acemoglu, D., Johnson, S., and Robinson, J.A. (2001). The Colonial Origins of Comparative Development: An Empirical Investigation. *American Economic Review*, 91(5), 1369–1401.

Acemoglu, Daron and Robinson, James A. *Economic Origins of Dictatorship and Democracy*. New York: Cambridge University Press, 2005.

Acemoglu, Daron and Robinson, James A. *Why Nations Fail: The Origins of Power, Prosperity, and Poverty*. New York: Crown Business, 2012.

Agence France-Presse. China Drives Growth in Patent Applications Worldwide. *Industry Week*, December 16, 2014. http://www.industryweek.com/global-economy/china-drives-growth-patent-applications-worldwide.

Allen, Robert C. *The British Industrial Revolution in Global Perspective*. Cambridge: Cambridge University Press, 2009.

Arrow, Kenneth J. The organization of economic activity: Issues pertinent to the choice of market versus non-market allocations, in *The analysis and evaluation of public expenditures: the PPB system; a compendium of papers submitted to the Subcommittee on Economy in Government of the Joint Economic Committee, Congress of the United States*. Washington, D.C.: Government Printing Office, 1969, pp. 47–64.

Ashton, Thomas S. *The Industrial Revolution, 1760–1830*. CUP Archive, Volume 38, 1970.

Azariadis, Costas, Kaas, Leo and Wen, Yi. Self-Fulfilling Credit Cycles. Working Paper, Federal Reserve Bank of St. Louis and University of Konstanz, 2015.

Beckert, Sven. *Empire of Cotton: A Global History*. Knopf, 2014.

Bell, Daniel A. *The China Model: Political Meritocracy and the Limits of Democracy*. Princeton University Press. 2015.

Benhibab, Jess, Wang, Pengfei and Wen, Yi. Sentiments and Aggregate Demand Fluctuations. *Econometrica* (forthcoming), Working Paper No. 2012–039B, Federal Reserve Bank of St. Louis, 2014.

Berlinger, Joshua. The 50 Most Dangerous Cities in the World. *Business Insider*, October 9, 2012. Available at http://www.businessinsider.com/most-dangerous-cities-in-the-world-2012-10.

Bernstein, William J. *A Splendid Exchange: How Trade Shaped the World*. Atlantic Monthly Press, 2008.

Boldrin, Michele and David K. Levine. *Against Intellectual Monopoly*. Cambridge University Press, 2008.

Boldrin, Michele, Levine David K. and Modica, Salvatore. A Review of Acemoglu and Robinson's *Why Nations Fail*. Unpublished Manuscript, 2014.

Bown, Stephen R. *Merchant Kings: When Companies Ruled the World, 1600– 1900*. New York: Macmillan, 2010.

Brandt, Loren, Ma, Debin and Rawski, Thomas G. From Divergence to Convergence: Reevaluating the History behind China's Economic Boom. Working Paper No. 158/12, London School of Economics, 2012.

Brandt, Loren and Rawski Thomas G. (eds). *China's Great Economic Transformation*. Cambridge University Press, 2008.

Breslin, Shaun. State Led Development in Historical Perspective: From Friedrich List to a Chinese Mode of Governance? Presented at *The Beijing Forum*, Beijing University, Beijing, November 2009.

Broadberry, Stephen and Gupta, Bishnupriya. Lancashire, India, and Shifting Competitive Advantage in Cotton Textiles, 1700–1850: The Neglected Role of Factor Prices. *The Economic History Review*, May 2009, 62(2), pp. 279– 305.

Byrne, Eileen. Tunisia Becomes Breeding Ground for Islamic State Fighters. The Guardian, October 13, 2014. Available at http://www.theguardian.com/world/2014/oct/13/tunisia-breeding-ground-islamic-state-fighters.

Caves, Douglas W. and Laurits R. Christensen. The Relative Efficiency of public and Private Firms in a Competitive Environment: the Case of Canadian Railroads. *The Journal of Political Economy*, 1980, pp. 958–976.

Cipolla, Carlo M. *Before the Industrial Revolution: European Society and Economy, 1000–1700*. W. W. Norton & Company, 1994.

Chandler, Alfred D., Jr. *The Visible Hand: The Managerial Revolution in American Business*, Cambridge: Harvard University Press, 1977.

Chang, Gordon G. *The Coming Collapse of China.* New York: Random House, 2001.

Chang, Ha-Joon. *Kicking Away the Ladder: Development Strategies in Historical Perspective.* London: Anthem Press, 2003.

Chang, Ha-Joon and Ajit Singh. Policy Arena: Can Large Firms be Run Efficiently Without being Bureaucratic? *Journal of International Development,* 1997, 9(6), pp. 865–875.

Chen, Ping. The Symmetry Assumption in Transaction Costs Approach. (2007).

Chen, Ping, ed. *Economic Complexity and Equilibrium Illusion: Essays on Market Instability and Macro Vitality.* Routledge, 2010.

Chow, Gregory C. *China's Economic Transformation.* John Wiley & Sons, 2015.

Clark, Gregory. Why isn't the Whole World Developed? Lessons from the Cotton Mills. *Journal of Economic History,* 1987, 47(1), pp. 141–173.

Clark, Gregory, The Agricultural Revolution and the Industrial Revolution: England, 1500–1912. Working Paper, University of California, Davis, 2002.

Clark, Gregory. *A Farewell to Alms: A Brief Economic History of the World.* USA: Princeton University Press, 2008.

Clark, Gregory. A Review Essay on the Enlightened Economy: An Economic History of Britain 1700–1850 by Joel Mokyr. *Journal of Economic Literature,* 2012, 50(1), pp. 85–95.

Clarkson, Leslie A. *Proto-Industrialization: The First Phase of Industrialization?* London: Macmillan, 1985.

Clarkson, Leslie A. 6 Ireland 1841: Pre-Industrial or Proto-Industrial; Industrializing or De-Industrializing? *European Proto-Industrialization: An Introductory Handbook,* 1996, 67.

Coase, Ronald and Wang, Ning. *How China Became Capitalist.* Palgrave Macmillan, 2013.

Coase, Ronald H. The Nature of the Firm. *Economica,* November 1937, 4(16), pp. 386–405.

Coury, Tarek and Wen, Yi. Global Indeterminacy in Locally Determinate Real Business Cycle Models. *International Journal of Economic Theory,* 2009, 5(1), pp. 49–60.

Dahl, Robert A. *Polyarchy: Participation and Opposition.* New Haven, CT: Yale University Press, 1971.

Dang, Jianwei and Motohashi, Kazuyuki. Patent Statistics: A Good Indicator for Innovation in China? Patent Subsidy Program Impacts on Patent Quality. *China Economic Review,* 2015, 35, pp. 137–155.

Davis, Ralph. The Rise of Protection in England, 1689–1786. *The Economic History Review,* 1966, 19(2), pp. 306–317.

Deane, Phyllis M. *The First Industrial Revolution.* Cambridge University Press, 1979.

Defoe, Daniel, *et al.* *A Tour Through the Whole Island of Great Britain.* Yale University Press, 1991.

Desmet, Klaus and Stephen L. Parente. The Evolution of Markets and the Revolution of Industry: A Unified Theory of Growth. *Journal of Economic Growth,* 2012, 17(3), pp. 205–234.

Diamond, Jared M. *Guns, Germs and Steel: A Short History of Everybody for the Last 13,000 Years.* Random House, 1998.

Díaz Frers, Luciana. Why did the Washington Consensus Policies Fail? Presented at the *Center for the International Private Enterprise,* 2014.

Encyclopedia.com. Putting-Out System. *International Encyclopedia of the Social Sciences,* 2008. Retrieved from http://www.encyclopedia.com/doc/1G2-3045302138.html.

Engels, Friedrich and John Burdon Sanderson Haldane. *Dialectics of Nature.* Ed. Ciemens Palme Dutt. New York: International Publishers, 1940.

Finer, S. E. *The History of Government.* Oxford University Press, Volume III, 1999.

Freeland, Chrystia. *Sale of the Century: Russia's Wild Ride from Communism to Capitalism.* Crown, 2000.

Fukuyama, Francis. *Political Order and Political Decay: From the Industrial Revolution to the Globalization of Democracy.* New York: Farrar, Strauss and Giroux, 2014.

Fytrou, Natali. World Food Crisis and the Arab Spring. 2014. Available at http://www.academia.edu/5743155/World_food_crisis_and_the_Arab_Spring.

Gallagher, Kevin. The End of the 'Washington Consensus.' *The Guardian,* 2011. Available at http://www.theguardian.com/commentisfree/cifamerica/2011/mar/07/china-usa.

Gates, Bill. A Stunning Statistic about China and Concrete. Gates Notes, June 25, 2014. Available at http://www.gatesnotes.com/About-Bill-Gates/Concrete-in-China.

Gerschenkron, Alexander. *Economic Backwardness in Historical Perspective.* Cambridge, MA: Belknap Press of Harvard University Press, 1962.

Gorrie, James R. *The China Crisis: How China's Economic Collapse Will Lead to a Global Depression.* John Wiley & Sons, 2013.

Greenfeld, Liah. *Nationalism: Five Roads to Modernity.* Harvard University Press, 1992.

Greenfeld, Liah. *The Spirit of Capitalism: Nationalism and Economic Growth.* Harvard University Press, 2009.

Gupta, Bishnupriya and Ma, Debin. Europe in an Asian Mirror: The Great Divergence, in Broadberry, Stephen and O'Rourke, Kevin (eds.), *The*

Cambridge economic history of modern Europe. New York: Cambridge University Press, 2010, pp. 264–284.

Hafeez, Seema. The efficacy of regulation in developing countries. United Nations, 2003.

Hansen, Gary D. and Prescott, Edward C. Malthus to Solow. *American Economic Review*, 2002, 92(4), pp. 1205–1217.

Harner, Stephen. Dealing with the Scourge of "Schadenfreude" in Foreign Reporting on China. China–U.S. Focus, October 3, 2014. Available at http://www.chinausfocus.com/culture-history/dealing-with-the-scourge-of-schadenfreude-in-foreign-reporting-on-china/.

Harrigan, Jane. Did Food Prices Plant the Seeds of the Arab Spring? *SOAS Inaugural Lecture Series*, 2011.

Harrigan, Jane. The Political Economy of Aid Flows to North Africa. WIDER Working Paper No. 72, World Institute for Development Economic Research, 2011.

Hegel, Georg Wilhelm Friedrich. *Phenomenology of Spirit. 1807. Trans. AV Miller.* Oxford: Oxford UP, 1977.

Hoppit, Julian. Patterns of Parliamentary Legislation, 1660–1800. *History Journal*, 1996, 39(1), pp. 109–131.

Huntington, Samuel P. *The Third Wave: Democratization in the Late Twentieth Century*. Norman OK, U.S.: University of Oklahoma Press, 1991.

Jacques, Martin. *When China Rules the World: The Rise of the Middle Kingdom and the End of the Western World*. London: Penguin Press, 2009.

Jacques, Martin. *When China Rules the World: The Rise of the Middle Kingdom and the Birth of a New Global Order*. Second Edition. London: Penguin Press, 2012.

Jiang, Kun and Wang, Susheng. A Contractual Analysis of State versus Private Ownership. Working Paper, 2015. Hong Kong University of Science and Technology.

Keynes, John M. *The General Theory of Employment, Interest, and Money*. New York: Harcourt, Brace & World, [1936] 1964.

Kole, Stacey R. and Harold J. Mulherin. The Government as a Shareholder: A Case from the United States 1. *The Journal of Law and Economics*, 1997, 40(1), pp. 1–22.

Kriedte, Peter, Medick, Hass and Schlumbohm, Jurgen. *Industrialization before Industrialization: Rural Industry in the Genesis of Capitalism*, translated by Beate Schmpp, with contributions from Herbert Kisch and Franklin F. Mendels, UK: Cambridge University Press, 1977.

Kynge, James. Uganda Turns East: Chinese Money will Build Infrastructure Says Museveni. Financial Times, October 21, 2014. Available at http://www.ft.com/cms/s/0/ab12d8da-5936-11e4-9546-00144feab7de.html.

Landes, David S. *The Wealth and Poverty of Nations: Why Some are So Rich and Some So Poor*. New York: W. W. Norton & Company, Inc., 1999.

Lau, Lawrence J., Yingyi, Qian, and Gerard, Roland. Reform Without Losers: An Interpretation of China's Dual-Track Approach to Transition. *Journal of Political Economy*, 2000, 108(1), pp. 120–143.

Law, Marc T. and Kim, Sukkoo. The Rise of the American Regulatory State: A View from the Progressive Era. *Handbook on the Politics of Regulation*, 113, 2011.

Lewis, Arthur. Economic Development with Unlimited Supplies of Labour. *The Manchester School*, 1954, 22(2), pp. 139–191.

Li, Eric Xi. A Tale of Two Systems, Presented at TEDGlobal, 2013. Available at http://blog.ted.com/2013/06/13/a-tale-of-two-systems-eric-x-li-at-tedglobal-2013/.

Li, Xiaopeng. *A Nation in Question: Understanding the Rise of China* (in Chinese: 这个国家会好吗？中国崛起的经济学分析). China Development Press, 2012.

Li, Xi, Liu, Xuewen and Wang, Yong. A Model of China's State Capitalism. Unpublished Working Paper, Hong Kong University of Science and Technology, 2014.

Lin, Justin Y. *Economic Development and Transition: Thought, Strategy, and Viability*. Cambridge University Press, 2009.

Lin, Justin Y. *Demystifying the Chinese Economy*. Cambridge University Press, 2011.

Lin, Justin Y. *New Structural Economics: A Framework for Rethinking Development and Policy*. World Bank Publications 2012.

Lin, Justin Y. *The Quest for Prosperity: How Developing Economies can Take Off*. Princeton University Press, 2013.

Lin, Justin Y., Cai, Fang and Li, Zhou. *The China Miracle*. Hong Kong: The Chinese University of Hong Kong, 1996.

Lipset, Seymour M. Some Social Requisites of Democracy: Economic Development and Political Legitimacy. *American Political Science Review*, 1959, 53(1), pp. 69–105.

Lipton, Michael. *Why Poor People Stay Poor: Urban Bias in Developing Countries*. London: Temple Smith, 1977.

List, Friedrich. *The Natural System of Political Economy*. London: Longmans, Green, and Co, [1841] 1909.

Long, Cheryl and Zhang, Xiaobo, Cluster-Based Industrialization in Financing and Performance, *Journal of International Economics*, 2011, 84(1), pp. 112–123.

Long, Cheryl and Zhang, Xiaobo, Patterns of China's Industrialization: Concentration, Specialization, and Clustering, *China Economic Review*, 2012, 23(3), pp. 593–612.

Lucas, Robert E. The Industrial Revolution: Past and Future. Federal Reserve Bank of Minneapolis, 2003.

Luo, Jinfeng and Wen, Yi. Institutions Do Not Rule: Reassessing the Driving Forces of Economic Development. Working Paper No. 2015-001A, Federal Reserve Bank of St. Louis, 2015.

Martin, Stephen and David, Parker. Privatization and Economic Performance Throughout the UK Business Cycle. *Managerial and Decision Economics,* 1995, 16(3), pp. 225–237.

Marx, Karl. *Capital, Vol. 1: A Critique of Political Economy.* New York: Vintage, 1867.

Marx, Karl and Engels, Friedrich. *Manifesto of the Communist Party.* Chapter 1. 1848.

Mas-Colell, Andreu, Michael Dennis Whinston and Jerry R. Green *Microeconomic Theory.* New York: Oxford University Press, 1995.

McCloskey, Deirdre N. *Bourgeois Dignity: Why Economics Can't Explain the Modern World.* Chicago: University of Chicago Press, 2010.

McKendrick, Neil, Brewer, John and Plumb, John H. *The Birth of a Consumer Society: The Commercialization of Eighteenth-Century England.* Bloomington, IN: Indiana University Press, 1982.

Mendels, Franklin F. Proto-industrialization: The First Phase of the Industrialization Process. *The Journal of Economic History,* 1972, 32(1), pp. 241–261.

Mendels, Franklin F. *Industrialization and Population Pressure in Eighteenth-Century Flanders.* New York: Arno Press, 1981.

Mokyr, Joel. *Industrialization in the Low Countries, 1795–1850.* New Haven: Yale University Press, 1976.

Mokyr, Joel. *The Institutional Origins of the Industrial Revolution.* Unpublished Manuscript, Northwestern University, 2008.

Mokyr, Joel. *The Enlightened Economy: An Economic History of Britain 1700–1850.* Yale University Press, 2009.

Morris, Charles R. *The Dawn of Innovation: The First American Industrial Revolution.* New York: Public Affairs, 2012.

Morris, Ian. *Why the West Rules-for Now: The Patterns of History and What They Reveal about the Future.* Profile books, 2010.

Murphy, Kevin M., Shleifer, Andrei and Vishny, Robert W. Industrialization and the Big Push. *Journal of Political Economy,* 1989, 97(5), pp. 1003–1026.

Naughton, Barry. *Growing Out of the Plan: Chinese Economic Reform, 1978–1993.* Cambridge University Press, 1995.

Naughton, Barry. *The Chinese Economy: Transitions and Growth.* MIT press, 2007.

Navarro, Peter, and Greg Autry. *Death by China: Confronting the Dragon — A Global Call to Action.* Pearson Prentice Hall, 2011.

Navy News. Dragons Be Here — As Largest Chinese Navy Visit to U.K. Begins. January 12, 2015. https://www.navynews.co.uk/archive/news/item/12225.

North, Douglas. *Structure and Change in Economic History*. New York: W. W. Norton, 1981.

North, Douglass C. and Thomas, Robert Paul. *The Rise of the Western World: A New Economic History*. New York: Cambridge University Press, 1973.

North, Douglass C. and Barry R. Weingast. Constitutions and Commitment: The Evolution of Institutions Governing Public Choice in Seventeenth-century England. *The Journal of Economic History*, 1989, 49(04), pp. 803–832.

North, Douglass C. and Wallis, John Joseph. *Violence and Social Orders: A Conceptual Framework for Interpreting Recorded Human History*. Cambridge University Press, 2009.

Ogilvie, Sheilagh and Cerman, Markus. *European Proto-Industrialization: An Introductory Handbook*. UK: Cambridge University Press, 1996.

Oi, Jean C. Fiscal Reform and the Economic Foundations of Local State Corporatism in China. *World Politics*, 1992, 45(1), pp. 99–126.

O'brien, Patrick, Trevor Griffiths, and Philip Hunt. Political Components of the Industrial Revolution: Parliament and the English Cotton Textile Industry, 1660–17741. *The Economic History Review*, 1991, 44(3), pp. 395–423.

O'Malley, Eoin. The Decline of Irish Industry in the 19th-Century. *The Economic and Social Review*, 1981, 13.

Paulson Papers on Investment. California Dreaming: How a Chinese Battery Firm Began Making Electric Buses in America. Paulson Institute. Case Study Series, June 2015.

Pintus, Patrick A. and Wen, Yi. Leveraged Borrowing and Boom-Bust Cycles. *Review of Economic Dynamics*, 2013, 16(4), pp. 617–633.

Polanyi, Karl. *The Great Transformation: The Political and Economic Origins of Our Time*. Beacon Press, 1944.

Pomeranz, Kenneth. *The Great Divergence: China, Europe, and the Making of the Modern World Economy*. Princeton University Press, 2001.

Pomeranz, Kenneth and Topik, Steven. *The World That Trade Created*. ME Sharpe, 3rd edition. 2013.

Pritchett, Lant and Summers, Lawrence H. Asiaphoria Meets Regression to the Mean. NBER Working Paper No. 20573, National Bureau of Economic Research, October 2014.

Qiu, Larry D. China's Textile and Clothing Industry. Mimeo, Hong Kong University of Science and Technology, 2005.

Rueschemeyer, Dietrich, Huber, Evelyne and Stephens, John D. *Capitalist Development and Democracy*. Chicago: University of Chicago Press, 1992.

Ramirez, Carlos D. Is Corruption in China "Out of Control"? A Comparison with the U.S. in Historical Perspective. *Journal of Comparative Economics*, February 2014, 42(1), pp. 76–91.

Rodrik, Dani. Goodbye Washington Consensus, Hello Washington Confusion? A Review of the World Bank's Economic Growth in the 1990s: Learning from a Decade of Reform. *Journal of Economic Literature*, December 2006, 44(4), pp. 973–987.

Rodrik, Dani. *One Economics, Many Recipes: Globalization, Institutions, and Economic Growth*. USA: Princeton University Press, 2008.

Roll, Eric. *An Early Experiment in Industrial Organization: Being a History of the Firm of Boulton & Watt, 1775–1805*. Frank Cass and Company, 1968.

Roosevelt, Theodore. 1899. Speech by Gov. Roosevelt: Famous Leader of the 'Rough Riders' Addresses the Assemblage on 'The Strenuous Life.' Chicago: Chicago Tribune, April 11, 1899, (1849–1985).

Rosenstein-Rodan, Paul. Problems of Industrialization of Eastern and South-Eastern Europe. *Economic Journal*, 1943, 53(210/211), pp. 202–211.

Rostow, Walt W. *The Stages of Economic Growth: A Non-communist Manifesto*. Cambridge University Press, 1960.

Rowland, Henry Augustus. A Plea for Pure Science. *Science*, 1883, 2(29), pp. 242–250. Published by: American Association for the Advancement of Science Stable URL: http://www.jstor.org/stable/1758976.

Schell, Orville and John Delury. *Wealth and Power: China's Long March to the Twenty-First Century*. Hachette UK, 2013.

Shammas, Carole. *The Pre-Industrial Consumer in England and America*. Oxford: Clarendon Press, 1990.

Sheng, Hua. On Private Land Property Rights, 2014, (in Chinese, available at http://www.360doc.com/content/14/1210/21/14561708_431886261.shtml.)

Shimposha, Toyo K. The industrialization and global integration of meiji Japan, in *Globalization of Developing Countries: Is Autonomous Development Possible?* Chapter 5, 2000, pp. 37–59.

Smith, Adam. *The Wealth of Nations* [*1776*]. na, 1937.

Stiglitz, Joseph. Challenging the Washington Consensus — an Interview with Lindsey Schoenfelder. *The Brown Journal of World Affairs*, May 2002, 9(2), pp. 33–40.

Stokey, Nancy L. A quantitative model of the British industrial revolution, 1780–1850. *Carnegie-Rochester Conference Series on Public Policy*. North-Holland, 2001, 55(1), pp. 55–109.

Studwell, Joe. *How Asia Works: Success and Failure in the World's Most Dynamic Region*. Grove Press, 2013.

The Economist. Tethered by History. July 5, 2014. Available at http://www.economist.com/news/briefing/21606286-failures-arab-spring-were-long-time-making-tethered-history.

The World Bank. Connecting to Compete 2014: Trade Logistics in the Global Economy — The Logistics Performance Index and Its Indicators, 2014.

Vernon-Wortzel, Heidi, and Lawrence H. Wortzel. Privatization: Not the Only Answer. World Development, 1989, 17(5), pp. 633–641.

Vogel, Ezra F. Deng Xiaoping and the Transformation of China. Cambridge, MA: Belknap Press of Harvard University Press, 2013.

Vries, Peer. State, Economy and the Great Divergence: Great Britain and China, 1680s–1850s. Bloomsbury Publishing, 2015.

Wallace, Anthony FC. Rockdale: The Growth of an American Village in the Early Industrial Revolution. University of Nebraska Press, 1978.

Weatherill, Lorna. Consumer Behavior and Material Culture, 1660–1760. London: Routledge, 1988.

Wen, Tiejun. Understanding the Sunan Model of Village Industries. 2011.

Wen, Yi and Wu, Jing. Withstanding the Great Recession like China. Working paper No. 2014-007, Federal Reserve Bank of St. Louis, 2014.

Williams, Eric. Capitalism and Slavery. UNC Press, 1944.

Wrigley, Edward A. Energy and the English Industrial Revolution. Cambridge University Press, 2010.

Wu, Jinglian. Understanding and Interpreting Chinese Economic Reform. Texere, 2005.

Xin, Wang. Village Development and Village Industrial Growth (in Chinese, 村庄发育、村庄工业的发生与发展: 苏南永联村记事 (1970–2002), 新望编著, 北京: 生活·读书·新知三联书店. 2004)

Xu, Chengang and Zhang, Xiaobo. The Evolution of Chinese Entrepreneurial Firms: Township-Village Enterprises Revisited, IFPRI Discussion Paper 00854, 2009.

Yang, Dennis Tao, Chen, Vivian Weijia and Monarch, Ryan. Rising Wages: Has China Lost its Global Labor Advantage? Pacific Economic Review 2010, 15(4), pp. 482–504.

Yang, Dennis Tao and Zhu, Xiaodong. Modernization of Agriculture and Long-Term Growth. Journal of Monetary Economics, 2013, 60(3), pp. 367–382.

Yang, Yufan. Industrial Cluster and Regional Brand: A Study of Gu Zhen's Light-Fixture Industrial Cluster. Guangzhou: Guangdong People Press House, 2010.

Zhang, Taisu. Property Rights in Land, Agricultural Capitalism, and the Relative Decline of Pre-Industrial China, Yale Law School, San Diego International Law Review, 2011, 13(1), p. 129.

Zhang, Weiwei. *The China Wave: Rise of a Civilizational State*. Hackensack, NJ: World Century Publishing Corporation, 2012.

Zhang, Yi and Zhang, Song-song. A Short History of China's Village Enterprises. 2001. (In Chinese: 张毅、张颂颂编著,《中国乡镇企业简史》, 中国农业出版社, 2001).

Zhou, Li. The Origin and Development of Rural Industrialization in China: A Case Study of Yong Village (1978–2004). 2005.

Zhu, Tian. Does China Lack Innovation? 2013. Available at http://www.ftchinese.com/story/001059724.

Zhu, Tian. Will China Fall into the Middle-Income Trap? 2013. Available at http://www.guancha.cn/ZhuTian/2014_10_17_274362.shtml.

Index

Printed in the United States
By Bookmasters